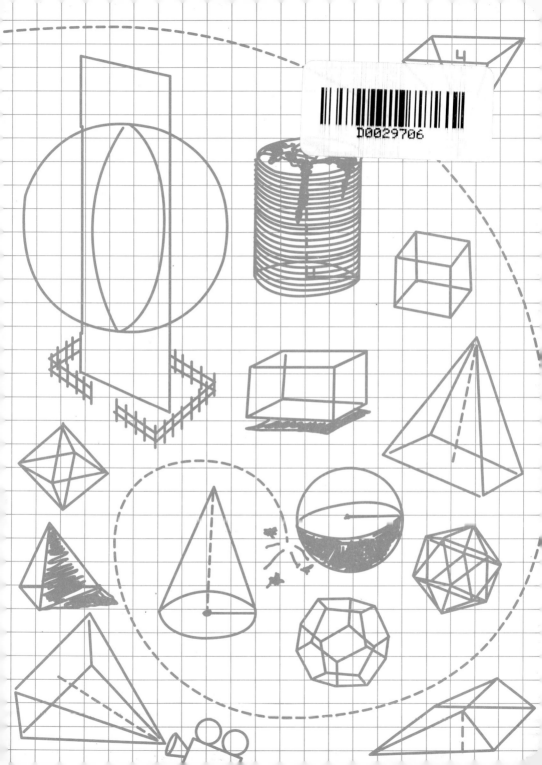

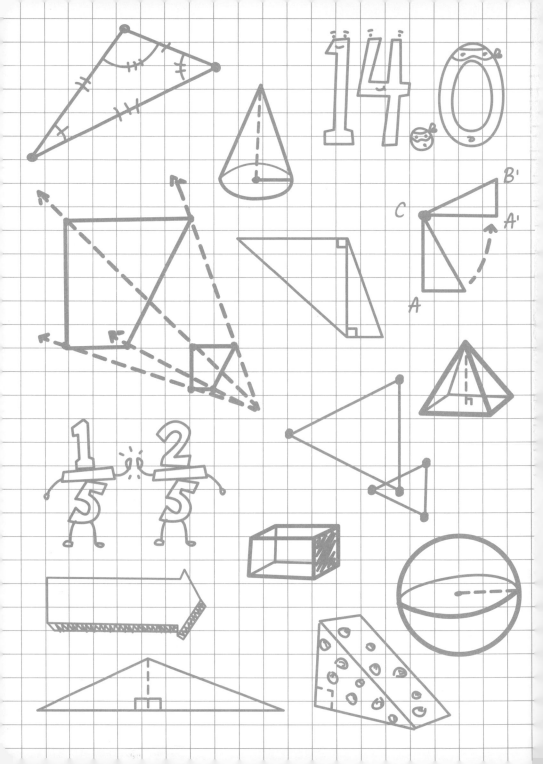

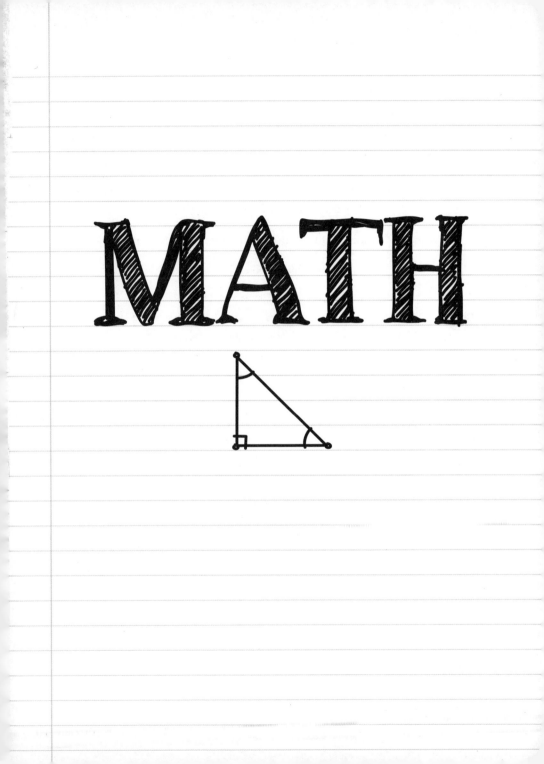

Library of Congress Cataloging-in-Publication Data is available.

ISBN 978-0-7611-6096-0

Writer Altair Peterson   Illustrator Chris Pearce
Series Designer Tim Hall   Designers Gordon Whiteside, Abby Dening
Editor Nathalie Le Du   Production Editor Jessica Rozler
Production Manager Julie Primavera
Concept by Raquel Jaramillo

Workman books are available at special discounts when purchased in bulk for premiums and sales promotions as well as for fund-raising or educational use. Special editions or book excerpts can also be created to specification. For details, contact the Special Sales Director at the address below, or send an email to specialmarkets@workman.com.

Workman Publishing Co., Inc.
225 Varick Street
New York, NY 10014-4381
workman.com

Printed in China

First printing August 2016

10 9 8 7 6 5 4

EVERYTHING YOU NEED TO ACE

MATH

IN ONE BIG FAT NOTEBOOK

Borrowed from the smartest kid in class
Double-checked by OUIDA NEWTON

WORKMAN PUBLISHING

NEW YORK

EVERYTHING YOU NEED TO KNOW TO ACE

MATH

HI!

These are the notes from my math class.
Oh, who am I? Well, some people said I was the
smartest kid in class.

I wrote everything you need to ace **MATH**, from
FRACTIONS to the COORDINATE PLANE,
and only the really important stuff in between—
you know, the stuff that's usually on the test!

$\frac{1}{2}$

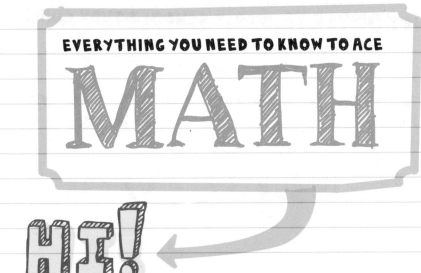

I tried to keep everything organized, so I almost always:

- Highlight vocabulary words in **YELLOW**.
- Color in definitions in green highlighter.
- Use BLUE PEN for important people, places, dates, and terms.
- Doodle a pretty sweet pie chart and whatnot to visually show the big ideas.

MMM...PIE

If you're not loving your textbook and you're not so great at taking notes in class, this notebook will help. It hits all the major points. (But if your teacher spends a whole class talking about something that's not covered, go ahead and write that down for yourself.)

ZZZ...WHAT?

Now that I've aced math, this notebook is **YOURS**. I'm done with it, so this notebook's purpose in life is to help **YOU** learn and remember just what you need to ace **YOUR** math class.

CONTENTS

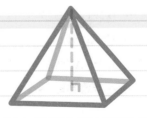

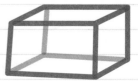

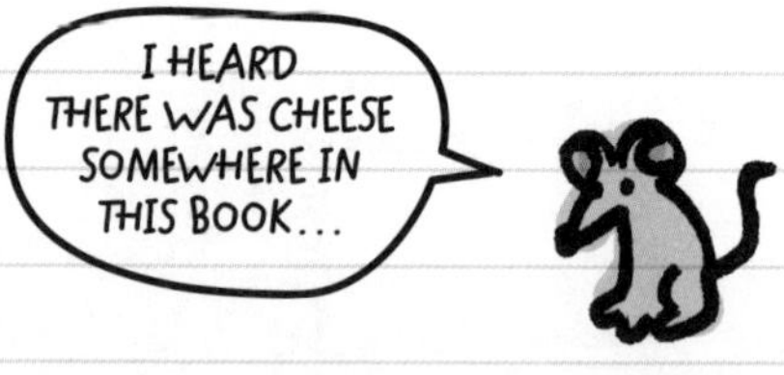
I HEARD THERE WAS CHEESE SOMEWHERE IN THIS BOOK...

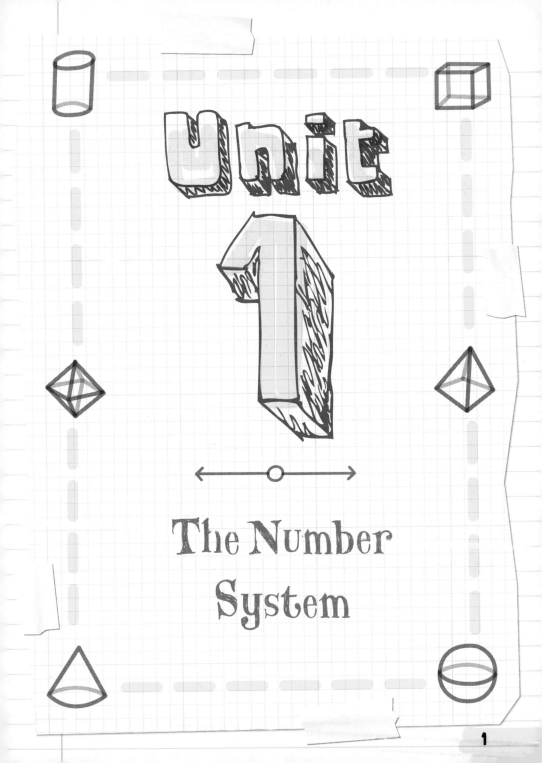

Unit 1

The Number System

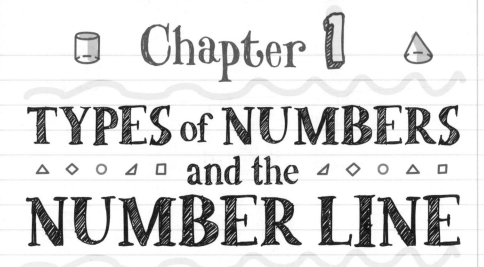

Chapter 1

TYPES of NUMBERS and the NUMBER LINE

There are many different types of numbers with different names. Here are the types of numbers used most often:

WHOLE NUMBERS: A number with no fractional or decimal part. Cannot be negative.

EXAMPLES: 0, 1, 2, 3, 4...

NATURAL NUMBERS: Whole numbers from 1 and up. Some teachers say these are all the "counting numbers."

EXAMPLES: 1, 2, 3, 4, 5...

INTEGERS: All whole numbers (including positive and negative whole numbers).
EXAMPLES: ... −4, −3, −2, −1, 0, 1, 2, 3, 4...

RATIONAL NUMBERS: Any number that can be written by dividing one integer by another—in plain English, any number that can be written as a fraction or ratio. (An easy way to remember this is to think of rational's root word "ratio.")

EXAMPLES: $\frac{1}{2}$, (which equals 0.5), 0.25 (which equals $\frac{1}{4}$), -7 (which equals $\frac{-7}{1}$), 4.12 (which equals $\frac{412}{100}$), $\frac{1}{3}$ (which equals $0.\bar{3}$)

THE LINE OVER THE 3 MEANS THAT IT REPEATS FOREVER!

−0.3333333333333333...

IRRATIONAL NUMBERS: A number that cannot be written as a simple fraction (because the decimal goes on forever without repeating).

("..." MEANS THAT IT CONTINUES ON FOREVER)

EXAMPLES: $3.14159265...$, $\sqrt{2}$

Every number has a decimal expansion. For example, 2 can be written $2.000...$ However, you can spot an irrational number because the decimal expansion goes on forever without repeating.

REAL NUMBERS: All the numbers that can be found on a number line. Real numbers can be large or small, positive or negative, decimals, fractions, etc.

EXAMPLES: 5, –17, 0.312, $\frac{1}{2}$, π, $\sqrt{2}$, etc.

Here's how all the types of numbers fit together:

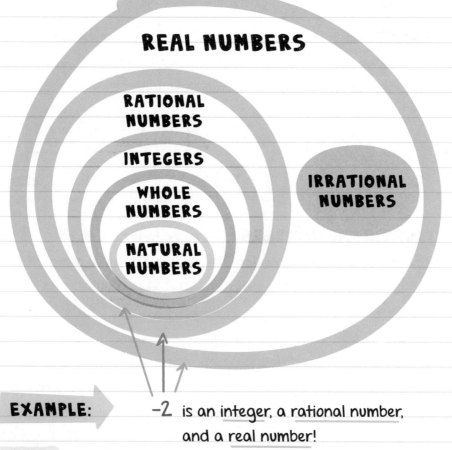

REAL NUMBERS

RATIONAL NUMBERS

INTEGERS

WHOLE NUMBERS

NATURAL NUMBERS

IRRATIONAL NUMBERS

EXAMPLE: –2 is an integer, a rational number, and a real number!

SOME OTHER EXAMPLES:

46 is natural, whole, an integer, rational, and real.

0 is whole, an integer, rational, and real.

$\frac{1}{4}$ is rational and real.

6.675 is rational and real. (TERMINATING DECIMALS or decimals that end are rational.)

$\sqrt{5}$ = 2.2360679775... is irrational and real. (Nonrepeating decimals that go on forever are irrational.)

RATIONAL NUMBERS AND THE NUMBER LINE

All rational numbers can be placed on a **NUMBER LINE**. A number line is a line that orders and compares numbers. Smaller numbers are on the left, and larger numbers are on the right.

EXAMPLE: Because 2 is larger than 1 and also larger than 0, it is placed to the right of those numbers.

EXAMPLE: Similarly, because -3 is smaller than -2 and also smaller than -1, it is placed to the left of those numbers.

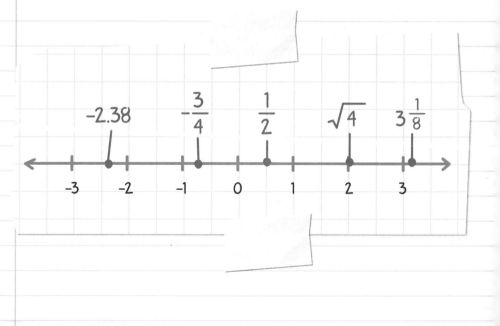

EXAMPLE: Not only can we place integers on a number line, we can put fractions, decimals, and all other rational numbers on a number line, too:

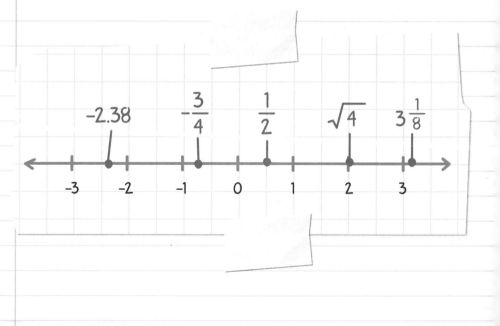

3333333333333333333...

STILL GOING!

CHECK YOUR KNOWLEDGE

For **1** through **8**, classify each number in as many categories as possible.

1. −3

2. 4.$\overline{5}$

3. −4.89375872537653487287439843098…

4. −9.7654321

5. 1

6. −$\dfrac{9}{3}$

7. $\sqrt{2}$

8. 5.$\overline{678}$

9. Is $\dfrac{1}{45}$ to the left or the right of 0 on a number line?

10. Is −0.001 to the left or the right of 0 on a number line?

ANSWERS

9

CHECK YOUR ANSWERS

1. Integer, rational, real

2. Rational, real

3. Irrational, real

4. Rational, real

5. Natural, whole, integer, rational, real

6. Integer, rational, real (because $-\dfrac{9}{3}$ can be rewritten as -3)

7. Irrational, real

8. Rational, real

9. To the right

10. To the left

Chapter 2

POSITIVE and NEGATIVE

△ ◇ ○ ◁ ◢ ▢ ▢ ○ △ ▢ ◢ ◇ ○ △ ▢

NUMBERS

POSITIVE NUMBERS are used to describe quantities greater than zero, and **NEGATIVE NUMBERS** are used to describe quantities less than zero. Often, positive and negative numbers are used together to show quantities that have opposite directions or values.

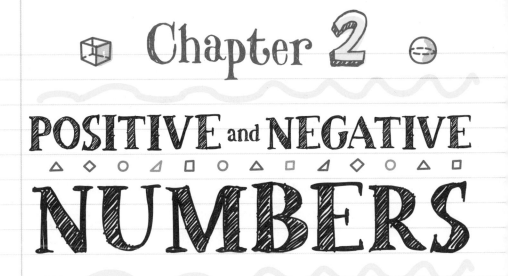

NEGATIVE

NEUTRAL

POSITIVE

All positive numbers just look like regular numbers (+4 and 4 mean the same thing). All negative numbers have a negative sign in front of them, like this: −4.

REMINDER:
All positive and negative whole numbers (without fractions or decimals) are integers.

As we know, all integers can be placed on a number line. If you put all integers on a number line, zero would be at the exact middle because zero is neither positive nor negative.

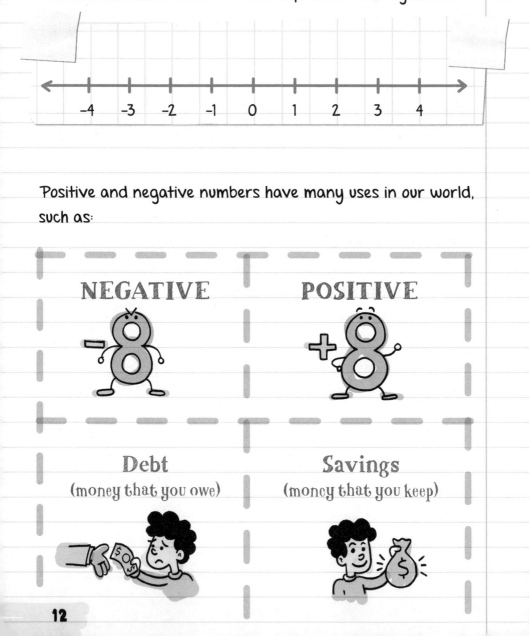

Positive and negative numbers have many uses in our world, such as:

NEGATIVE

POSITIVE

Debt
(money that you owe)

Savings
(money that you keep)

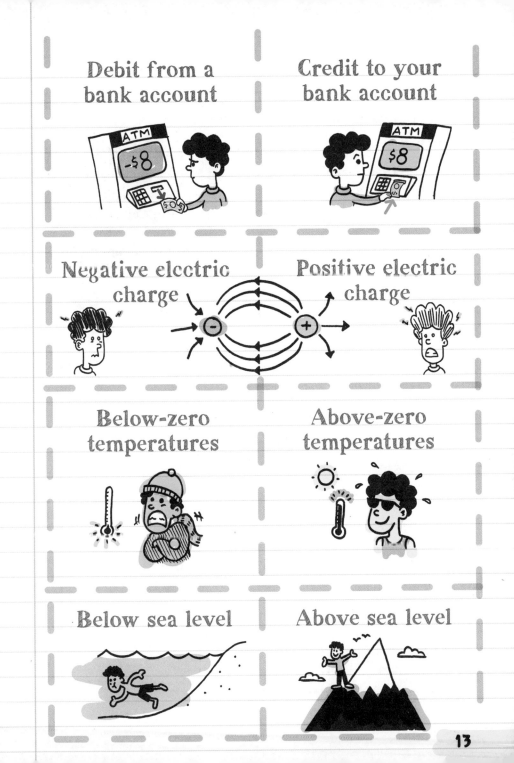

Debit from a bank account

Credit to your bank account

Negative electric charge

Positive electric charge

Below-zero temperatures

Above-zero temperatures

Below sea level

Above sea level

13

On a horizontal number line: Numbers to the left of zero are negative, and numbers to the right of zero are positive. Numbers get larger as they move to the right, and smaller as they move to the left. We draw **ARROWS** on each end of a number line to show that the numbers keep going (all the way to **INFINITY** and negative infinity!).

INFINITY
Something that is endless, unlimited, or without bounds

THE SYMBOL FOR INFINITY IS ∞.

$$\longleftarrow \quad \overset{-5}{|} \quad \overset{-4}{|} \quad \overset{-3}{|} \quad \overset{-2}{|} \quad \overset{-1}{|} \quad \overset{0}{|} \quad \overset{1}{|} \quad \overset{2}{|} \quad \overset{3}{|} \quad \overset{4}{|} \quad \overset{5}{|} \quad \longrightarrow$$

Positive (+) and negative (−) signs are called **OPPOSITES**, so +5 and −5 are also called opposites. They are both the same number of spaces or the same distance from zero on the number line, but on "opposite" sides.

On a vertical number line (such as a thermometer), numbers above zero are positive, and numbers below zero are negative.

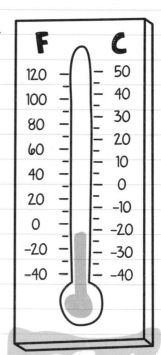

EXAMPLE: What is the opposite of 8?

-8 ←

EXAMPLE: Devin borrows $2 from his friend Stanley. Show the amount that Devin owes as an integer.

-2 ←

The **OPPOSITES OF OPPOSITES PROPERTY** says that the opposite of the opposite of a number is the number itself!

EXAMPLE: What is the opposite of the opposite of -16?

The opposite of -16 is 16. The opposite of 16 is -16.

So the opposite of the opposite of -16 is -16 ← (which is the same as itself).

CHECK YOUR KNOWLEDGE

For **1** through **5**, write the integer that represents each quantity.

1. A submarine is 200 feet below sea level.

2. A helicopter is 525 feet above the landing pad.

3. The temperature is 8 degrees below zero.

4. Griselda owes her friend Matty $17.

5. Matty has $1,250 in his savings account.

6. Show the location of the opposite of 2 on the number line.

```
<----+----+----+----+----+----+---->
    -2   -1    0    1    2
```

7. What is the opposite of -100?

8. Draw a number line that extends from -3 to 3.

9. What is the opposite of the opposite of 79?

10. What is the opposite of the opposite of -47?

ANSWERS

CHECK YOUR ANSWERS

1. -200

2. +525 (or 525)

3. -8

4. -17

5. +1,250 (or 1,250)

6.
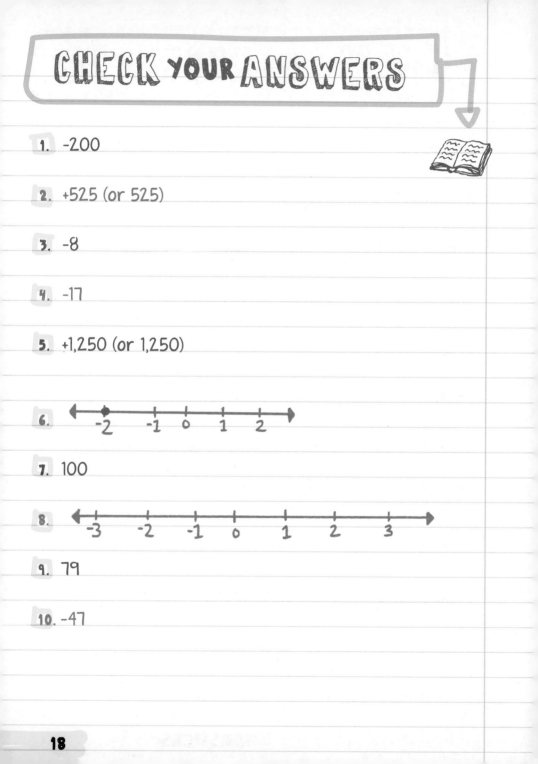

7. 100

8.

9. 79

10. -47

Chapter 3

ABSOLUTE VALUE

The **ABSOLUTE VALUE** of a number is its distance from zero (on the number line). Thus, the absolute value is always positive. We indicate absolute value by putting two bars around the number.

EXAMPLE: $|-4|$

$|-4|$ is read "the absolute value of -4." Because -4 is 4 spaces from zero on the number line, the absolute value is 4.

EXAMPLE: $|9|$

$|9|$ is read "the absolute value of 9." Because 9 is 9 spaces from zero on the number line, the absolute value is 9.

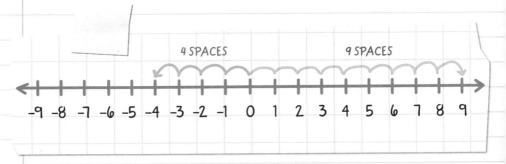

Absolute value bars are also grouping symbols, so you must complete the operation inside them first, then take the absolute value.

EXAMPLE: $|5-3| = |2| = 2$

Sometimes, there are positive or negative symbols outside an absolute value bar. Think: inside, then outside—first take the absolute value of what is inside the bars, then apply the outside symbol.

EXAMPLE: $-|6| = -6$

(The absolute value of 6 is 6. Then we apply the negative symbol on the outside of the absolute value bars to get the answer -6.)

NOW, THIS CHANGES EVERYTHING.

EXAMPLE: $-|-16| = -16$

(The absolute value of -16 is 16. Then we apply the negative symbol on the outside of the absolute value bars to get the answer -16.)

A number in front of the absolute value bars means multiplication (like when we use parentheses).

EXAMPLE: $2|-4|$ (The absolute value of -4 is 4.)

$2 \cdot 4 = 8$ (Once you have the value inside the absolute value bars, you can solve normally.)

Multiplication can be shown in a few different ways—not just with **x**. All of these symbols mean multiply:

$$2 \times 4 = 8$$
$$2 \cdot 4 = 8$$
$$(2)(4) = 8$$
$$2(4) = 8$$

If you use **VARIABLES**, you can put variables next to each other or put a number next to a variable to indicate multiplication, like so:

$$ab = 8$$
$$3x = 15$$

VARIABLE: a letter or symbol used in place of a quantity we don't know yet

CHECK YOUR KNOWLEDGE

Evaluate 1 through 8.

1. $|-19|$

2. $|49|$

3. $|-4.5|$

4. $\left|-\dfrac{1}{5}\right|$

5. $|7-3|$

6. $|1 \cdot 5|$

7. $-|65|$

8. $-|-9|$

9. Johanne has an account balance of -$56.50. What is the absolute value of his debt?

10. A valley is 94 feet below sea level. What is the absolute value of the elevation difference between the valley and the sea level?

ANSWERS ➤   23

CHECK YOUR ANSWERS

1. 19

2. 49

3. 4.5

4. $\dfrac{1}{5}$

5. 4

6. 5

7. −65

8. −9

9. 56.50

10. 94

Chapter 4

FACTORS and GREATEST COMMON FACTOR

FACTORS are integers you multiply together to get another integer.

EXAMPLE: What are the factors of 6?

2 and 3 are factors of 6, because $2 \times 3 = 6$.
1 and 6 are also factors of 6, because $1 \times 6 = 6$.

So, the factors of 6 are: 1, 2, 3, and 6.

When finding the factors of a number, ask yourself, "What numbers can be multiplied together to give me this number?"

> I AM EVERYWHERE!

Every number greater than 1 has at least two factors, because every number can be divided by 1 and itself!

EXAMPLE: What are the factors of 10?
(Think: "What can be multiplied together to give me 10?")

1 · 10
2 · 5

The factors of 10 are 1, 2, 5, and 10.

> Even though 5 x 2 also equals 10, these numbers have already been listed, so we don't need to list them again.

EXAMPLE: Emilio needs to arrange chairs for a drama club meeting at his school. There are 30 students coming. What are the different ways he can arrange the chairs so that each row has the same number of chairs?

1 row of 30 chairs
2 rows of 15 chairs
3 rows of 10 chairs
5 rows of 6 chairs
30 rows of 1 chair

THIS IS THE SAME AS SAYING, "FIND THE FACTORS OF 30."

The factors of 30 are 1, 2, 3, 5, 6, 10, 15, and 30. The product of each pair of numbers is 30.

Here are some shortcuts to find an integer's factors:

⭐ An integer is divisible by 2 if it ends in an even number.

EXAMPLE: 10, 92, 44, 26, and 8 are all divisible by 2 because they end in an even number.

⭐ An integer is divisible by 3 if the sum of its digits is divisible by 3.

EXAMPLE: 42 is divisible by 3 because $4 + 2 = 6$, and 6 is divisible by 3.

⭐ An integer is divisible by 5 if it ends in 0 or 5.

EXAMPLE: 10, 65, and 2,320 are all divisible by 5 because they end in either 0 or 5.

⭐ An integer is divisible by 9 if the sum of the digits is divisible by 9.

EXAMPLE: 297 is divisible by 9 because $2 + 9 + 7 = 18$, and 18 is divisible by 9.

⭐ An integer is divisible by 10 if it ends in 0.

EXAMPLE: 50, 110, and 31,330 are all divisible by 10 because they end in 0.

Prime Numbers

A **PRIME NUMBER** is a number that has only two factors (the number itself and 1). Some examples of prime numbers are 2, 3, 7, and 13.

2 IS ALSO THE ONLY EVEN PRIME NUMBER.

Common Factors

Any factors that are the same for two (or more) numbers are called COMMON FACTORS.

EXAMPLE: What are the common factors of 12 and 18?
The factors for 12 are 1, 2, 3, 4, 6, 12.
The factors for 18 are 1, 2, 3, 6, 9, 18.
The common factors of 12 and 18 (factors that both 12 and 18 have in common) are 1, 2, 3, and 6.

The largest factor that both numbers share is called the **GREATEST COMMON FACTOR**, or **GCF** for short. The GCF of 12 and 18 is 6.

EXAMPLE: What is the GCF of 4 and 10?

Factors of 4 are 1, 2, 4.
Factors of 10 are 1, 2, 5, 10.

So the GCF of 4 and 10 is 2.

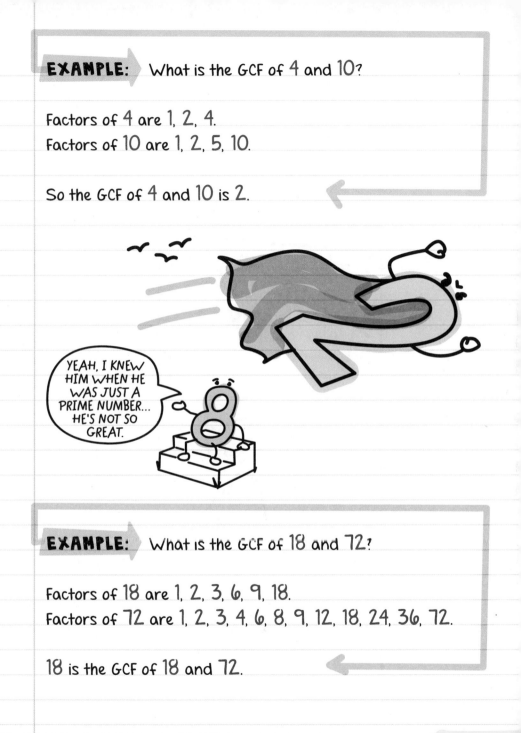

YEAH, I KNEW HIM WHEN HE WAS JUST A PRIME NUMBER... HE'S NOT SO GREAT.

EXAMPLE: What is the GCF of 18 and 72?

Factors of 18 are 1, 2, 3, 6, 9, 18.
Factors of 72 are 1, 2, 3, 4, 6, 8, 9, 12, 18, 24, 36, 72.

18 is the GCF of 18 and 72.

CHECK YOUR KNOWLEDGE

1. What are the factors of 12?

2. What are the factors of 60?

3. Is 348 divisible by 2?

4. Is 786 divisible by 3?

5. Is 936 divisible by 9?

6. Is 3,645,211 divisible by 10?

7. Find the greatest common factor of 6 and 20.

8. Find the greatest common factor of 33 and 74.

9. Find the greatest common factor of 24 and 96.

10. Sara has 8 red-colored pens and 20 yellow-colored pens. She wants to create groups of pens such that there are the same number of red-colored pens and yellow-colored pens in each group and there are no pens left over. What is the greatest number of groups that she can create?

ANSWERS

CHECK YOUR ANSWERS

1. 1, 2, 3, 4, 6, and 12

2. 1, 2, 3, 4, 5, 6, 10, 12, 15, 20, 30, and 60

3. Yes, because 348 ends in an even number.

4. Yes, because 7 + 8 + 6 = 21, and 21 is divisible by 3.

5. Yes, because 9 + 3 + 6 = 18, and 18 is divisible by 9.

6. No, because it does not end in a 0.

7. 2

8. 1

9. 24

10. 4 groups. (Each group has 2 red-colored pens and 5 yellow-colored pens.)

Chapter 5

MULTIPLES AND LEAST COMMON MULTIPLE

When we multiply a number by any whole number (that isn't 0), the product is a **MULTIPLE** of that number. Every number has an infinite list of multiples.

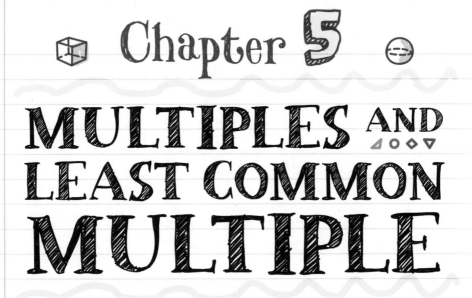

EXAMPLE: What are the multiples of 4?

$4 \times 1 = 4$
$4 \times 2 = 8$
$4 \times 3 = 12$
$4 \times 4 = 16$

and so on...forever!

The multiples of 4 are 4, 8, 12, 16...

Any multiples that are the same for two (or more) numbers are called **COMMON MULTIPLES**.

EXAMPLE: What are the multiples of 2 and 5?
The multiples of 2 are 2, 4, 6, 8, 10, 12, 14, 16, 18, 20...
The multiples of 5 are 5, 10, 15, 20...

Up until this point, 2 and 5 have the multiples 10 and 20 in common.

What is the smallest multiple that both 2 and 5 have in common? The smallest multiple is 10. We call this the **LEAST COMMON MULTIPLE**, or **LCM**.

To find the LCM of two or more numbers, list the multiples of each number in order from least to greatest until you find the first multiple they both have in common.

EXAMPLE: Find the LCM of 9 and 11.
The multiples of 9 are 9, 18, 27, 36, 45, 54, 63, 72, 81, 99, 108...
The multiples of 11 are 11, 22, 33, 44, 55, 66, 77, 88, 99, 110...

99 is the first multiple 9 and 11 have in common, so the LCM of 9 and 11 is 99.

Sometimes, it's easier to start with the bigger number. Instead of listing all of the multiples of 9 first, start with the multiples of 11, and ask yourself, "Which of these numbers is divisible by 9?"

EXAMPLE: Susie signs up to volunteer at the animal shelter every 6 days. Luisa signs up to volunteer at the shelter every 5 days. If they both sign up to volunteer on the same day, when is the first day that Susie and Luisa will work together?

THIS IS THE SAME AS SAYING, "FIND THE LCM FOR 5 AND 6."

Susie will work on the following days: 6th, 12th, 18th, 24th, and 30th...

30 is the first number divisible by 5, so the LCM is 30.

The first day that Susie and Luisa will work together is on the 30th day.

35

1. List the first five multiples of 3.

2. List the first five multiples of 12.

3. Find the LCM of 5 and 7.

4. Find the LCM of 10 and 11.

5. Find the LCM of 4 and 6.

6. Find the LCM of 12 and 15.

7. Find the LCM of 18 and 36.

8. Kirk goes to the gym every 3 days. Deshawn goes to the gym every 4 days. If they join the gym on the same day, when is the first day that they'll be at the gym together?

9. Betty and Jane have the same number of coins. Betty sorts her coins in groups of 6, with no coins left over. Jane sorts her coins in groups of 8, with no coins left over. What is the least possible amount of coins that each of them has?

10. Bob makes flower bouquets. Each bouquet must have 3 white flowers and 7 red flowers. If Bob uses all of his white flowers and all of his red flowers, what is the least possible number of bouquets that Bob could make?

CHECK YOUR ANSWERS

1. 3, 6, 9, 12, 15

2. 12, 24, 36, 48, 60

3. 35

4. 110

5. 12

6. 60

7. 36

8. On the 12th day

9. 24 coins

10. 21 bouquets

Chapter 6

FRACTION BASICS:

□ ◇ ○ ◁ ◻ ◇ ○ △ ◻ ◇

TYPES OF FRACTIONS, AND ADDING AND SUBTRACTING FRACTIONS

FRACTION BASICS

Fractions are real numbers that represent a part of a whole. A fraction bar separates the part from the whole like so:

$$\frac{\text{PART}}{\text{WHOLE}}$$

The "part" is the **NUMERATOR**, and the "whole" is the **DENOMINATOR**.

For example, suppose you cut a whole pizza into 6 pieces and eat 5 of the pieces. The "part" you have eaten is 5, and the "whole" you started with is 6. Therefore, the amount you ate is $\frac{5}{6}$ of the pizza.

If 3 people shared a pizza cut into 8 slices, each person would get 2 pieces, and 2 pieces would be left over. These left over two are called the **REMAINDER**.

REMAINDER
part, quantity, or number left over after division

There are 3 types of fractions:

1. **Proper fractions:** The numerator is smaller than the denominator.

EXAMPLES: $\dfrac{5}{6}, \dfrac{2}{3}, \dfrac{1}{1,000}, -\dfrac{4}{27}$

2. **Improper fractions:** The numerator is bigger than, or equal to, the denominator.

EXAMPLES: $\dfrac{10}{3}, \dfrac{8}{8}, -\dfrac{25}{5}$

3. **Mixed numbers:** There is a whole number and a fraction.

EXAMPLES: $2\dfrac{2}{3}, 18\dfrac{1}{8}, -9\dfrac{5}{7}$

CONVERTING MIXED NUMBERS and IMPROPER FRACTIONS

Remember! To CHANGE A MIXED NUMBER TO AN IMPROPER FRACTION, you will first multiply and then add.

EXAMPLE: To change the mixed number $3\frac{1}{5}$ to an improper fraction, we first calculate $3 \times 5 = 15$ and then $+ 1$, so that the improper fraction is $\frac{16}{5}$.

To CHANGE AN IMPROPER FRACTION TO A MIXED NUMBER, you divide the numerator by the denominator. Ask yourself: "How many times does the denominator go into the numerator? What remainder do I have left over?"

EXAMPLE: To change the improper fraction $\frac{23}{8}$ to a mixed number, we calculate:

$23 \div 8 = 2\,R7$, so the mixed number is $2\frac{7}{8}$.

"R" STANDS FOR REMAINDER.

> If you get an answer that is an improper fraction, always convert it into a mixed number for your final answer. Some teachers take off points if you don't!

SIMPLIFYING FRACTIONS

Sometimes, the numerator and denominator will have common factors. You can **SIMPLIFY** them by dividing the numerator and the denominator by the greatest common factor. Some teachers call this "**CROSS-REDUCING**," "simplifying," or "**CANCELING**." Whatever you call it, it's a shortcut!

EXAMPLE: $\frac{6}{10}$ can be simplified to $\frac{3}{5}$ because 2 is the GCF of 6 and 10.

$$\frac{6}{10} = \frac{6 \div 2}{10 \div 2} = \frac{3}{5}$$

EXAMPLE: $\frac{20}{8}$ can be simplified to $\frac{5}{2}$ because the GCF of 20 and 8 is 4.

$$\frac{20}{8} = \frac{20 \div 4}{8 \div 4} = \frac{5}{2}$$

> Most teachers want you to simplify your answers if possible, so get in the habit!

ADDING FRACTIONS

If we want to add fractions together, the denominators must be the same.

EXAMPLE: $\frac{1}{5} + \frac{3}{5} = \frac{4}{5}$

In the sum, the denominator stays the same and you add the numerator. For example, you have two identical candy bars, and you cut each into 5 pieces. You give your little brother 1 piece from the first candy bar, and you give your sister 2 pieces from the second candy bar. How much of a whole candy bar did you give away?

You gave 1 of the 5 pieces of the first candy bar to your brother = $\frac{1}{5}$.

You gave 2 of the 5 pieces of the second candy bar to your sister = $\frac{2}{5}$.

Now, add them together: $\frac{1}{5} + \frac{2}{5} = \frac{3}{5}$ (The denominator stays the same, and you add the numerators.)

COOL DENOMINATOR!   PUT IT UP THERE!

Because both candy bars are the same size and are cut into the same number of pieces, you keep the denominator as 5 and add the numerators to get the answer of $\frac{3}{5}$.

> **YOU CAN REMEMBER WITH THIS RHYME:**
> Denominator's the same—keep it in the game!
> Add up the top, simplify, and stop!

MATH IS DELICIOUS.

44

SUBTRACTING FRACTIONS

The same idea applies to subtraction—the denominators must be the same (both wholes must be the same size) in order to subtract.

EXAMPLE: $\dfrac{8}{9} - \dfrac{7}{9} = \dfrac{1}{9}$ (The denominator stays the same, and you subtract the numerators.)

ADDING and SUBTRACTING FRACTIONS with DIFFERENT DENOMINATORS

In order to add or subtract fractions with different denominators, you just have to make their denominators the same! We can do that by finding the LCM of the denominators.

How to add or subtract fractions with unlike denominators:

1. Find the LCM of both denominators. (Some teachers call this the **LEAST COMMON DENOMINATOR**, or **LCD** for short.)

EXAMPLE: $\dfrac{2}{5} + \dfrac{1}{4}$

The LCM of 5 and 4 is 20.

2. Convert the numerators. (Some teachers call this **RENAMING** the numerators.)

$$\frac{2 \cdot 4}{5 \cdot 4} = \frac{8}{20}$$

5 times what number equals 20? 4. So, you must also multiply the numerator by 4 to convert the numerator.

$$\frac{1 \cdot 5}{4 \cdot 5} = \frac{5}{20}$$

4 times what number equals 20? 5. So, you must also multiply the numerator by 5 to convert the numerator.

3. Add or subtract, and simplify if necessary.

$$\frac{2}{5} + \frac{1}{4} = \frac{8}{20} + \frac{5}{20} = \frac{13}{20}$$

EXAMPLE: $\dfrac{4}{7} - \dfrac{1}{3}$

The LCM of 7 and 3 is 21.

$$\frac{4 \times 3}{7 \times 3} = \frac{12}{21}$$

$$\frac{1 \times 7}{3 \times 7} = \frac{7}{21}$$

$$\frac{4}{7} - \frac{1}{3} = \frac{12}{21} - \frac{7}{21} = \frac{5}{21}$$

CHECK YOUR KNOWLEDGE

Calculate. Simplify each answer if possible.

1. $\dfrac{1}{8} + \dfrac{2}{8}$

2. $\dfrac{7}{11} - \dfrac{4}{11}$

3. $\dfrac{3}{5} + \dfrac{3}{5}$

4. $\dfrac{9}{10} - \dfrac{4}{10}$

5. $\dfrac{13}{15} - \dfrac{4}{15}$

6. $\dfrac{3}{5} - \dfrac{1}{2}$

7. $\dfrac{4}{5} - \dfrac{1}{10}$

8. $\dfrac{8}{9} - \dfrac{3}{6}$

9. $\dfrac{1}{2} - \dfrac{3}{8}$

10. $\dfrac{5}{6} - \dfrac{3}{8}$

ANSWERS

CHECK YOUR ANSWERS

1. $\dfrac{3}{8}$

2. $\dfrac{3}{11}$

3. $\dfrac{6}{5} = 1\dfrac{1}{5}$

4. $\dfrac{5}{10} = \dfrac{1}{2}$

5. $\dfrac{9}{15} = \dfrac{3}{5}$

6. $\dfrac{1}{10}$

7. $\dfrac{7}{10}$

8. $\dfrac{7}{18}$

9. $\dfrac{1}{8}$

10. $\dfrac{11}{24}$

Chapter 7

MULTIPLYING AND DIVIDING FRACTIONS

MULTIPLYING FRACTIONS

Unlike when you add and subtract fractions, the denominators do not have to be the same. To multiply fractions, first multiply the numerators. Then multiply the denominators. Simplify your answer if necessary. That's it!

EXAMPLE: $\dfrac{3}{5} \times \dfrac{4}{7} = \dfrac{12}{35}$

Sometimes, when multiplying fractions, you might see that a numerator and a denominator will have common factors. You can simplify them before multiplying in the same way that we simplify fractions. Some teachers call this "**CROSS-REDUCING**" or "**CANCELING**." Whatever you call it, it's a shortcut!

EXAMPLE: $\dfrac{1}{\cancel{4}_{1}} \cdot \dfrac{\cancel{8}^{2}}{9} = \dfrac{2}{9}$ (The GCF of 8 and 4 is 4.)

EXAMPLE: A recipe calls for $\frac{4}{5}$ cup of chocolate milk, but you want to cut the recipe in half. How much chocolate milk do you need?

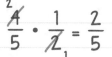

$$\frac{\overset{2}{\cancel{4}}}{5} \cdot \frac{1}{\underset{1}{\cancel{2}}} = \frac{2}{5}$$

DIVIDING FRACTIONS

To divide fractions,
follow these steps:

1. Flip the second fraction to make its **RECIPROCAL**.

2. Change the division sign to multiplication.

3. Multiply.

EXAMPLE: $\frac{3}{5} \div \frac{8}{9} = \frac{3}{5} \cdot \frac{9}{8} = \frac{27}{40}$

A **RECIPROCAL** of a number is another number that, when multiplied together, their product is **1**. In plain English—any number multiplied by its reciprocal equals **1**.

$$\frac{8}{1} \times \frac{1}{8} = 1$$

$$\frac{2}{3} \times \frac{3}{2} = 1$$

To find the reciprocal, flip the fraction.

Don't forget that when you are multiplying or dividing mixed numbers, you must convert them to improper fractions first!

EXAMPLE: $2\frac{1}{3} \div 1\frac{1}{4}$

$$\frac{7}{3} \div \frac{5}{4} = \frac{7}{3} \times \frac{4}{5} = \frac{28}{15} = 1\frac{13}{15}$$

1. $\dfrac{3}{4} \cdot \dfrac{1}{2}$

2. $\dfrac{7}{10} \cdot 1\dfrac{1}{3}$

3. $\dfrac{4}{5} \cdot \dfrac{1}{8}$

4. A machine pumps $4\dfrac{1}{2}$ gallons of water every hour. How many gallons of water does it pump after $2\dfrac{2}{3}$ hours?

5. Billy jogs $\dfrac{4}{5}$ kilometer every minute. How many kilometers does he jog after $6\dfrac{1}{8}$ minutes?

6. $\dfrac{5}{7} \div \dfrac{1}{2}$

7. $\dfrac{7}{8} \div \dfrac{2}{9}$

8. $9\dfrac{1}{2} \div 3\dfrac{1}{5}$

9. How many $\dfrac{3}{4}$-ounce spoonfuls of sugar are in a $5\dfrac{1}{2}$-ounce bowl?

10. How much chocolate will each person get if 3 people share $\dfrac{4}{5}$ pound of chocolate equally?

ANSWERS

CHECK YOUR ANSWERS

1. $\dfrac{3}{8}$

2. $\dfrac{14}{15}$

3. $\dfrac{1}{10}$

4. 12 gallons

5. $4\dfrac{9}{10}$ kilometers

6. $1\dfrac{3}{7}$

7. $3\dfrac{15}{16}$

8. $2\dfrac{31}{32}$

9. $7\dfrac{1}{3}$ spoonfuls

10. $\dfrac{4}{15}$ pound

WE NEED **HALF** OF THAT CHOCOLATE MILK.

NO PROBLEM.

Chapter 8

ADDING AND SUBTRACTING DECIMALS

When adding and subtracting numbers with decimals, line the decimal points up exactly on top of each other. The digits to the left of the decimal point (such as the ones, tens, and hundreds) should all line up with each other; the digits to the right of the decimal point (such as the tenths, hundredths, and thousandths) should also be aligned. Then you can add as you normally would and bring the decimal point straight down.

EXAMPLE: Find the sum of 6.45 and 23.34.

$$
\begin{array}{r}
6.45 \\
+23.34 \\
\hline
29.79
\end{array}
$$

Any time you add a whole number and a decimal, include the "invisible" decimal point to the right of the whole number.

> When adding money, everything to the left of the decimal point represents whole dollars, and everything to the right represents cents, or parts of a dollar.

Do the same for subtraction—align the decimal points of each number, subtract, and drop down the decimal point.

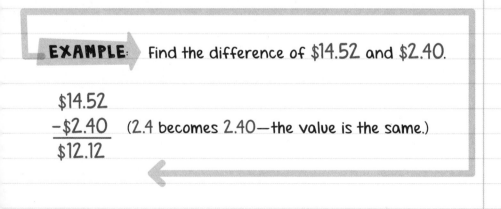

EXAMPLE: Find the difference of $14.52 and $2.40.

```
 $14.52
-$2.40     (2.4 becomes 2.40—the value is the same.)
 $12.12
```

CHECK YOUR KNOWLEDGE

1. $5.89 + $9.23

2. 18.1876 + 4.3215

3. 6 + 84.32

4. 1,234.56 + 8,453.234

5. 8.573 + 2.2 + 17.01

6. $67.85 − $25.15

7. 100 − 6.781

8. 99.09 − 98.29

9. 14.327.81 − 2.6387

10. Justin goes to the mall with $120. He spends $54.67 on clothes, $13.49 on school supplies, and $8.14 on lunch. How much does he have left?

ANSWERS

CHECK YOUR ANSWERS

1. $15.12

2. 22.5091

3. 90.32

4. 9,687.794

5. 27.783

6. $42.70

7. 93.219

8. 0.8

9. 14,325.1718

10. $43.70

Chapter 9

MULTIPLYING
△○◇▽□○◇□△○◇□○△
DECIMALS

When multiplying decimals, you don't need to line up the decimals. In fact, you don't have to think about the decimal point until the very end.

Steps for multiplying decimals:

1. Multiply the numbers as though they were whole numbers.

2. Include the decimal point in your answer—the number of decimal places in the answer is the same as the total number of digits to the right of the decimal point in each of the factors.

INTEGERS YOU ARE MULTIPLYING

EXAMPLE: 4.24 x 2.1

$$
\begin{array}{r}
4.24 \\
\times 2.1 \\
\hline
424 \\
848 \\
\hline
8904
\end{array}
$$

YOU DON'T
NEED TO LINE
← UP DECIMALS!

The total number of decimal places in 4.24 and 2.1 is 3, so the answer is 8.904.

Let's try it again:

EXAMPLE: Bruce jogs 1.2 kilometers per minute. If he jogs for 5.8 minutes, how far does he jog?

$$
\begin{array}{r}
1.2 \\
\times 5.8 \\
\hline
96 \\
60 \\
\hline
696
\end{array}
$$

The total number of decimal places in 1.2 and 5.8 is 2, so the answer is 6.96 kilometers.

When counting decimal places, don't be fooled by zeros at the end—they don't count.

0.30 ← CAN'T BE COUNTED

0.30 = 0.3 (only 1 decimal point)

1. 5.6×6.41

2. $(3.55)(4.82)$

3. $0.350 \cdot 0.40$

4. $(9.8710)(3.44)$

5. $(1.003)(2.4)$

6. 310×0.0002

7. 0.003×0.015

8. The price of fabric is \$7.60 per meter. Lance bought 5.5 meters of fabric. What was the total cost?

9. Each centimeter on a map represents 3.2 meters. How many meters do 5.04 centimenters represent?

10. A gallon of gas costs \$2.16. Rob buys 13.5 gallons of gas. How much did he pay?

ANSWERS

CHECK YOUR ANSWERS

1. 35.896

2. 17.111

3. 0.14

4. 33.95624

5. 2.4072

6. 0.062

7. 0.000045

8. $41.80

9. 16.128 meters

10. $29.16

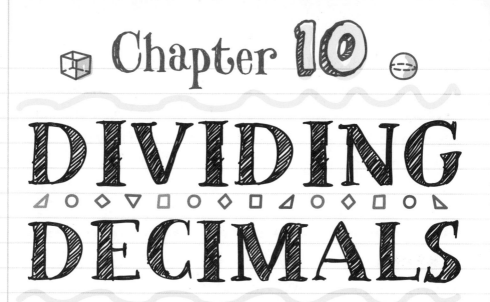

Chapter 10

DIVIDING
△ ○ ◇ ▽ □ ○ ◇ □ △ ○ ◇ □ ○ ▷
DECIMALS

You can divide decimals easily by simply making them into whole numbers. You do that by multiplying both the **DIVIDEND** and **DIVISOR** by the same power of ten. Because the new numbers are proportional to the original numbers, the answer is the same!   CORRESPONDING IN SIZE

EXAMPLE: $2.5 \div 0.05 = (2.5 \times 100) \div (0.05 \times 100)$
$= 250 \div 5 = 50$

The **DIVIDEND** is the number that is being divided.
The **DIVISOR** is the number that "goes into" the dividend.
The answer to a division problem is called the **QUOTIENT**.

$\dfrac{\text{dividend}}{\text{divisor}} = \text{quotient}$, OR dividend ÷ divisor = quotient,

$$\text{OR divisor} \overline{)\text{dividend}}^{\text{quotient}}$$

Multiply both decimal numbers by 100, because the decimal needs to move two places in order for both the dividend and divisor to become whole numbers. Remember, every time you multiply by another power of ten, the decimal moves one more space to the right!

Let's try another example:

EXAMPLE: A car drives 21.6 miles in 2.7 hours. How many miles does it travel each hour?

$$\frac{21.6}{2.7} = \frac{21.6 \times 10}{2.7 \times 10} = \frac{216}{27} = 8 \text{ miles}$$

Don't be thrown off if you see decimals being divided like this:

$$2.7\overline{)21.6}$$

The process is the same—multiply both numbers by 10 in order for both terms to become whole numbers:

$$2.7\overline{)21.6} = 27\overline{)216}^{\,8 \text{ miles}}$$

$\times 10 \quad \times 10$

1. $7.5 \div 2.5$

2. $18.4 \div 4.6$

3. $102.84 \div 0.2$

4. $1,250 \div 0.05$

5. $\dfrac{3.98}{0.4}$

6. $\dfrac{0.27}{0.4}$

7. $\dfrac{1.5}{3.75}$

8. $\dfrac{1.054}{0.02}$

9. A machine pumps 8.4 gallons of water every 3.2 minutes. How many gallons does the machine pump each minute?

10. Will swims a total of 45.6 laps in 2.85 hours. How many laps does he swim each hour?

ANSWERS ➤

CHECK YOUR ANSWERS

1. 3

2. 4

3. 514.2

4. 25,000

5. 9.95

6. 0.675

7. 0.4

8. 52.7

9. 2.625 gallons

10. 16 laps

Chapter 11

ADDING POSITIVE AND NEGATIVE NUMBERS

To add positive and negative numbers, you can use a number line or use absolute value.

TECHNIQUE #1: USE a NUMBER LINE

Draw a number line and begin at **ZERO**.

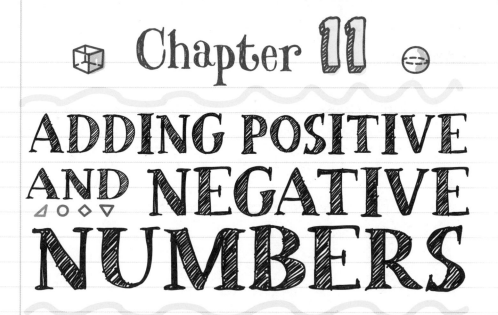

For a **NEGATIVE** (-) number, move that many spaces to the left.

For a **POSITIVE** (+) number, move that many spaces to the right.

Wherever you end up is the answer!

EXAMPLE: -5 + 4

Begin at zero. Because -5 is negative, move 5 spaces to the left.

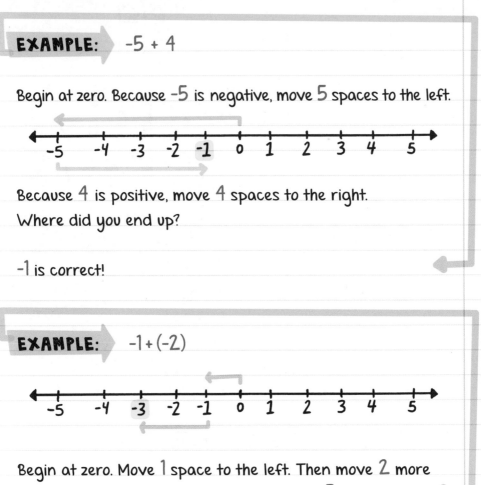

Because 4 is positive, move 4 spaces to the right.
Where did you end up?

-1 is correct!

EXAMPLE: -1 + (-2)

Begin at zero. Move 1 space to the left. Then move 2 more
spaces to the left. Where did you end up? -3

> The sum of a number and its opposite always equals zero.
> For example, 4 + -4 = 0. Think about it like this: if you take
> four steps forward, then four steps backward, you end up
> exactly where you began, so you've moved zero spaces!

TECHNIQUE #2:
USE ABSOLUTE VALUE

If you need to add larger numbers, you probably don't want to draw a number line. So, look at the signs and decide what to do:

> If the signs of the numbers you are adding are the same, they are alike (they go in the same direction), so you can add those two numbers together and keep their sign.

EXAMPLE: $-1 + (-2)$

Both -1 and -2 are negative, so they are alike. We add them together and keep their sign to get -3.

If the signs of the numbers you are adding are different, subtract the absolute value of each of the two numbers. Which number had a higher absolute value? The answer will have the same sign that this number had at the beginning.

To remember all this, try singing this to the tune of "Row, Row, Row Your Boat."

*Same sign: keep and add!
Different sign: subtract!
Keep the sign of the
larger amount,
then you'll be exact!*

EXAMPLE: -10 + 4

-10 and 4 have different signs, so subtract the absolute value, like so: $|-10| - |4| = 10 - 4 = 6$.

-10 had the higher absolute value, so the answer is also negative: -6.

EXAMPLE: -35 + 100

-35 + 100 = 65   (Different sign, so we have to subtract! +100 had the higher absolute value, so the answer is also positive.)

EXAMPLE: The temperature in Wisconsin was -8 degrees Fahrenheit in the morning. By noon, it had risen by 22 degrees Fahrenheit. What was the temperature at noon? Use integers to solve.

-8 + 22 = 14

The temperature at noon was 14 degrees Fahrenheit.

1. $-8 + 8$

2. $-22 + -1$

3. $-14 + 19$

4. $28 + (-13)$

5. $-12 + 3 + -8$

6. $-54 + -113$

7. $-546 + 233$

8. $1,256 + (-4,450)$

9. It's 0 degrees outside at midnight. The temperature of the air drops 20 degrees in the morning hours, then gains 3 degrees as soon as the sun comes up. What is the temperature after the sun comes up?

10. Denise owes her friend Jessica $25. She pays her back $17. How much does she still owe?

ANSWERS

69

CHECK YOUR ANSWERS

1. 0

2. -23

3. 5

4. 15

5. -17

6. -167

7. -313

8. -3,194

9. -17 degrees

10. She owes $8 (-$8).

Chapter 12

SUBTRACTING POSITIVE AND NEGATIVE NUMBERS

NEXT UP: learning to subtract positive and negative numbers. We already know that subtraction and addition are "opposites" of each other. So, we can use this shortcut:

Change a subtraction problem to an addition problem by using the additive inverse, or opposite!

EXAMPLE: $5 - 4$

The additive inverse of 4 is -4, which we can change to an addition problem, like so: $5 - 4 = 5 + (-4)$.

$5 + (-4) = 1$

EXAMPLE: 7 – 10

The additive inverse of 10 is –10.

7 – 10 = 7 + (–10)

7 + (–10) = –3

EXAMPLE: 3 – (–1)

The additive inverse of –1 is 1.

3 – (–1) = 3 + 1 = 4

3 + 1 = 4

EXAMPLE: A bird is flying 42 meters above sea level. A fish is swimming 12 meters below sea level. How many meters apart are the bird and the fish?

The bird's height is 42.

The fish's height is –12.

To find the difference, we should subtract:

42 – (–12) = 42 + 12 = 54

Answer: They are 54 meters apart.

EXAMPLE: –3 – 14 = –3 + (–14) = –17

EXAMPLE: –4 – (–9) + 8 = –4 + 9 + 8 = 13

1. $5 - (-3)$

2. $16 - (-6)$

3. $-3 - 9$

4. $-8 - 31$

5. $-14 - (-6)$

6. $-100 - (-101)$

7. $11 - 17$

8. $84 - 183$

9. $-12 - (-2) + 10$

10. The temperature at 2:00 p.m. is 27 degrees. At 2:00 a.m., the temperature has fallen to -4 degrees. What is the difference in temperature from 2:00 p.m. to 2:00 a.m.?

ANSWERS

CHECK YOUR ANSWERS

1. 8

2. 22

3. -12

4. -39

5. -8

6. 1

7. -6

8. -99

9. 0

10. 31 degrees

Chapter 13

MULTIPLYING AND DIVIDING POSITIVE AND NEGATIVE NUMBERS

Multiply or divide the numbers, then count the number of negative signs.

If there are an **ODD NUMBER** of negative numbers, the answer is **NEGATIVE.**

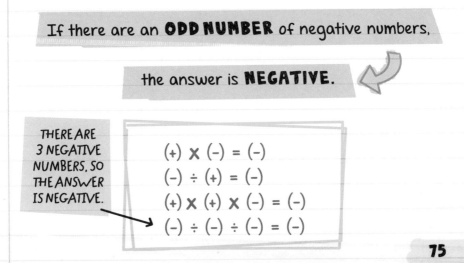

THERE ARE 3 NEGATIVE NUMBERS, SO THE ANSWER IS NEGATIVE.

$$(+) \times (-) = (-)$$
$$(-) \div (+) = (-)$$
$$(+) \times (+) \times (-) = (-)$$
$$(-) \div (-) \div (-) = (-)$$

If there are an **EVEN NUMBER** of negative numbers,

the answer is **POSITIVE**.

THERE ARE 2 NEGATIVE NUMBERS, SO THE ANSWER IS POSITIVE.

$(-) \times (-) = (+)$
$(-) \div (-) = (+)$
$(-) \times (+) \times (-) = (+)$

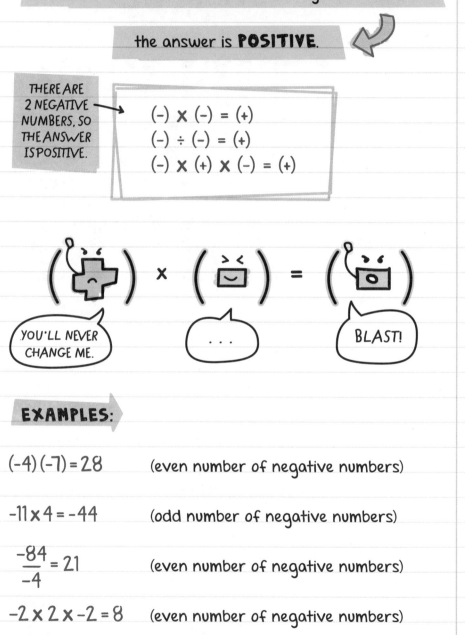

YOU'LL NEVER CHANGE ME.

. . .

BLAST!

EXAMPLES:

$(-4)(-7) = 28$ (even number of negative numbers)

$-11 \times 4 = -44$ (odd number of negative numbers)

$\dfrac{-84}{-4} = 21$ (even number of negative numbers)

$-2 \times 2 \times -2 = 8$ (even number of negative numbers)

1. $(-2)(-8)$

2. $9 \cdot -14$

3. -20×-18

4. 100×-12

5. Joe drops a pebble into the sea. The pebble drops 2 inches every second. How many inches below sea level does it drop after 6 seconds?

6. $66 \div (-3)$

7. $-119 \div -119$

8. $\dfrac{27}{-3}$

9. $\dfrac{-9}{3} \div -1$

10. Last week, Sal's business lost a total of $126. If he lost the same amount of money on each of the 7 days, how much money did he lose each day?

ANSWERS

77

CHECK YOUR ANSWERS

1. 16

2. −126

3. 360

4. −1,200

5. 12 inches (or −12)

6. −22

7. 1

8. −9

9. 3

10. He lost $18 each day (or −$18).

Chapter 14

INEQUALITIES

An inequality is a mathematical sentence that is used to compare quantities and contains one of the following signs:

$$a < b \text{ or "a is less than b"}$$
$$a > b \text{ or "a is greater than b"}$$
$$a \neq b \text{ or "a is not equal to b"}$$

OPEN SIDE > VERTEX SIDE

When using an inequality sign to compare two amounts, place the sign in between the numbers with the "open" side toward the greater amount and the "vertex" side toward the lesser amount.

You can use a number line to compare quantities. Numbers get smaller the farther you go to the left, and larger the farther you go to the right. Whichever number is farther to the left is "less than" the number on its right.

> THE MATH MONSTER ALWAYS WANTS TO EAT THE GREATER AMOUNT!

EXAMPLE: Compare -2 and 4.

-2 is farther to the left than 4, so -2 < 4.

We can also reverse this expression
and say that 4 > -2.

-2 < 4 is the same as 4 > -2.

Remember that any negative number is always less
than zero, and any positive number is always greater
than zero and all negative numbers.

Just like when we add or subtract fractions with different denominators, we have to make the denominators the same when comparing fractions.

EXAMPLE: Compare $-\dfrac{1}{2}$ and $-\dfrac{1}{3}$.

The LCM of 2 and 3 is 6.

$$-\frac{1 \cdot 3}{2 \cdot 3} = -\frac{3}{6}$$

$$-\frac{1 \cdot 2}{3 \cdot 2} = -\frac{2}{6}$$

Compare $-\dfrac{3}{6}$ and $-\dfrac{2}{6}$.

$-\dfrac{3}{6} < -\dfrac{2}{6}$ therefore $-\dfrac{1}{2} < -\dfrac{1}{3}$

There are two other inequality symbols you should know:

> $a \leq b$ or "a is less than or equal to b"
>
> $a \geq b$ or "a is greater than or equal to b"

EXAMPLE: $x \leq 3$, which means x can equal any number less than or equal to 3.

3 and any number to the left of 3 will make this number sentence true. The value of x could be 3, 2, 1, 0, -1, and so on. But x could not be 4, 5, 6, and so on.

EXAMPLE: $x \geq -\dfrac{1}{2}$

$-\dfrac{1}{2}$ and any number to the right of $-\dfrac{1}{2}$ will make this sentence true. The value of x could be 0, $\dfrac{1}{2}$, 1, and so on. But x could not be -1, $-1\dfrac{1}{2}$, and so on.

CHECK YOUR KNOWLEDGE

1. Compare -12 and 8.

2. Compare -14 and -15.

3. Compare 0 and -8.

4. Compare 0.025 and 0.026.

5. Compare $\dfrac{2}{5}$ and $\dfrac{4}{5}$.

6. Compare $-\dfrac{2}{3}$ and $-\dfrac{1}{2}$.

7. If $y \leq -4$, list 3 values that y could be.

8. If $m \geq 0$, list 3 values that m could NOT be.

9. Which is warmer: $-5°C$ or $-8°C$?

10. Fill in the blanks: Whichever number is farther to the left on a number line is ____ ____ the number on its right.

ANSWERS 83

CHECK YOUR ANSWERS

1. -12 < 8 or 8 > -12

2. -14 > -15 or -15 < -14

3. 0 > -8 or -8 < 0

4. 0.025 < 0.026 or 0.026 > 0.025

5. $\dfrac{4}{5} > \dfrac{2}{5}$

6. $-\dfrac{1}{2} > -\dfrac{2}{3}$

7. -4 and/or any number less than -4, such as -5, -6, etc.

8. Any number less than 0, such as -1, -2, -3, etc.

9. -5°C

10. Less than

#7 and #8 have more than one correct answer.

Unit 2

Ratios, Proportions, and Percents

Chapter 15

RATIOS

A **RATIO** is a comparison of two quantities. For example, you might use a ratio to compare the number of students who have cell phones to the number of students who don't have cell phones. A ratio can be written a few different ways.

The ratio 3 to 2 can be written:

$3:2$ or $\dfrac{3}{2}$ or 3 to 2

Use "a" to represent the first quantity and "b" to represent the second quantity. The ratio a to b can be written:

$a:b$ or $\dfrac{a}{b}$ or a to b

> A fraction can also be a ratio.

EXAMPLES: Five students were asked if they have a cell phone. Four said yes and one said no. What is the ratio of students who do not have cell phones to students who do?

1:4 or $\frac{1}{4}$ or 1 to 4.   (Another way to say this is, "For every 1 student who does not have a cell phone, there are 4 students who do have a cell phone.")

What is the ratio of students who have cell phones to total number of students asked?

4:5 or $\frac{4}{5}$ or 4 to 5.

EXAMPLE: Julio opens a small bag of jelly beans and counts them. He counts 10 total. Among those 10, there are 2 green jelly beans and 4 yellow jelly beans. What is the ratio of green jelly beans to yellow jelly beans? And what is the ratio of green jelly beans to total number of jelly beans?

The ratio of green jelly beans to yellow jelly beans in fraction form is $\frac{2}{4}$. That can be simplified to $\frac{1}{2}$.

So, for every 1 green jelly bean, there are 2 yellow jelly beans.

The ratio of green jelly beans to the total amount is $\frac{2}{10}$.

That can be simplified to $\frac{1}{5}$.

So, 1 out of every 5 jelly beans in the bag is green.

Just like you simplify fractions,
you can also simplify ratios!

Ratios are often used to make **SCALE DRAWINGS**—
a drawing that is similar to an actual object
or place but bigger or smaller.

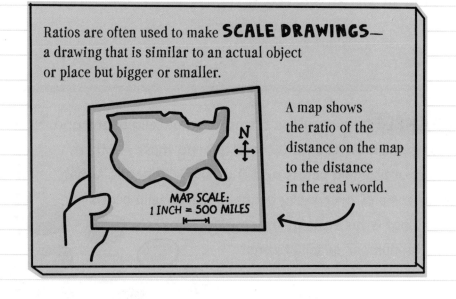

MAP SCALE:
1 INCH = 500 MILES

A map shows
the ratio of the
distance on the map
to the distance
in the real world.

CHECK YOUR KNOWLEDGE

For **1** through **6**, write each ratio as a fraction. Simplify if possible.

1. 2:9

2. 42:52

3. 5 to 30

4. For every 100 apples, 22 apples are rotten.

5. 16 black cars to every 2 red cars

6. 19:37

For **7** through **10**, write a ratio in the format of $a:b$ to describe each situation.

7. Of the 27 people surveyed, 14 live in apartment buildings.

8. In the sixth grade, there are 8 girls to every 10 boys.

9. Exactly 84 out of every 100 homes have a computer.

10. Lucinda bought school supplies for class. She bought 8 pens, 12 pencils, and 4 highlighters. What was the ratio of pens to total items?

ANSWERS

1. $\dfrac{2}{9}$

2. $\dfrac{21}{26}$

3. $\dfrac{1}{6}$

4. $\dfrac{11}{50}$

5. $\dfrac{8}{1}$

6. $\dfrac{19}{37}$

7. 14:27

8. 8:10 or 4:5

9. 21:25

10. 8:24 or 1:3

Chapter 16

UNIT RATE
AND UNIT PRICE

A **RATE** is a special kind of ratio where the two amounts being compared have different units. For example, you might use rate to compare 3 cups of flour to 2 teaspoons of sugar. The units (cups and teaspoons) are different.

A **UNIT RATE** is a rate that has 1 as its denominator. To find a unit rate, set up a ratio as a fraction and then divide the numerator by the denominator.

EXAMPLE: A car can travel 300 miles on 15 gallons of gasoline. What is the unit rate per gallon of gasoline?

← MEANS DIVIDE

$$300 \text{ miles} : 15 \text{ gallons} = \frac{300 \text{ miles}}{15 \text{ gallons}} = 20 \text{ miles per gallon}$$

The unit rate is 20 miles per gallon.

This means the car can travel 20 miles on 1 gallon of gasoline.

EXAMPLE: An athlete can swim $\frac{1}{2}$ mile every $\frac{1}{3}$ hour. What is the unit rate of the athlete?

In plain English: How many miles per hour can the athlete swim?

$$\frac{1}{2} \text{ mile} : \frac{1}{3} \text{ hour} = \frac{\frac{1}{2}}{\frac{1}{3}} = \frac{1}{2} \times \frac{3}{1} = \frac{3}{2}$$

$$= 1\frac{1}{2} \text{ miles per hour}$$

When the unit rate describes a price, it is called **UNIT PRICE**. When you're calculating unit price, be sure to put the price in the numerator!

EXAMPLE: Jacob pays $1.60 for 2 bottles of water. What is the unit price of each bottle?

$$\$1.60 : 2 \text{ bottles or } \frac{1.60}{2} = \$0.80$$

The unit price is $0.80 per bottle.

CHECK YOUR KNOWLEDGE

For **1** through **10**, find the unit rate or unit price.

1. My mom jogs 30 miles in 5 hours.

2. We swam 100 yards in 2 minutes.

3. Juliette bought 8 ribbons for $1.52.

4. He pumped 54 gallons in 12 minutes.

5. It costs $2,104.50 to purchase 122 soccer balls.

6. A runner sprints $\frac{1}{2}$ of a mile in $\frac{1}{15}$ hour.

7. Linda washes 26 bowls per 4 minutes.

8. Safira spends $47 for 12 gallons of gas.

9. Nathaniel does 240 push-ups in 5 minutes.

10. A team digs 12 holes every 20 hours.

ANSWERS ➤ 93

1. 6 miles per hour

2. 50 yards per minute

3. $0.19 per ribbon

4. 4.5 gallons per minute

5. $17.25 per soccer ball

6. $7\frac{1}{2}$ miles per hour

7. 6.5 bowls per minute

8. $3.50 per gallon of gas

9. 48 push-ups per minute

10. 0.6 holes per hour

Chapter 17

PROPORTIONS

A **PROPORTION** is a number sentence where two ratios are equal. For example, someone cuts a pizza into 2 equal pieces and eats 1 piece. The ratio of pieces that person ate to the original pieces of pizza is $\frac{1}{2}$. The number $\frac{1}{2}$ is the same ratio as if that person instead cut the pizza into 4 equal pieces and ate 2 pieces.

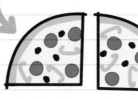

$$\frac{1}{2} = \frac{2}{4}$$

You can check if two ratios form a proportion by using cross products. To find cross products, set the two ratios next to each other, then multiply diagonally. If both products are equal to each other, then the two ratios are equal and form a proportion.

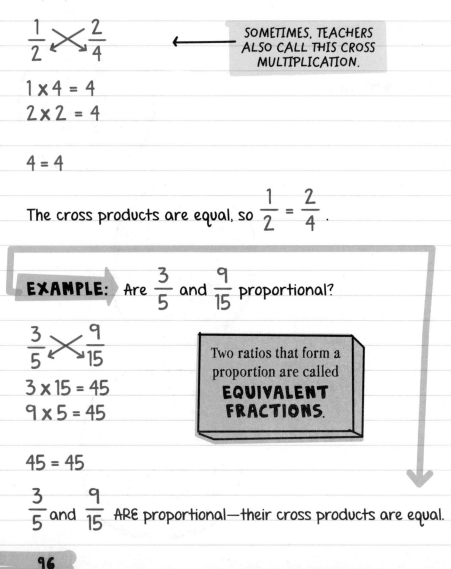

$\dfrac{1}{2} \times \dfrac{2}{4}$

SOMETIMES, TEACHERS ALSO CALL THIS CROSS MULTIPLICATION.

$1 \times 4 = 4$
$2 \times 2 = 4$

$4 = 4$

The cross products are equal, so $\dfrac{1}{2} = \dfrac{2}{4}$.

EXAMPLE: Are $\dfrac{3}{5}$ and $\dfrac{9}{15}$ proportional?

$\dfrac{3}{5} \times \dfrac{9}{15}$

Two ratios that form a proportion are called **EQUIVALENT FRACTIONS**.

$3 \times 15 = 45$
$9 \times 5 = 45$

$45 = 45$

$\dfrac{3}{5}$ and $\dfrac{9}{15}$ ARE proportional—their cross products are equal.

96

You can also use a proportion to **FIND AN UNKNOWN QUANTITY**. For example, you are making lemonade, and the recipe says to use 5 cups of water for every lemon you squeeze. How many cups of water do you need if you have 6 lemons?

First, set up a ratio: $\dfrac{5 \text{ cups}}{1 \text{ lemon}}$

Second, set up a ratio for what you are trying to figure out. Because you don't know how many cups are required for 6 lemons, use **X** for the amount of water.

$\dfrac{X \text{ cups}}{6 \text{ lemons}}$

Third, set up a proportion by setting the ratios equal to each other:

$$\dfrac{5 \text{ cups}}{1 \text{ lemon}} \quad \dfrac{X \text{ cups}}{6 \text{ lemons}}$$

NOTICE THAT THE UNITS ACROSS FROM EACH OTHER MATCH.

Last, use cross products to find the missing number!

$1 \cdot X = 5 \times 6$
$1 \cdot X = 30$ (Divide both sides by 1 so you can get **X** alone.)

$X = 30$

You need 30 cups for 6 lemons!

EXAMPLE: You drive 150 miles in 3 hours. At this rate, how far would you travel in 7 hours?

$$\frac{150 \text{ miles}}{3 \text{ hours}} = \frac{x \text{ miles}}{7 \text{ hours}}$$

$150 \cdot 7 = 3 \cdot x$

$1{,}050 = 3x$ (Divide both sides by 3 so you can get x alone.)

$350 = x$

You'll travel 350 miles in 7 hours.

> Whenever you see "at this rate," set up a proportion!

Sometimes, a proportion stays the same, even in different scenarios. For example, Tim runs $\frac{1}{2}$ a mile, and then he drinks 1 cup of water. If Tim runs 1 mile, he needs 2 cups of water. If Tim runs 1.5 miles, he needs 3 cups of water (and so on). The proportion stays the same, and we multiply by the same number in each scenario (in this case, we multiply by 2). This is known as the **CONSTANT OF PROPORTIONALITY** or the **CONSTANT OF VARIATION** and is closely related to unit rate (or unit price).

EXAMPLE: A recipe requires 6 cups of water for 2 pitchers of fruit punch. The same recipe requires 15 cups of water for 5 pitchers of fruit punch. How many cups of water are required to make 1 pitcher of fruit punch?

We set up a proportion:

$$\frac{6 \text{ cups}}{2 \text{ pitchers}} = \frac{x \text{ cups}}{1 \text{ pitcher}} \quad \text{or} \quad \frac{15 \text{ cups}}{5 \text{ pitchers}} = \frac{x \text{ cups}}{1 \text{ pitcher}}$$

By solving for x in both cases, we find out that the answer is always 3 cups.

We can also see unit rate by using a table. With the data from the table, we can set up a proportion:

EXAMPLE: Daphne often walks laps at the track. The table below describes how much time she walks and how many laps she finishes. How many minutes does Daphne walk per lap?

Total minutes walking	28	42
Total number of laps	4	6

$$\frac{28 \text{ minutes}}{4 \text{ laps}} = \frac{x \text{ minutes}}{1 \text{ lap}} \quad \text{or} \quad \frac{42 \text{ minutes}}{6 \text{ laps}} = \frac{x \text{ minutes}}{1 \text{ lap}}$$

Solving for x, we find out that the answer is 7 minutes.

CHECK YOUR KNOWLEDGE

1. Do the ratios $\frac{3}{4}$ and $\frac{6}{8}$ form a proportion? Show why or why not with cross products.

2. Do the ratios $\frac{4}{9}$ and $\frac{6}{11}$ form a proportion? Show why or why not with cross products.

3. Do the ratios $\frac{4}{5}$ and $\frac{12}{20}$ form a proportion? Show why or why not with cross products.

4. Solve for the unknown: $\frac{3}{15} = \frac{9}{x}$.

5. Solve for the unknown: $\frac{8}{5} = \frac{y}{19}$. Answer in decimal form.

6. Solve for the unknown: $\frac{m}{6.5} = \frac{11}{4}$. Answer in decimal form.

7. In order to make the color pink, a painter mixes 2 cups of white paint with 5 cups of red. If the painter wants to use 4 cups of white paint, how many cups of red paint will she need to make the same color pink?

8. Four cookies cost $7. At this rate, how much will 9 cookies cost?

9. Three bagels cost $2.67. At this rate, how much will 10 bagels cost?

10. It rained 3.75 inches in 15 hours. At this rate, how much will it rain in 35 hours? Answer in decimal form.

CHECK YOUR ANSWERS

1. Yes, because $\dfrac{3}{4} \times \dfrac{6}{8}$ $3 \times 8 = 24$
   $6 \times 4 = 24$
   $24 = 24$

2. No, because $\dfrac{4}{9} \times \dfrac{6}{11}$ $4 \times 11 = 44$
   $6 \times 9 = 54$
   $44 \neq 54$

3. No, because $\dfrac{4}{5} \times \dfrac{12}{20}$ $4 \times 20 = 80$
   $12 \times 5 = 60$
   $80 \neq 60$

4. $x = 45$

5. $y = 30.4$

6. $m = 17.875$

7. 10 cups

8. $15.75

9. $8.90

10. 8.75 inches

Chapter 18

CONVERTING

△ ○ ◇ ▽ ▢ ○ ◇ ▢ △ ○ ◇ ▢ ○ △

MEASUREMENTS

Sometimes, we want to change one type of measurement unit (such as inches) to another unit (such as feet). This is called **CONVERTING MEASUREMENTS**.

STANDARD SYSTEM of MEASUREMENT

In the U.S., we use the **STANDARD SYSTEM** of measurement. Here are some standard system measurements and their equivalent units:

> ### Length
> 12 inches (in) = 1 foot (ft)
> 3 feet (ft) = 1 yard (yd)
> 1,760 yards (yd) = 1 mile (mi)

Weight

1 pound (lb) = 16 ounces (oz)

1 ton (t) = 2,000 pounds (lb)

Capacity

1 tablespoon (tbsp) = 3 teaspoons (tsp)

1 fluid ounce (oz) = 2 tablespoons (tbsp)

1 cup (c) = 8 fluid ounces (oz)

1 pint (pt) = 2 cups (c)

1 quart (qt) = 2 pints (pt)

1 gallon (gal) = 4 quarts (qt)

When converting between measurements, set up a proportion and solve.

EXAMPLE: How many quarts are there in 10 pints?

We already know that 1 quart is the same as 2 pints, so we use this ratio:

$$\frac{x \text{ quarts}}{10 \text{ pints}} = \frac{1 \text{ quart}}{2 \text{ pints}}$$

We cross multiply to find the answer is 5 quarts.

EXAMPLE: How many pints are there in 64 fluid ounces?

We can use ratios and proportions, and repeat this process until we end up with the right units. We already know that there are 8 fluid ounces in 1 cup, so we change from fluid ounces to cups first.

$$\frac{x \text{ cups}}{64 \text{ fluid ounces}} = \frac{1 \text{ cup}}{8 \text{ fluid ounces}}$$

We cross multiply to find the answer is 8 cups.

Next, we change 8 cups to pints.

We already know that there are 2 cups in 1 pint, so we set up another proportion:

$$\frac{x \text{ pints}}{8 \text{ cups}} = \frac{1 \text{ pint}}{2 \text{ cups}}$$

MAKE SURE YOUR UNITS ALWAYS MATCH HORIZONTALLY.

We cross multiply to find the answer is 4 pints.

METRIC SYSTEM of MEASUREMENT

Most other countries use the **METRIC SYSTEM** of measurement. Here are some metric system measurements and their equivalent units:

WE ALSO USE THE METRIC SYSTEM IN SCIENCE CLASS!

Length
10 millimeters (mm) = 1 centimeter (cm)

100 centimeters (cm) = 1 meter (m)

1,000 meters (m) = 1 kilometer (km)

Weight
1,000 milligrams (mg) = 1 gram (g)

1,000 grams (g) = 1 kilogram (kg)

When converting between measurements, set up a proportion and solve.

EXAMPLE: How many centimeters are there in 2 kilometers?

We can use ratios and proportions because we already know that there are 1,000 meters in 1 kilometer:

$$\frac{x \text{ meters}}{2 \text{ kilometers}} = \frac{1,000 \text{ meters}}{1 \text{ kilometer}}$$

We cross multiply to find the answer is 2,000 meters.

Next, we change 2,000 meters to centimeters.

We already know that there are 100 centimeters in 1 meter, so we set up another proportion:

$$\frac{x \text{ centimeters}}{2,000 \text{ meters}} = \frac{100 \text{ centimeters}}{1 \text{ meter}}$$

We cross multiply to find the answer is 200,000 cm.

CONVERTING BETWEEN MEASUREMENT SYSTEMS

Sometimes, we want to change one type of measurement unit (such as inches) to another unit (such as centimeters). When we change units from the standard system to the metric system or vice versa, we are **CONVERTING BETWEEN MEASUREMENT SYSTEMS**.

Here are some of the **COMMON CONVERSIONS OF STANDARD TO METRIC**:

> **Length**
> 1 inch (in) = 2.54 centimeters (cm)
> 3.28 feet (ft) = 1 meter (m) (approximately)
> 1 yard (yd) = 0.9144 meter (m)
> 1 mile (mi) = 1.61 kilometers (km) (approximately)

Weight

1 ounce (oz) = 28.349 grams (g) (approximately)

1 pound (lb) = 453.592 grams (g) (approximately)

1 pound (lb) = 0.454 kilograms (kg) (approximately)

Capacity

1 fluid ounce (fl oz) = 29.574 milliliters (ml) (approximately)

1 pint (pt) = 473.177 milliliters (ml) (approximately)

1 pint (pt) = 0.473 liters (l) (approximately)

1 gallon (gal) = 3.785 liters (l) (approximately)

When converting between measurement systems, just set up a proportion and solve.

EXAMPLE: How many gallons are in 12 liters?

First, set up a proportion with the unknown quantity as x.

$$\frac{1 \text{ gallon}}{3.785 \text{ liters}} = \frac{x \text{ gallons}}{12 \text{ liters}}$$

Next, use cross products to find the missing number.

$$3.785x = 12$$

(Divide both sides by 3.785 to isolate x on one side of the equal sign.)

x = approximately 3.17 gallons

So, there are roughly 3 gallons in 12 liters!

CHECK YOUR KNOWLEDGE

For **1** through **8**, fill in the blanks.

1. 26 feet = _____ inches

2. _____ gallons = 24 quarts

3. 30 teaspoons = _____ fluid ounces

4. _____ millimeters = 0.08 kilometers

5. 30 centimeters = _____ inches

6. 4.5 miles = _____ feet

7. _____ grams = 36 ounces

8. 5.25 pints = _____ liters

9. While hiking a trail that is 7 miles long, you see a sign that says, "Distance you've traveled: 10,000 feet." How many feet remain in the hike?

10. Mount Everest, on the border of Nepal, is 8,848 meters tall, while Chimborazo in Ecuador is 6,310 meters tall. What is the difference in elevation between the two mountains in feet?

ANSWERS ➤

1. 312

2. 6

3. 5

4. 80,000

5. Approximately 11.81

6. 23,760

7. Approximately 1,020.564

8. Approximately 2.48325

9. 26,960

10. Approximately 8,325.64

Chapter 19

PERCENT

△ ○ ◇ ▽ ▢ ○ ◇ ▢ △ ○ ◇ ▢ ○ △

PERCENT means "per hundred." Percentages are ratios that compare a quantity to 100. For example, 33% means "33 per hundred" and can also be written $\frac{33}{100}$ or 0.33.

> **SHORTCUT:** Any time you have a percent, you can put the number over 100 and get rid of the % sign. Don't forget to simplify the fraction if possible!

EXAMPLES of a percent as a fraction:

$$3\% = \frac{3}{100}$$

$$25\% = \frac{25}{100} = \frac{1}{4}$$

EXAMPLES of a fraction as a percent:

$$\frac{11}{100} = 11\%$$

$$\frac{1}{5} = \frac{20}{100} = 20\%$$

↰ THIS IS A PROPORTION!

$$65\% = \frac{65}{100} = 0.65 \qquad 6.5\% = \frac{6.5}{100} = 0.065$$

To turn a fraction into a percent, divide the **NUMERATOR** (top of the fraction) by the **DENOMINATOR** (bottom of the fraction).

> **SHORTCUT:** When dividing by 100, just move the decimal point two spaces to the left!

EXAMPLE:

$$\frac{14}{50} = 14 \div 50 = 0.28 = 28\%$$

(Once you get the decimal form of the answer, move the decimal two spaces to the right, then include the % sign at the end.)

REMEMBER:
Any number that doesn't have a decimal point has an "invisible" decimal point at the far right of the number: 14 is the same as 14.0.

WE ARE INVISIBLE! WE LURK IN THE SHADOWS! RIGHT, ZERO?

RIGHT, BOSS!

LET'S TRY IT AGAIN:

Five out of every eight albums that Latrell owns are jazz.
What percentage of his music collection is jazz?

$$\frac{5}{8} = 5 \div 8 = 0.625$$

(Move the decimal two spaces
to the right and include
a percent sign.)

Jazz makes up 62.5% of Latrell's music collection.

Alternative method: You can also solve
problems like this by setting up a proportion, like this:

$$\frac{5}{8} \qquad \frac{x}{100}$$

$8 \cdot x = 5 \cdot 100$

$8 \cdot x = 500$ (Divide both sides by 8 so you can
get x alone.)

$x = 62.5 \longrightarrow$ 62.5% of Latrell's music is jazz.

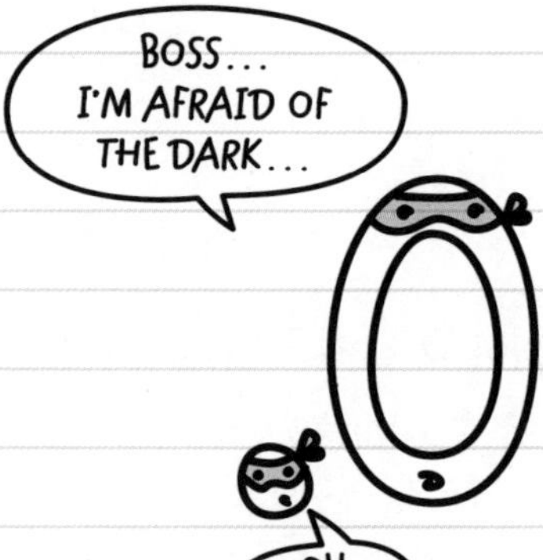
BOSS...
I'M AFRAID OF
THE DARK...
OH,
BROTHER.

1. Write 45% as a fraction.

2. Write 68% as a fraction.

3. Write 275% as a fraction. ← YOU CAN WRITE YOUR ANSWER AS AN IMPROPER FRACTION OR A MIXED NUMBER.

4. Write 8% as a decimal.

5. Write 95.4% as a decimal.

6. Write 0.003% as a decimal.

7. $\dfrac{6}{20}$ is what percent?

8. $\dfrac{15}{80}$ is what percent?

9. In the school election, Tammy received 3 out of every 7 votes. What percent of the votes was this (approximate to the nearest percent)?

10. If you get 17 out of 20 questions correct on your next test, what percent of the test did you answer incorrectly?

ANSWERS ➤

CHECK YOUR ANSWERS

1. $\dfrac{45}{100} = \dfrac{9}{20}$

2. $\dfrac{68}{100} = \dfrac{17}{25}$

3. $\dfrac{275}{100} = \dfrac{11}{4}$ or $2\dfrac{3}{4}$

4. 0.08

5. 0.954

6. 0.00003

7. 30%

8. 18.75%

9. Approximately 43%

10. 15%

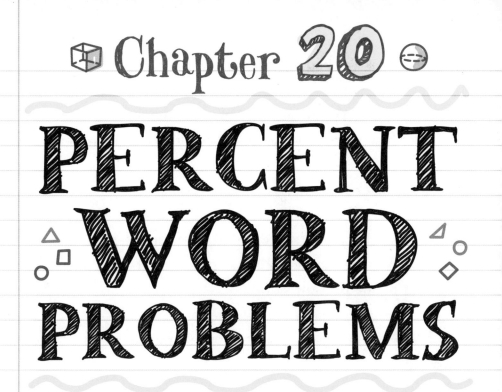

Chapter 20

PERCENT WORD PROBLEMS

The key to solving percent word problems is to translate the word problem into mathematical symbols first. Remember these steps, and solving them becomes much easier:

STEP 1: Find the word "is." Put an equal sign above it. This becomes the center of your equation.

STEP 2: Everything that comes before the word "is" can be changed into math symbols and written to the left of the equal sign. Everything that comes after the word "is" should be written to the right of the = sign.

STEP 3: Look for key words:

 "What" or "What number" means an unknown number. Represent the unknown number with a variable like X.

 "Of" means "multiply."

Percents can be represented as decimals, so if you see % move the decimal two spaces to the left and get rid of the percent sign.

STEP 4: Now you have your number sentence, so do the math!

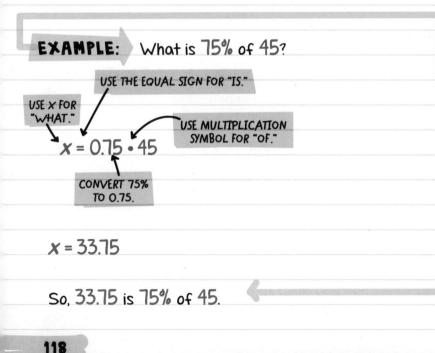

EXAMPLE: What is 75% of 45?

USE THE EQUAL SIGN FOR "IS."

USE X FOR "WHAT."

USE MULTIPLICATION SYMBOL FOR "OF."

$$X = 0.75 \cdot 45$$

CONVERT 75% TO 0.75.

$$X = 33.75$$

So, 33.75 is 75% of 45.

EXAMPLE: 13 is what percent of 25?

13 = x • 25   (Divide both sides by 25 to get x alone.)

0.52 = x   (To convert 0.52 to a percent, move the
decimal two spaces to the right and
include the % sign.)

52% = x

So, 13 is 52% of 25.

Don't forget to double-check your math, read
through the word problem again, and think
about whether your answer makes sense.

EXAMPLE: 4 is 40% of what number?

4 = 0.40 • x   (Divide both sides by 0.4
to get x alone.)

10 = x

So, 4 is 40% of 10.

EXAMPLE: What percentage of 5 is 1.25?

$x \cdot 5 = 1.25$

$x = 0.25$

So, 25% of 5 is 1.25.

CHECK YOUR KNOWLEDGE

1. What is 45% of 60?

2. What is 15% of 250?

3. What is 3% of 97?

4. 11 is what percent of 20?

5. 2 is what percent of 20?

6. 17 is what percent of 25?

7. 35 is 10% of what number?

8. 40 is 80% of what number?

9. 102,000 is 8% of what number?

10. George wants to buy a new bike, which costs $280. So far, he has earned $56. What percent of the total price has he already earned?

ANSWERS

CHECK YOUR ANSWERS

1. 27

2. 37.5

3. 2.91

4. 55%

5. 10%

6. 68%

7. 350

8. 50

9. 1,275,000

10. George has already earned 20% of the total price.

Chapter 21

TAXES AND FEES
○ ◇ ▽

TAXES

TAXES are fees charged by the government to pay for creating and taking care of things that we all share, like roads and parks. **SALES TAX** is a fee charged on something purchased. The amount of sales tax we pay is usually determined by a percentage.

> The tax rate stays the same, even as the price of things change. So the more something costs, the more taxes we have to pay. That's a proportion!

> Sales taxes are charged by your state and city so that they can provide their own services to the people like you who live in your state. Sales tax rates vary from state to state.

For example, an 8% sales tax means we pay an extra 8 cents for every 100 cents ($1) we spend. Eight percent can also be written as a ratio (8:100) or fraction $\left(\frac{8}{100}\right)$.

EXAMPLE: You want to buy a sweater that costs $40, and your state's sales tax is 8%. How much will the tax be? (There are three different ways to figure out how much you will pay.)

Method 1: Multiply the cost of the sweater by the percent to find the tax.

STEP 1: Change 8% to a decimal.

8% = 0.08

STEP 2: Multiply 0.08 and 40.

40 x 0.08 = 3.2

So, the tax will be $3.20.

Don't forget to include a dollar sign and use standard dollar notation when writing your final answer.

Method 2: Set up a proportion and solve to find the tax.

STEP 1: $8\% = \dfrac{8}{100}$

STEP 2: Set your tax equal to the proportional ratio with the unknown quantity.

$$\dfrac{8}{100} = \dfrac{x}{40}$$

STEP 3: Cross multiply to solve.

$100x = 320$
$x = 3.2$

So, the tax will be $3.20.

Method 3: Create an equation to find the answer.

STEP 1: Make a question: "What is 8% of $40?"

STEP 2: Translate the word problem into mathematical symbols.

$x = 0.08 \times 40$
$x = 3.2$

So, the tax will be $3.20.

Finding the Original Price

You can also find the original price if you know the final price and the percent of tax.

EXAMPLE: You bought new headphones. The receipt says that the total cost of headphones is $53.99, including an 8% sales tax. What was the original price of the headphones without the tax?

STEP 1: Add the percent of the cost of the headphones and the percent of the tax to get the total cost percent.

> YOU PAID FULL PRICE, SO THE COST OF THE HEADPHONES IS 100% OF THE ORIGINAL PRICE.

$100\% + 8\%$ tax $= 108\%$

STEP 2: Convert the percent to a decimal.

$108\% = 1.08$

STEP 3: Solve for the original price.

$53.99 = 1.08 \cdot x$ (Divide both sides by 1.08 to get x alone.)

$x = 49.99$ (rounding to the nearest cent)

The original cost of the headphones was $49.99.

FEES

Other types of fees can work like a tax—the amount of the fee can be determined by a percentage of something else.

EXAMPLE: A bike rental company charges a 17% late fee whenever a bike is returned late. If the regular rental fee is $65, but you return the bike late, what is the late fee, and what is the total that you have to pay? (Let's use Method 1 from before.)

I WAS... ONLY A FEW... MINUTES LATE!

17% = 0.17 $\longrightarrow$ 65 x 0.17 = 11.05

So, the late fee is $11.05.

To get the total that you have to pay, you add the late fee to the original rental price.

$11.05 + $65 = $76.05

So, you have to pay $76.05.

Finding the Original Price

You can also find the original price if you know the final price and the percent of the fee.

EXAMPLE: You rent a snowboard for the day, but have such a blast that you lose track of time and return the board late. The receipt says that the total cost of the rental was $66.08 including a 12% late fee. What was the original price of the snowboard rental without the fee?

STEP 1: Add the percent of the cost of the rental and the percent of the fee to get the total cost percent:

> YOU PAID FULL PRICE, SO THE COST OF THE SNOWBOARD RENTAL IS 100% OF THE ORIGINAL PRICE.

$$100\% + 12\% \text{ tax} = 112\%$$

STEP 2: Convert the percent to a decimal.

$$112\% = 1.12$$

STEP 3: Solve for the original price.

$$66.08 = 1.12 \cdot x$$

$$x = 59$$

The original cost of the snowboard rental was $59.00.

CHECK YOUR KNOWLEDGE

1. Complete the following table. Round answers to the nearest cent.

	8% Sales Tax	8.5% Sales Tax	9.25% Sales Tax
Book $12.00			
Total Price (with tax)			
Board game $27.50			
Total Price (with tax)			
Television $234.25			
Total Price (with tax)			

2. You buy your favorite band's new album. The receipt says that the total cost of the album is $11.65, including a 6% sales tax. What was the original price of the album without the tax?

ANSWERS

1.

	8% Sales Tax	8.5% Sales Tax	9.25% Sales Tax
Book $12.00	$0.96	$1.02	$1.11
Total Price (with tax)	$12.96	$13.02	$13.11
Board game $27.50	$2.20	$2.34	$2.54
Total Price (with tax)	$29.70	$29.84	$30.04
Television $234.25	$18.74	$19.91	$21.67
Total Price (with tax)	$252.99	$254.16	$255.92

2. $10.99

Chapter 22

DISCOUNTS AND MARKUPS ◁ ○ ◇ ▽

DISCOUNTS

Stores use **DISCOUNTS** to get us to buy their products. In any mall or store, you will often see signs such as

But don't be swayed by signs and commercials that promise to save you money. Calculate how much you will save to decide for yourself whether it's a good deal or not.

> Other words and phrases that mean you will save money (and that you subtract the discount from the original price): savings, price reduction, markdown, sale, clearance.

Calculating a discount is like calculating tax, but because you are saving money, you subtract it from the original price.

EXAMPLE: A new hat costs $12.50. A sign in the window at the store says, "**ALL ITEMS 20% OFF.**" What is the discount off of the hat, and what is the new price of the hat?

Method 1: Find out the value of the discount and subtract it from the original price.

STEP 1: Change the percent discount to a decimal.
20% = 0.20

STEP 2: Multiply the decimal by the original amount to get the discount.
0.20 x $12.50 = $2.50

STEP 3: Subtract the discount from the original price.
$12.50 – $2.50 = $10

The new price of the hat is $10.00.

Method 2: Create an equation to find the answer.

STEP 1: Write a question: "What is 20% of $12.50?"

STEP 2: Translate the word problem into mathematical symbols.
$x = 0.20 \cdot 12.50$
$x = 2.5$

STEP 3: Subtract the discount from the original price.

$12.50 - $2.50 = $10

The new price of the hat is $10.00.

What if you are lucky enough to get an additional discount after the first? Just deal with one discount at a time!

EXAMPLE: Valery's Videos is selling all games at a 25% discount. However, you also have a membership card to the store, which gives you an additional 15% off. What will you end up paying for $100 worth of video games?

Let's deal with the first discount:
25% = 0.25
0.25 x $100 = $25

So, the first discount is $25.
$100 - $25 = $75

The first discounted price is $75.

Now, we can calculate the additional 15% discount from the membership card.

$15\% = 0.15$

$0.15 \times \$75 = \$11.25$

(DON'T FORGET THAT THE SECOND DISCOUNT IS ADDITIONAL, SO IT'S CALCULATED BASED ON THE FIRST DISCOUNTED PRICE—**NOT** THE ORIGINAL PRICE.)

So, the second discount is $11.25.

$\$75 - \$11.25 = \$63.75$

The final price is $63.75. That's a pretty good deal!

Finding the Original Price

You can also find the original price if you know the final price and the discount.

EXAMPLE: A video game is on sale for 30% off of the regular price. If the sale price is $41.99, what was the original price?

STEP 1: Subtract the percent of the discount from the percent of the original cost:

$100\% - 30\% = 70\%$

UNLIKE THE EXAMPLES IN THE LAST CHAPTER, YOU DID NOT PAY FULL PRICE—YOU PAID **ONLY** 70% OF THE ORIGINAL PRICE. SWEET DEAL!

STEP 2: Convert the percent to a decimal.

$70\% = 0.7$

STEP 3: Solve for the original price.

$41.99 = 0.7 \cdot x$ (Divide both sides by 0.7 to get x alone.)

$x = 59.99$ (rounding to the nearest cent)

The original price of the video game was $59.99.

Finding the Percent Discount

Similarly, you can also find the percent discount if you know the final price and the original price.

EXAMPLE: Julie paid $35 for a shirt that is on sale. The original price was $50. What was the percent discount?

$35 = x \cdot 50$ (Divide both sides by 50 to get x alone.)

$x = 0.7$ (This tells us Julie paid 70% of the original price for the shirt.)

$1 - 0.7 = 0.3$ (We need to subtract the percent paid from the original price to find the percent discount.)

The discount was 30% off of the original price.

MARKUPS

Stores often offer discounts during sales. But if they did that all the time, they would probably go out of business. In fact, stores and manufacturers usually increase the price of their products to make a profit. These increases are known as **MARKUPS**.

EXAMPLE: A video game costs $40 to make. To make a profit, a manufacturer marks it up 20%. What is the markup amount? What is the new price of the game?

Method 1: Find out the value of the markup.
STEP 1: Change the percent discount to a decimal.
20% = 0.20

STEP 2: Multiply the decimal by the original cost. This is the markup.
0.20 x $40 = $8

STEP 3: Add the markup price to the original cost.
$40 + $8 = $48

The new price of the game is $48.

Method 2: Create an equation to find the answer.
STEP 1: Write a question: "What is 20% of $40?"

STEP 2: Translate the word problem into mathematical symbols.
$x = 0.20 \cdot 40 \longrightarrow x = 8$

STEP 3: Add the markup price to the original cost.
$40 + $8 = $48
The new price of the game is $48.

Finding the Original Cost

Just like when you calculate for tax and fees, you can also find the original cost if you know the final price and the markup.

EXAMPLE: A bakery charges $5.08 for a cake. In order to make a profit, the store marks up its goods by 70%. What is the original cost of the cake?

STEP 1: Add the percent of the original cost of the cake and the percent of the markup to get the total cost percent:
100% + 70% = 170%

> YOU PAID THE FULL ORIGINAL COST PLUS THE STORE'S MARKUP, SO THE COST OF THE CAKE IS ACTUALLY 170% OF THE ORIGINAL COST.

STEP 2: Convert the percent to a decimal.
170% = 1.7

STEP 3: Solve for the original cost.
5.08 = 1.7 • x

x = 2.99 (rounding to the nearest cent)

The original cost of the cake was $2.99.

1. A computer has a price tag of $300. The store is giving you a 15% discount for the computer. Find the discount and final price of the computer.

2. Find the discount and final price when you receive 20% off a pair of pants that costs $48.00.

3. A bike is on sale for 45% off of the regular price. If the sale price is $299.75, what was the original price?

4. At a clothing store, a sign in the window says, "Clearance sale: 15% off all items." You find a shirt you like with an original price of $30.00; however, a sticker on the tag says, "Take an additional 10% off the final price." How much will this shirt cost after the discounts are taken?

5. You want to buy a new truck. At dealership A, the truck you want costs $14,500, but they offer you a 10% discount. You find the same truck at dealership B, where it costs $16,000, but they offer you a 14% discount. Which dealership is offering you a better deal?

6. A manufacturer makes a bookshelf that costs $50. The price at the store is increased by a markup of 8%. Find the markup amount and the new price.

7. A bike mechanic makes a bike for $350. A bike shop then marks it up by 15%. What is the markup amount? What is the new price?

8. A supermarket charges $3.24 for a carton of milk. They mark up the milk by 35% in order to make a profit. What is the original cost of the milk?

9. Phoebe wants to buy a TV. Store #1 sells the TV for $300. Store #2 has a TV that costs $250, but marks up the price by 25%. From which store should Phoebe buy the TV?

10. A furniture store has a bed that costs $200 in stock. It decreased the price by 30%. It then marked up the price by 20%. What is the new price of the bed?

ANSWERS 139

CHECK YOUR ANSWERS

1. Discount = $45; New Price = $255

2. Discount = $9.60; New Price = $38.40

3. Original price = $545

4. $22.95

5. Dealership A's truck will cost $13,050.
   Dealership B's truck will cost $13,760.
   Dealership A is the better deal.

6. Markup = $4; New Price = $54

7. Markup = $52.50; New Price = $402.50

8. Original Price = $2.40

9. Store #1 = $300; Store #2 = $312.50.
   Phoebe should buy the TV from Store #1.

10. Original price = $200; Discount Amount = $60;
    New price after discount = $140. Markup Amount = $28;
    New price after the markup = $168

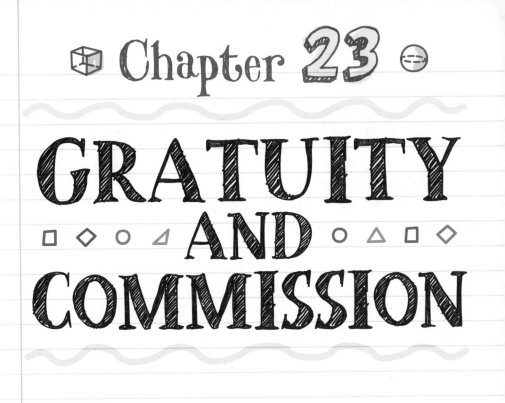

Chapter 23

GRATUITY AND COMMISSION

A **GRATUITY** is a "tip"—a gift, usually in the form of money that you give someone in return for his or her service. We usually talk about tips and gratuity in regard to servers at restaurants. A **COMMISSION** is a fee paid to someone for his or her services in helping to sell something to a customer. We usually talk about commissions in regard to salespeople at stores. In both cases, how much you pay usually depends on the total cost of the meal or item you purchased. You can calculate gratuity and commission just like sales tax.

Again, the more your bill is, the more the gratuity or commission will be— they have a proportional relationship.

EXAMPLE OF GRATUITY: At the end of a meal, your server brings the final bill, which is $25. You want to leave a 15% gratuity. How much is the tip in dollars, and how much should you leave in total?

15% = 0.15
$25 x 0.15 = $3.75

The tip is $3.75.

$25 + 3.75 = $28.75

The total you should leave is $28.75.

EXAMPLE OF COMMISSION: My sister got a summer job working at her favorite clothing store at the mall. Her boss agreed to pay 12% commission on her total sales. At the end of her first week, her sales totaled $3,500. How much did she earn in commission?

12% = 0.12

$3,500 x 0.12 = $420.00

She earned $420.

Alternative method: You can also solve these problems by setting up proportions, like this:

$$\frac{12}{100} = \frac{x}{3,500}$$

$100x = 42,000$

$x = 420

CHECK YOUR KNOWLEDGE

1. The Lee family eats dinner at a restaurant for a total bill of $45. They decide to give a tip of 18%. How much tip will they give?

2. A saleswoman will receive 35% commission of her total sales. She makes a total of $6,000. What is the commission that she will receive?

3. A business pays a catering company $875 for a special event. The business decides to give the catering company a tip of 25%. How much is the tip, and how much does the business pay in total to the catering company?

4. Mr. and Mrs. Smith pay their babysitter a total of $70. They also decide to give a tip of 32%. How much is the tip, and how much do Mr. and Mrs. Smith pay the babysitter?

5. If you give your hairdresser a 10% tip on a $25 haircut, how much will the total cost be?

6. The bill for dinner at Zolo's Restaurant is $32.75. You decide to leave a 17% gratuity. What is the total amount of money that you will pay?

7. Julio gets a job selling motor scooters and is paid 8% commission on all his sales. At the end of the week, Julio's sales are $5,450. How much has he earned in commission?

8. Amber's boss tells her that she can choose whether she wants to be paid 12% commission or a flat fee (one-time payment) of $500. Her total sales for the period are $3,950. Which should she select?

9. Mauricio and Judith are salespeople at different stores, and both are paid on commission. Mauricio earns 8% commission on his total sales, and Judith earns 9.5% commission. Last month, Mauricio sold $25,000, while Judith sold $22,000. Who earned more?

10. Luke is a waiter at a restaurant. He receives an 18% tip from a group whose bill is $236. Mary is an electronics salesperson next door. She receives a 12% commission from selling a total of $380 worth of electronics equipment. Who received more money?

ANSWERS

CHECK YOUR ANSWERS

1. $8.10

2. $2,100

3. Tip = $218.75; Total = $1,093.75

4. Tip = $22.40; Total = $92.40

5. $27.50

6. $38.32

7. $436

8. Amber's commission would be $474, so she should choose the $500 flat fee.

9. Mauricio earned $2,000 in commission, and Judith earned $2,090 in commission. Judith earned more.

10. Luke received a tip of $42.48. Mary received a commission of $45.60. So, Mary received more money than Luke.

Chapter 24

SIMPLE INTEREST

INTEREST is a fee that someone pays in order to borrow money. Interest functions in two ways:

1. A bank may pay you interest if you put your money into a savings account. Depositing your money in the bank makes the bank stronger and allows them to lend money to other people, so they pay you interest for that service.

2. You may pay interest to a bank if you borrow money from them—it's a fee they charge so that you can use somebody else's money before you have your own.

You need to know three things to determine the amount of interest that must be paid (if you are the **BORROWER**) or earned (if you are the **LENDER**):

1. **PRINCIPAL**: The amount of money that is being borrowed or loaned

2. **INTEREST RATE**: The percentage that will be paid for every year the money is borrowed or loaned

3. **TIME**: The amount of time that money will be borrowed or loaned

---

If you are given weeks, months, or days, write a fraction to calculate interest in terms of years.

EXAMPLES:

9 months $= \frac{9}{12}$ year   80 days $= \frac{80}{365}$ year   10 weeks $= \frac{10}{52}$ year

---

Once you have determined the principal, rate, and time, you can use this **SIMPLE INTEREST FORMULA**:

$$\text{interest} = \text{principal} \times \text{interest rate} \times \text{time}$$

$$I = P \cdot R \cdot T$$

> **BALANCE** is the total amount when you add the interest and beginning principal together.

EXAMPLE: You deposit $200 into a savings account that offers a 5% interest rate. How much interest will you have earned at the end of 3 years?

Principal (P) = $200
Rate (R) = 5% = 0.05
Time (T) = 3 years

> ALWAYS CHANGE A PERCENT TO A DECIMAL WHEN CALCULATING!

Simple interest can also be thought of like a ratio.

$$5\% \text{ interest} = \frac{5}{100}$$

So, for every $100 you deposit, the bank will pay you $5 each year. Then you multiply $5 by the number of years.

Now, substitute these numbers into the formula, and solve!

$I = P \cdot R \cdot T$
$I = (\$200)(0.05)(3)$
$I = 30$

INTERESTING...

After 3 years, you would earn an extra $30. Not bad for just letting your money sit in a bank for a few years!

EXAMPLE: In order to purchase your first used car, you need to borrow $11,000. Your bank agrees to loan you the money for 5 years if you pay 3.25% interest each year. How much interest will you have paid after the 5 years? What will be the total cost of the car?

$P = \$11,000$
$R = 3.25\% = 0.0325$
$T = 5 \text{ years}$

$I = P \cdot R \cdot T$

$I = (\$11,000)(0.0325)(5)$

$I = \$1,787.50$

You'll have to pay $1,787.50 in interest alone!

With this in mind, what will be the total price of the car?

$\$11,000 + \$1,787.50 = \$12,787.50$

The car will cost $12,787.50 in total.

EXAMPLE: Joey has $3,000. He deposits it in a bank that offers an annual interest rate of 4%. How long does he need to leave it in the bank in order to earn $600 in interest?

$I = \$600$
$P = \$3,000$
$R = 4\%$ (use .04)
$T = x$

$I = P \cdot R \cdot T$

(In this case, we know what the interest will be, but we don't know the length of time. We use x to represent time and fill in all the other information we know.)

$\$600 = \$3,000(.04)T$

$\$600 = \$120T$ ← (Divide both sides by 120 to get T by itself.)

$5 = T$

So, Joey will earn $600 after 5 years.

HAS IT BEEN 5 YEARS YET?

IT'S BEEN 2 HOURS.

For **1** through **5**: Enrique deposits $750 into a savings account that pays 4.25% annual interest. He plans to leave the money in the bank for 3 years.

1.   What is the principal?

2.   What is the interest rate? (Write your answer as a decimal.)

3.   What is the time?

4.   How much interest will Enrique earn after 3 years? (Round up to the nearest cent.)

5.   What will be Enrique's balance after 3 years?

For **6** through **9**: Sabrina gets a car loan for $7,500 at 6% interest for 3 years.

6.   How much interest will she pay over the 3 years?

7. Mario also gets a car loan for $7,500; however, his interest rate is 6% for 5 years. How much interest will Mario pay over the 5 years?

8. How much more interest does Mario pay than Sabrina in order to borrow the same amount of money at the same interest rate over 5 years instead of 3?

9. What does your answer for #8 tell you about borrowing money?

10. Complete the following chart:

INTEREST	PRINCIPAL	INTEREST RATE	TIME
	$2,574.50	5.5%	2 years
$2,976.00	$6,200.00	12%	

ANSWERS

CHECK YOUR ANSWERS

1. $750

2. 0.0425

3. 3 years

4. $95.63

5. $845.63

6. $1,350

7. $2,250

8. $900

9. The longer you borrow money, the more interest you must pay.

10.

INTEREST	PRINCIPAL	INTEREST RATE	TIME
$283.20	$2,574.50	5.5%	2 years
$2,976.00	$6,200.00	12%	4 years

Chapter 25

PERCENT RATE OF CHANGE

Sometimes, it is difficult to tell whether a change in the amount of something is a big deal or not. We use **PERCENT RATE OF CHANGE** to show how much an amount has changed in relation to the original amount. Another way to think about it is simply as the rate of change expressed as a percent.

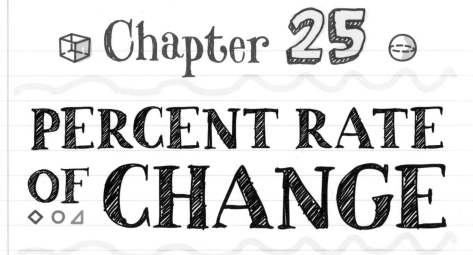

When the original amount goes **UP**, we calculate percent **INCREASE**.

When the original amount goes **DOWN**, we calculate percent **DECREASE**.

To calculate the percent rate of change:

First, set up this ratio: $$\frac{\text{CHANGE IN QUANTITY}}{\text{ORIGINAL QUANTITY}}$$

(The "change in quantity" is the difference between the original and new quantity.)

Second, divide.

Last, move the decimal two spaces to the right and add your % symbol.

EXAMPLE: A store purchases T-shirts from a factory for $20 each and sells them to customers for $23. What is the percent increase in price?

$$\frac{23-20}{20} = \frac{3}{20} = 0.15 = 15\% \text{ increase}$$

EXAMPLE: On your first history test, you get 14 questions correct. On your second test, you don't study as much, so you get only 10 questions correct. What is the percent decrease from your first to your second test?

$$\frac{14-10}{14} = \frac{4}{14} = \frac{2}{7} = 0.29 = 29\% \text{ decrease}$$

Remember to reduce fractions whenever possible to make your calculations easier.

FOR PERCENTAGES, ROUND TO THE NEAREST HUNDREDTH PLACE.

CHECK YOUR KNOWLEDGE

For **1** through **5**: Are the following rates of change percent increases or decreases?

1. 7% to 17%

3. 5.0025% to 5.0021%

2. 87.5% to 36.2%

4. $92\frac{1}{2}\%$ to $92\frac{1}{5}\%$

5. 31.5% to 75%

6. Find the percent increase or decrease from 8 to 18.

7. Find the percent increase or decrease from 0.05 to 0.03.

8. Find the percent increase or decrease from 2 to 2,222.

9. A bike store purchases mountain bikes from the manufacturer for $250 each. They then sell the bikes to their customers for $625. What percent of change is this?

10. While working at the taco shop, Gerard noticed that on Sunday they sold 135 tacos. However, the next day, they sold only 108. What percent of change happened from Sunday to Monday?

ANSWERS

1. Increase

2. Decrease

3. Decrease

4. Decrease

5. Increase

6. 125% increase

7. 40% decrease

8. 111,000% increase

9. 150% increase

10. 20% decrease

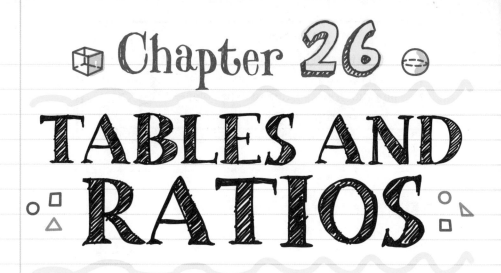

Chapter 26

TABLES AND RATIOS

We can use tables to compare ratios and proportions. For example, Sue runs laps around a track. Her coach records the time below:

NUMBER OF LAPS	TOTAL MINUTES RUN
2	6 minutes
5	15 minutes

What if Sue's coach wanted to find out how long it would take her to run 1 lap? If her speed remains constant, this is easy to calculate, because we have already learned how to find unit rate!

We can set up this proportion: $\dfrac{1}{x} = \dfrac{2}{6}$

Another option is to set up this proportion: $\dfrac{1}{x} = \dfrac{5}{15}$

The answer is 3 minutes.

EXAMPLE: Linda and Tim are racing around a track.
Their coach records their times below.

Linda

NUMBER OF LAPS	TOTAL MINUTES RUN
1	?
2	8 minutes
6	24 minutes

Tim

NUMBER OF LAPS	TOTAL MINUTES RUN
1	?
3	15 minutes
4	20 minutes

If each runner's speed stays constant, how would their coach find out who runs faster? Their coach must complete the table and find out how much time it would take Tim to run 1 lap and how much time it would take Linda to run 1 lap, and then compare them. The coach can find out the missing times with proportions:

LINDA:

$$\frac{1}{x} = \frac{2}{8}$$

$$x = 4$$

So, it takes Linda 4 minutes to run 1 lap.

TIM:

$$\frac{1}{x} = \frac{3}{15}$$

$$x = 5$$

So, it takes Tim 5 minutes to run 1 lap.
Linda runs faster than Tim!

WOO-HOO!

Nathalie, Patty, Mary, and Mino are picking coconuts. They record their times in the table below. Fill in the missing numbers (assuming their rates ater proportional).

1. Nathalie

NUMBER OF COCONUTS	MINUTES
1	
5	30
	48

2. Patty

NUMBER OF COCONUTS	MINUTES
1	
2	14
6	

3. Mary

NUMBER OF COCONUTS	MINUTES
1	
	4
8	16

4. Mino

NUMBER OF COCONUTS	MINUTES
1	
	20
9	36
	40

5. Who picked 1 coconut in the least amount of time?

CHECK YOUR ANSWERS

1. Nathalie

NUMBER OF COCONUTS	MINUTES
1	6
5	30
8	48

2. Patty

NUMBER OF COCONUTS	MINUTES
1	7
2	14
6	42

3. Mary

NUMBER OF COCONUTS	MINUTES
1	2
2	4
8	16

4. Mino

NUMBER OF COCONUTS	MINUTES
1	4
5	20
9	36
10	40

5. Mary picked 1 coconut in the least amount of time: 2 minutes.

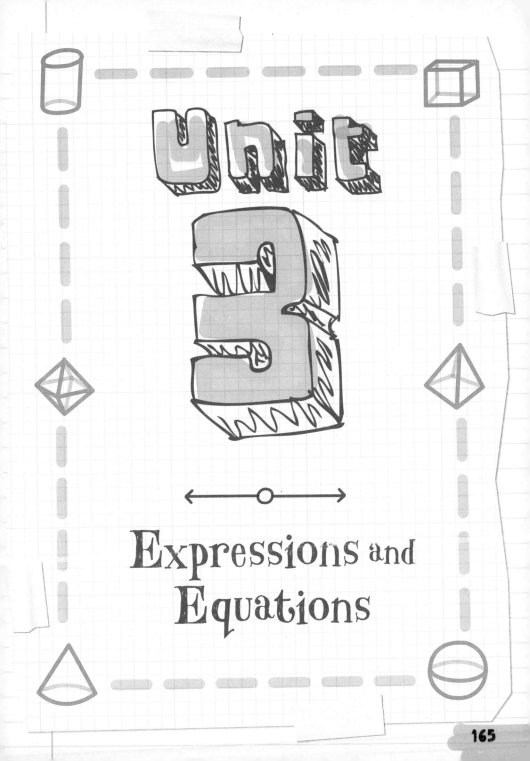

Unit 3

Expressions and Equations

Chapter 27

EXPRESSIONS

○ ◇ △ □ ◁ ◻ ○ ◇ ▽ ◻ △ ○

In math, an **EXPRESSION** is a mathematical phrase that contains numbers, **VARIABLES** (letters or symbols used in place of a quantity we don't know yet), and/or operators (such as + and −).

EXAMPLES:

$x + 5$ $3m - 2$ $\dfrac{a}{-b}$

$44k$ $59 + -3$

Sometimes, an expression allows us to do calculations to find out what quantity the variable is.

EXAMPLE: When Georgia runs, she runs a 6-mile loop each day. We don't know how many days she runs, so we'll call that number "d." So, now we can say that Georgia runs $6d$ miles. (In other words, $6d$ is the expression that represents how much Georgia runs each week.)

When a number is attached to a variable, like $6d$, you multiply the number and the variable. Any number that is used to multiply a variable (in this case 6) is called the **COEFFICIENT**.

A **CONSTANT** is a number that stays fixed in an expression (it stays "constant"). For example, in the expression $6x + 4$, the constant is 4.

An expression is made up of one or more **TERMS**—a number by itself or the product of a number and variable (or more than one variable). Each term is separated by an addition calculation symbol. In the expression $6x + 4$, there are two terms: $6x$ and 4.

> **TERM**
> a number by itself or the product of a number and variable(s). Terms in a math sentence are separated by a ✦ or ⎯ symbol.

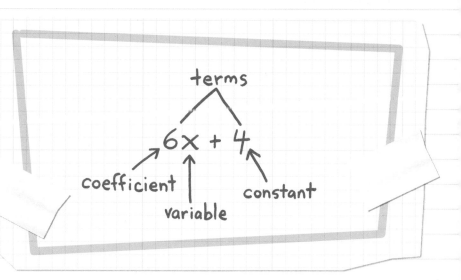

terms
$$6x + 4$$
coefficient
variable
constant

EXAMPLE: Name the variable, terms, coefficient, and constant of $8y - 2$.

The variable is y.

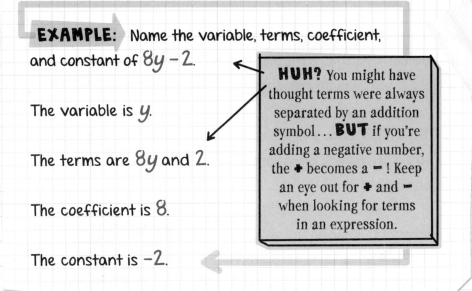

HUH? You might have thought terms were always separated by an addition symbol... **BUT** if you're adding a negative number, the **+** becomes a **−**! Keep an eye out for **+** and **−** when looking for terms in an expression.

The terms are $8y$ and 2.

The coefficient is 8.

The constant is -2.

Operators tell us what to do. Addition (+), subtraction (−), multiplication (×), and division (÷) are the most common operators. Word problems that deal with expressions use words instead of operators. Here's a quick translation:

OPERATION	OPERATOR	KEY WORDS
sum	+	greater than more than plus added to increased by

OPERATION	OPERATOR	KEY WORDS
difference	–	less than decreased by subtracted from fewer
product	×	times multiplied by of
quotient	÷	divided by per

EXAMPLE: "14 increased by g" = $14 + g$

EXAMPLE: "17 less than h" = $h - 17$
(Be careful! Any time you are translating "less than," the second number in the word problem is written first in the expression!)

EXAMPLE: "The product of -7 and x" = $-7 \cdot x$
This can also be written $(-7)(x)$ or $-7(x)$ or $-7x$.

EXAMPLE: "The quotient of 99 and w" = $99 \div w$
This can also be written $\dfrac{99}{w}$.

CHECK YOUR KNOWLEDGE

For **1** through **3**, name the variable(s), coefficient(s), and/or constant(s), if applicable.

1. $3y$

2. $5x + 11$

3. $-52m + 6y - 22$

For **4** and **5**, list the terms.

4. $2{,}500 + 11t - 3w$

5. $17 + d(-4)$

For **6** through **10**, write the expression.

6. 19 less than y

7. The quotient of 44 and 11

8. The product of -13 and k

9. Katherine drives 27 miles to work each day. Last Wednesday, she had to run some errands and drove a few extra miles. Write an expression that shows how many miles she drove on Wednesday. (Use *x* as your variable.)

10. There is a hip-hop dance contest on Saturday nights at a club. Because there was a popular DJ playing, the organizers expected 2 times the amount of people. The organizers also invited an extra 30 people from out of town. Write an expression that shows how many people they can expect to come to the event. (Use *x* as your variable.)

CHECK YOUR ANSWERS

1. Variable: y; Coefficient: 3; No constants

2. Variable: x; Coefficient: 5; Constant: 11

3. Variables: m, y; Coefficient: -52; 6 Constant: -22

4. 2,500, 11t, -3w

5. 17, $d(-4)$

6. $y - 19$

7. $44 \div 11$ or $\dfrac{44}{11}$

8. -13k

9. $27 + x$

10. $2x + 30$

Chapter 28

PROPERTIES

○ ◇ △ ▢ ◿ ▢ ▢ ○ ◇ ▽ ▢ ◣ ○

Properties are like a set of math rules that are always true. They often help us solve equations. Here are some important ones:

The **IDENTITY PROPERTY OF ADDITION** looks like this: $a + 0 = a$. It says that if you add zero to any number, that number stays the same.

EXAMPLE: $5 + 0 = 5$

The **IDENTITY PROPERTY OF MULTIPLICATION** looks like this: $a \times 1 = a$. It says that if you multiply any number by 1, that number stays the same.

EXAMPLE: $7 \times 1 = 7$

The **COMMUTATIVE PROPERTY OF ADDITION** looks like this: $a + b = b + a$. It says that when adding two (or more) numbers, you can add them in any order and the answer will be the same.

EXAMPLE: $3 + 11 = 11 + 3$ (Both expressions equal 14.)

The **COMMUTATIVE PROPERTY OF MULTIPLICATION** looks like this: $a \cdot b = b \cdot a$. It says that when multiplying two (or more) numbers, you can multiply them in any order and the answer will be the same.

EXAMPLE: $-5 \cdot 4 = 4 \cdot -5$ (Both expressions equal -20.)

DON'T FORGET: The commutative properties only work with addition and multiplication; they do NOT work with subtraction and division!

When talking about properties, your teacher or textbook may use the term **EQUIVALENT EXPRESSIONS**, which simply means that the math sentences have equal value. For example, $3 + 11 = 11 + 3$. (They are equivalent expressions.)

The **ASSOCIATIVE PROPERTY OF ADDITION** looks like this: $(a + b) + c = a + (b + c)$. It says that when adding three different numbers, you can change the order that you add them by moving the parentheses and the answer will still be the same.

EXAMPLE: $(2 + 5) + 8 = 2 + (5 + 8)$

(Both expressions equal 15.)

The **ASSOCIATIVE PROPERTY OF MULTIPLICATION** looks like this: $(a \cdot b) \cdot c = a \cdot (b \cdot c)$. It says that when multiplying three different numbers, you can change the order that you multiply them by moving the parentheses and the answer will still be the same.

EXAMPLE: $(2 \cdot 5) \cdot 8 = 2 \cdot (5 \cdot 8)$

(Both expressions equal 80.)

DON'T FORGET: The associative properties only work with addition and multiplication; they do NOT work with subtraction and division!

The **DISTRIBUTIVE PROPERTY OF MULTIPLICATION OVER ADDITION** looks like this: $a(b + c) = ab + ac$. It says that adding two numbers inside parentheses, then multiplying that sum by a number outside the parentheses is equal to first multiplying the number outside the parentheses by each of the numbers inside the parentheses and then adding the two products together.

> The **DISTRIBUTIVE PROPERTY** allows us to simplify an expression by taking out the parentheses.

EXAMPLE: $2(4 + 6) = 2 \cdot 4 + 2 \cdot 6$

(You "distribute" the "$2 \cdot$" across the terms inside the parentheses. Both expressions equal 20.)

EXAMPLE: $7(x + 8) =$

> Think about catapulting the number outside the parentheses inside to simplify.

$$7 \quad 7$$
$$(x + 8) = 7(x) + 7(8) = 7x + 56$$

The **DISTRIBUTIVE PROPERTY OF MULTIPLICATION OVER SUBTRACTION** looks like this: $a(b - c) = ab - ac$. It says that subtracting two numbers inside parentheses, then multiplying that difference times a number outside the parentheses is equal to first multiplying the number outside the parentheses by each of the numbers inside the parentheses and then subtracting the two products.

EXAMPLE: $9(5 - 3) = 9(5) - 9(3)$

(Both expressions equal 18.)

EXAMPLE: $6(x - 8) =$

$$(x - 8) = 6(x) - 6(8) = 6x - 48$$

FACTORING is the reverse of the distributive property. Instead of getting rid of parentheses, factoring allows us to include parentheses (because sometimes it's simpler to work with an expression that has parentheses).

EXAMPLE: Factor $15y + 12$.

STEP 1: Ask yourself, "What is the greatest common factor of both terms?" In the above case, the GCF of $15y$ and 12 is 3. ($15y = 3 \cdot 5 \cdot y$ and $12 = 3 \cdot 4$)

STEP 2: Divide all terms by the GCF and put the GCF on the outside of the parentheses.

$$15y + 12 = 3(5y + 4)$$

> You can always check your answer by using the **DISTRIBUTIVE PROPERTY**. Your answer should match the expression you started with!

EXAMPLE: Factor $12a + 18$.

The GCF of $12a$ and 18 is 6. So, we divide all terms by 6 and put it outside of the parentheses.

$$12a + 18 = 6(2a + 3)$$

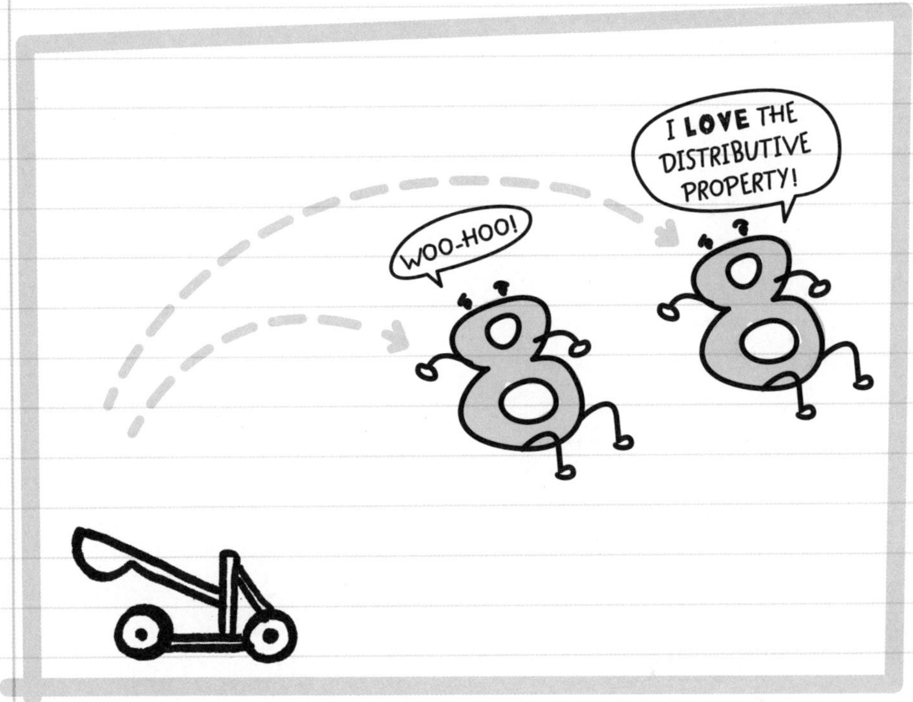
WOO-HOO!
I LOVE THE DISTRIBUTIVE PROPERTY!

CHECK YOUR KNOWLEDGE

In each blank space below, use the property listed to write an equivalent expression.

PROPERTY	EXPRESSION	EQUIVALENT EXPRESSION
Identity Property of Addition	6	
Identity Property of Multiplication	y	
Commutative Property of Addition	$6 + 14$	
Commutative Property of Multiplication	$8 \cdot m$	
Associative Property of Addition	$(x + 4) + 9$	
Associative Property of Multiplication	$7 \cdot (r \cdot 11)$	
Distributive Property of Multiplication over Addition	$5(v + 22)$	
Distributive Property of Multiplication over Subtraction	$8(7 - w)$	
Factor	$18x + 6$	
Factor	$14 - 35z$	

1. Distribute $3(x + 2y - 5)$.

2. Distribute $\frac{1}{2}(4a - 3b - c)$.

3. Factor $6x + 10y + 18$.

4. Factor $3g - 12h - 99j$.

5. Mr. Smith asks Johnny to solve $(12 - 8) - 1$. Johnny says that he can use the Associative Property and rewrite the problem as $12 - (8 - 1)$. Do you agree with Johnny? Why or why not?

ANSWERS

CHECK YOUR ANSWERS

PROPERTY	EXPRESSION	EQUIVALENT EXPRESSION
Identity Property of Addition	6	$6 + 0$
Identity Property of Multiplication	y	$y \cdot 1$ or $1y$
Commutative Property of Addition	$6 + 14$	$14 + 6$
Commutative Property of Multiplication	$8 \cdot m$	$m \cdot 8$
Associative Property of Addition	$(x + 4) + 9$	$x + (4 + 9)$
Associative Property of Multiplication	$7 \cdot (r \cdot 11)$	$(7 \cdot r) \cdot 11$
Distributive Property of Multiplication over Addition	$5(v + 22)$	$5v + 110$
Distributive Property of Multiplication over Subtraction	$8(7 - w)$	$56 - 8w$
Factor	$18x + 6$	$6(3x + 1)$
Factor	$14 - 35z$	$7(2 - 5z)$

1. $3x + 6y - 15$

2. $2a - \dfrac{3}{2}b - \dfrac{1}{2}c$

3. $2(3x + 5y + 9)$

4. $3(g - 4h - 33j)$

5. No, Johnny is wrong because the Associative Property does not work with subtraction—the order in which you subtract matters.

Chapter 29

LIKE TERMS

A term is a number by itself or the product of a number and variable (or more than one variable).

EXAMPLES:

5 (a number by itself)

x (a variable)

$7y$ (a number and a variable)

$16\,mn^2$ (a number and more than one variable)

In an expression, terms are separated by an addition calculation, which may appear as a positive or negative sign.

EXAMPLES:

$5x + 3y + 12$ (The terms are $5x$, $3y$, and 12.)

$3g^2 + 47h - 19$ (The terms are $3g^2$, $47h$, and -19.)

↖ ALTHOUGH THIS MAY LOOK LIKE A SUBTRACTION SYMBOL, YOU'RE ACTUALLY ADDING A NEGATIVE NUMBER.

We **COLLECT LIKE TERMS** (also called **COMBINING LIKE TERMS**) to simplify an expression—meaning, we rewrite the expression so that it contains fewer numbers, variables, and operations. Basically, you make it look more "simple."

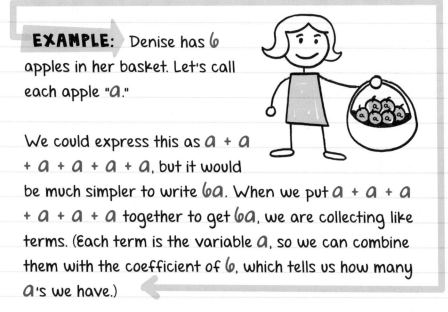

EXAMPLE: Denise has 6 apples in her basket. Let's call each apple "a."

We could express this as $a + a + a + a + a + a$, but it would be much simpler to write $6a$. When we put $a + a + a + a + a + a$ together to get $6a$, we are collecting like terms. (Each term is the variable a, so we can combine them with the coefficient of 6, which tells us how many a's we have.)

When combining terms with the same variable, add the coefficients.

EXAMPLE:
Denise now has 6 apples in her pink basket, 1 apple in her purple basket, and 7 apples in her white basket.

We could express this as $6a + a + 7a$ but it would be much simpler to write $14a$.

A variable without a coefficient actually has a coefficient of 1. So "m" really means "$1m$" and "k^3" really means "$1k^3$." (Remember the identity property of multiplication!)

EXAMPLE: $9x - 3x + 5x$
(When there is a "$-$" sign in front of the term, we have to subtract.)
$9x - 3x + 5x = 11x$

If two terms do NOT have the exact same variable, they cannot be combined.

EXAMPLE: $7m + 3y - 2m + y + 8$
(The $7m$ and $-2m$ combine to make $5m$, the $3y$ and y combine to make $4y$, and the constant 8 does not combine with anything.)
$7m + 3y - 2m + y + 8 = 5m + 4y + 8$

REMEMBER: A term with a variable cannot be combined with a constant.

$3ab$ can combine with $4ba$, because the **commutative property of multiplication** tells us that ab and ba are equivalent!

SORRY—
WE'RE JUST
NOT A GOOD
COMBO.

4y

8

When simplifying, we often put the term with the greatest exponent first, and we put the constant last. This is called **DESCENDING ORDER**.

Also, mathematicians tend to put their variables in alphabetical order!

EXAMPLE: $7m^2 + 2m - 6$

In order to combine like terms, the variables have to be exactly the same. So, $4y$ cannot combine with $3y^2$ because $3y^2$ really means $3 \cdot y \cdot y$, so the terms are not alike.

Sometimes, we need to use the distributive property first and then collect like terms.

EXAMPLE: $3x + 4(x + 3) - 1$

$3x + 4(x + 3) - 1$ First, use the distributive property to catapult the 4 over the parentheses.

$= 3x + 4x + 12 - 1$ Next, collect like terms.

$= 7x + 11$ This is as simple as you can make this expression!

CHECK YOUR KNOWLEDGE

For **1** through **3**, list the terms in each expression.

1. $4t^3 + 9y + 1$

2. $11gh - 6t + 4$

3. $z + mn - 4v^2$

For **4** through **5**, list the coefficients and the constant in each expression.

4. $2m^5 + 3y - 1$

5. $19x^5 - 55y^2 + 11$

For **6** through **10**, simplify each expression.

6. $7x + 11x$

7. $12y - 5y + 19$

8. $3t + 6z - 4t + 9z + z$

9. $19mn + 6x^2 + 2nm$

10. $5x + 3(x + 1) + 2x - 9$

ANSWERS

CHECK YOUR ANSWERS

1. $4t^3$, $9y$, 1

2. $11gh$, $-6t$, 4

3. z, mn, $-4v^2$

4. Coefficients: 2, 3; Constant: -1

5. Coefficients: 19, -55; Constant: 11

6. $18x$

7. $7y + 19$

8. $-t + 16z$

9. $6x^2 + 21mn$

10. $10x - 6$

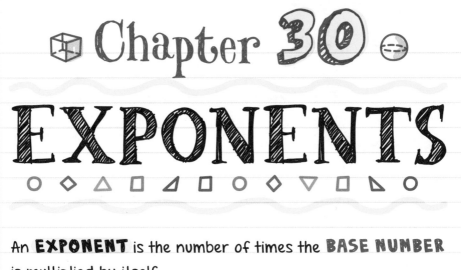

⬡ Chapter 30 ⊜

EXPONENTS
○ ◇ △ □ ◿ ◻ ○ ◇ ▽ □ ◣ ○

An **EXPONENT** is the number of times the **BASE NUMBER** is multiplied by itself.

EXAMPLE: 4^3

4 is the base number. The small, raised number 3 to the right of the base number indicates the number of times the base number is multiplied by itself.

Therefore: $4^3 = 4 \times 4 \times 4 = 64$.

4^3 is read "four to the third power."

> **COMMON MISTAKE:**
> The expression 4^3 does NOT mean 4×3.

Things to remember about exponents:

1. Any base without an exponent has an "invisible" exponent of 1.

EXAMPLE: $8 = 8^1$

2. Any base with an exponent 0, equals 1.

EXAMPLE: $6^0 = 1$

3. Be careful when calculating negative numbers with exponents.

EXAMPLE:

$$-3^2 = -(3^2) = -(3 \times 3) = -9 \text{ VS. } (-3)^2 = (-3) \times (-3) = 9$$

Always LOOK AT WHAT IS NEXT TO THE EXPONENT:
In the first example, the number 3 is next to the exponent.
So, only the 3 is being raised to the second power.

In the second example, the parentheses is next to the exponent, so we raise *everything* inside the parentheses to the second power. The -3 is inside the parentheses and, therefore, -3 is raised to the second power.

Simplifying Expressions with Exponents

You can simplify expressions with more than one exponent by combining the exponents—the only requirement is that the base must be the same. It looks like this:

$$x^a \cdot x^b = x^{a+b}$$
$$x^a \div x^b = x^{a-b}$$

THAT'S **39,060** MORE POWER THAN THE AVERAGE 5!

When multiplying powers with the same base, write the base once, and then add the exponents!

EXAMPLE: $5^2 \cdot 5^6 = 5^{2+6} = 5^8$

If you want to check that this works, try the long way:
$$5^2 \cdot 5^6 = 5 \cdot 5 \cdot 5 \cdot 5 \cdot 5 \cdot 5 \cdot 5 \cdot 5 = 5^8$$

When dividing powers with the same base, write the base once and subtract the exponents!

EXAMPLE: $7^6 \div 7^2 = 7^{6-2} = 7^4$

If you want to check that this works, try the long way:
$$\frac{7^6}{7^2} = \frac{7 \cdot 7 \cdot 7 \cdot 7 \cdot 7 \cdot 7}{7 \cdot 7} = 7^4$$

(We can cancel out two of the 7s on top and both on the bottom because anything divided by itself equals 1.)

$$\frac{7^6}{7^2} = \frac{7 \cdot 7 \cdot 7 \cdot 7 \cdot \cancel{7} \cdot \cancel{7}}{\cancel{7} \cdot \cancel{7}} = 7^4$$

Let's try it with variables:

EXAMPLE: $x^2 \cdot 2y \cdot x^4$ To simplify, we keep the base (x) and add the exponents $2 + 4$.

$$= x^6 \cdot 2y$$

← CAN ALSO BE WRITTEN AS $2x^6 y$

EXAMPLE: $3a^9 \div 7a^5$ To simplify $a^9 \div a^5$, we keep the base (a) and subtract the exponents $9 - 5$.

$$= 3a^4 \div 7$$

DON'T FORGET THAT YOU CAN ALSO FORMAT THIS QUESTION LIKE A FRACTION IF IT MAKES THE SOLUTION EASIER TO SEE. $\dfrac{3a^9}{7a^5}$

When there is an exponent inside parentheses and another outside the parentheses, this is called a **POWER OF A POWER**. A power of a power can be simplified by multiplying the exponents. It looks like this:

$$(v^a)^b = v^{a \cdot b}$$

Mnemonic for "Power of a Power: Multiply Exponents":

Powerful Orangutans Propelled Multiple Elephants.

EXAMPLE: $(4^2)^3 = 4^{2 \cdot 3} = 4^6$

> If you want to check that this works, try the long way:
> $(4^2)^3 = 4^2 \times 4^2 \times 4^2 = 4 \times 4 \times 4 \times 4 \times 4 \times 4 = 4^6$

EXAMPLE:

$(3x^7y^4)^2 = 3^{1 \cdot 2} \cdot x^{7 \cdot 2} \cdot y^{4 \cdot 2} = 3^2 \cdot x^{14} \cdot y^8 = 9x^{14}y^8$

(Don't forget: Any base without an exponent has an "invisible" exponent of 1.)

Negative Exponents

What about if you see a **NEGATIVE EXPONENT**? You can easily calculate a negative exponent by using reciprocals.

A negative exponent in the numerator becomes a positive exponent when moved to the denominator. It looks like this:

$$x^{-m} = \frac{1}{x^m}$$

193

See a negative exponent?
MOVE IT! If it's in the numerator, move it to the denominator and vice versa. Then you can lose the negative sign!

EXAMPLE: $3^{-3} = \dfrac{1}{3^3} = \dfrac{1}{27}$

And the opposite is true: A negative exponent in the denominator becomes a positive exponent when moved to the numerator. It looks like this:

$$\frac{1}{x^{-m}} = x^m$$

EXAMPLE: $\dfrac{1}{5^{-2}} = 5^2 = 25$

EXAMPLE: $\dfrac{x^5 y^{-3}}{x^{-4}y^4}$

Turn y^{-3} into y^3 by moving it to the denominator.
Turn x^{-4} into x^4 by moving it to the numerator.

The new expression is $\dfrac{x^5 \cdot x^4}{y^3 \cdot y^4}$.

It simplifies to $\dfrac{x^9}{y^7}$.

CHECK YOUR KNOWLEDGE

Simplify each of the following:

1. 5^3

2. $14m^0$

3. -2^4

4. $x^9 \cdot x^5$

5. $4x^2 \cdot 2y \cdot -3x^5$

6. $\dfrac{t^9}{t}$

7. $\dfrac{-15x^4 y^2}{5x^3 y^2}$

8. $(10^3)^2$

9. $(8m^3 n)^3$

10. $\dfrac{y^5 z^{-2}}{y^2 z^6}$

CHECK YOUR ANSWERS

1. 125

2. 14

3. −16

4. x^{14}

5. $-24x^7y$

6. t^8

7. $-3x$

8. 10^6 or 1,000,000

9. $512m^9n^3$

10. $\dfrac{y^3}{z^8}$

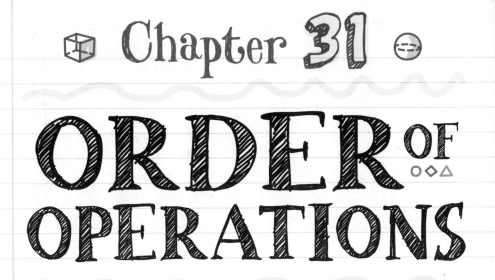

Chapter 31

ORDER OF OPERATIONS

The **ORDER OF OPERATIONS** is an order agreed upon by all mathematicians (and math students!) that should be closely followed. Follow this order:

1ST Any calculations inside parentheses or brackets should be done first. (This includes all grouping symbols, such as ( ), { }, and [ ].)

2ND Exponents, roots, and absolute value are calculated left to right.

3RD Multiplication and division—whichever comes first when you calculate left to right.

4TH Addition and subtraction—whichever comes first when you calculate left to right.

Lots of people use the mnemonic "Please Excuse My Dear Aunt Sally" for **PEMDAS** (Parentheses, Exponents, Multiplication, Division, Addition, and Subtraction) to remember the order of operations, but it can be VERY misleading. You can do division before multiplication as long as you are calculating from left to right—the same thing goes for addition and subtraction. Also, because other calculations like roots and absolute value aren't included, PEMDAS isn't totally foolproof.

EXAMPLE: $4 + 3 \cdot 2$ First, multiply the 3 and 2 together.

$= 4 + 6$ Then add.
$= 10$

EXAMPLE: $6 + (12 \div 4) \cdot 2$ Start with the calculation inside the parentheses first.

$= 6 + (3) \cdot 2$ Next, multiply the 3 and 2 together.

$= 6 + 6$ Then add.
$= 12$

EXAMPLE: $3^2 - 4(6 + 1) - 2$ Start with the exponent and the calculations inside the parentheses.

$= 9 - 4(7) - 2$ Next, multiply.

$= 9 - 28 - 2$ Last, subtract from left to right.

$= -21$

Whenever you have two sets of parentheses or brackets nested inside one another, CALCULATE THE INNERMOST SET OF PARENTHESES OR BRACKETS FIRST, then work outward.

EXAMPLE: $[14 \div (9 - 2) + 1] \cdot 6$ Start with the calculations inside the innermost parentheses: $9 - 2 = 7$.

$= [14 \div 7 + 1] \cdot 6$ Next, divide inside the brackets: $14 \div 7 = 2$.

$= [2 + 1] \cdot 6$ Then, add inside the brackets: $2 + 1 = 3$.

$= 3 \cdot 6$
$= 18$

For **1**, fill in the blanks:

According to the order of operations, follow this order: First, do any calculations inside parentheses or _____ . (This includes all grouping symbols, such as ( ), { }, and [ ].) Then, calculate exponents, roots, and _____. Next, do multiplication and division (it doesn't matter whether you do _____ or multiplication first, as long as you calculate from _____ to _____). Then, do addition and subtraction (it doesn't matter whether you do subtraction or _____ first as long as you calculate from _____ to _____).

For **2** through **10**, simplify the following expressions:

2. $4 + 8 \cdot 2$

3. $2 + 6 + 8^2$

4. $9 + (9 - 4 \cdot 2)$

5. $4^2 + (19 - 15) \cdot 3$

6. $(-4)(-2) + 2(6 + 5)$

7. $(6 - 3)^2 - (4 + -3)^3$

8. $|6 - 8| + [(2 + 5) \cdot 3]^2$

9. $\dfrac{27}{-3} + (12 \div 4)^3$

10. $[6 \cdot 4(15 \div 5)] + [2^2 + (1 \cdot -5)]$

CHECK YOUR ANSWERS

1. brackets; absolute value; division; left; right; addition; left; right

2. 20

3. 72

4. 10

5. 28

6. 30

7. 8

8. 443

9. 18

10. 71

Chapter 32

SCIENTIFIC

◦ ◇ △ ☐ ◿ ☐ ◻ ◯ ◇ ▽ ☐ ◹ △ ◯

NOTATION

We usually write numbers in **STANDARD NOTATION**.

EXAMPLE: 2,300,000

NOT VERY SCIENTIFIC.

SCIENTIFIC NOTATION is a shorthand way of writing numbers that are often very small or large by using powers of 10.

EXAMPLE: 2.3×10^6

I APPROVE!

(which is the same as 2,300,000)

In scientific notation, the first number is greater than or equal to 1, but less than 10. The second number is a power of 10.

EXAMPLE of a very **LARGE** number:
$$7.4 \times 10^9 = 7,400,000,000$$

EXAMPLE of a very small number:
$$7.4 \times 10^{-9} = 0.0000000074$$

To CONVERT A NUMBER FROM SCIENTIFIC NOTATION TO
STANDARD NOTATION:

> If the exponent on the 10 is positive, move the
> decimal that many spaces to the **RIGHT**.

> If the exponent on the 10 is negative, move the
> decimal that many spaces to the **LEFT**.

EXAMPLE: Convert 8.91×10^7 to standard notation.

8.91×10^7 ⟵   The exponent 7 is positive, so move
                      the decimal seven spaces to the right
$89,100,000$ (and fill with zeros).

EXAMPLE: Convert 4.667×10^{-6} to standard notation.

4.667×10^{-6} ⟵   The exponent 6 is negative, so move
                      the decimal six spaces to the left
0.000004667 (and fill with zeros).

To CONVERT A POSITIVE NUMBER FROM STANDARD
NOTATION TO SCIENTIFIC NOTATION, count how many
places you have to move the decimal point so that there is
only a number between 1 and 10 that remains. The number
of spaces that you move the decimal point is related to the
exponent of 10.

If the standard notation number is greater than 1, the exponent of 10 will be **POSITIVE**.

EXAMPLE: Convert 3,320,000 to scientific notation.

3,320,000 Move the decimal point six spaces to get a number between 1 and 10: 3.32.

3.32×10^6 The standard notation number (3,320,000) is greater than 1, so the exponent of 10 is positive 6.

If the standard notation number is less than 1, the exponent of 10 will be **NEGATIVE**.

EXAMPLE: Convert 0.0007274 to scientific notation.

0.0007274 Move the decimal point four spaces to get a number between 1 and 10: 7.274.

7.274×10^{-4} The standard notation number (0.0007274) is less than 1, so the exponent of 10 is negative 4.

You can use scientific notation with negative numbers, too. For example, changing **−360** to scientific notation would be: **-3.6×10^2**. You simply count how many places you have to move the decimal point so that there is only a number between 0 and −10 that remains.

Calculating Numbers in Scientific Notation

To MULTIPLY NUMBERS IN SCIENTIFIC NOTATION, remember our shortcut for multiplying powers with the same base. Just write the base once and add the exponents.

EXAMPLE: $(2 \times 10^4)(3 \times 10^5)$

$= 2 \cdot 10^4 \cdot 3 \cdot 10^5$ Keep the base 10 and add the exponents: $10^{4+5} = 10^9$.

$= 2 \times 3 \times 10^9$

$= 6 \times 10^9$

To DIVIDE NUMBERS IN SCIENTIFIC NOTATION, remember our shortcut for dividing powers with the same base. Just write the base once and subtract the exponents.

EXAMPLE: $\dfrac{8 \times 10^9}{4 \times 10^6}$

$= \dfrac{8}{4} \times \dfrac{10^9}{10^6}$ $\Big\{$ Keep the base 10 and subtract the exponents: $10^{9-6} = 10^3$.

$= 2 \times 10^3$

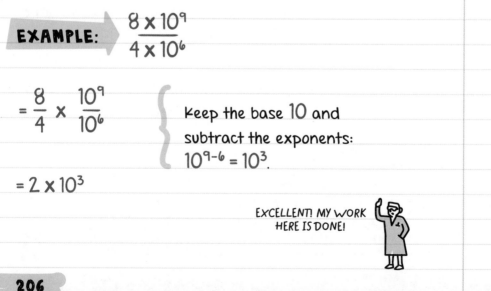

EXCELLENT! MY WORK HERE IS DONE!

CHECK YOUR KNOWLEDGE

1. Convert 2.29×10^5 to standard notation.

2. Convert 8.44×10^{-3} to standard notation.

3. Convert 1.2021×10^{-9} to standard notation.

4. Convert 4,502,000 to scientific notation.

5. Convert 67,000,000,000 to scientific notation.

6. Convert 0.00005461 to scientific notation.

For **7** through **11**, evaluate:

7. $(4.6 \times 10^3)(2.1 \times 10^2)$

8. $(2 \times 10^{-5})(3.3 \times 10^{-2})$

9. $(4 \times 10^4)(3 \times 10^3)$

10. $\dfrac{9 \times 10^7}{1.8 \times 10^3}$

11. $\dfrac{3.64 \times 10^5}{2.6 \times 10^{-2}}$

ANSWERS

CHECK YOUR ANSWERS

1. 229,000

2. 0.00844

3. 0.0000000012021

4. 4.502×10^6

5. 6.7×10^{10}

6. 5.461×10^{-5}

7. 9.66×10^5

8. 6.6×10^{-7}

9. $12 \times 10^7 = 1.2 \times 10^8$

10. 5×10^4

11. 1.4×10^7

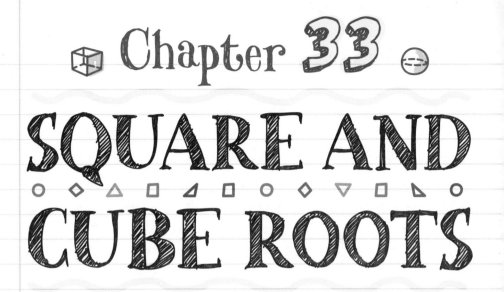

Chapter 33

SQUARE AND CUBE ROOTS

SQUARE ROOTS

When we **SQUARE** a number, we raise it to the power of 2.

EXAMPLE: 3^2 (Read aloud as "three squared.")

$3^2 = 3 \times 3 = 9$

The opposite of squaring a number is to take a number's **SQUARE ROOT**. The square root of a number is indicated by putting it inside a **RADICAL SIGN**, or $\sqrt{}$.

EXAMPLE: $\sqrt{16}$ (Read aloud as "square root of 16.")

$\sqrt{16} = \sqrt{4 \times 4} = 4$ and $\sqrt{16} = \sqrt{-4 \times -4} = 4$

> When simplifying a square root, ask yourself,
> "What number times itself equals the number
> inside the radical sign?"

Perfect Squares

I'M PERFECT!

$\sqrt{16}$ is also a **PERFECT SQUARE**, which is a number that is the square of an integer.

When you find the square root of a perfect square, it is a positive or negative whole number—in this case ± 4. The $\pm$ means "positive or negative" ($4 \cdot 4 = 16$ and $-4 \cdot -4 = 16$).

EXAMPLE: 4 is a perfect square.

$\sqrt{4} = \pm 2$ ($2 \cdot 2 = 4$ and $-2 \cdot -2 = 4$)

EXAMPLE: 1 is a perfect square.

$\sqrt{1} = \pm 1$ ($1 \cdot 1 = 1$ and $-1 \cdot -1 = 1$)

EXAMPLE: $\frac{1}{4}$ is a perfect square.

$\sqrt{\frac{1}{4}} = \pm\frac{1}{2} \left(\frac{1}{2} \cdot \frac{1}{2} = \frac{1}{4} \text{ and } -\frac{1}{2} \cdot -\frac{1}{2} = \frac{1}{4} \right)$

If a number under the radical sign is NOT a perfect square, it is an irrational number.

EXAMPLE: $\sqrt{7}$ is irrational.

WHO ARE YOU CALLING IRRATIONAL?

EXAMPLE: $\sqrt{10}$ is irrational.

CUBE ROOTS

When we **CUBE** a number, we raise it to the power of 3.

EXAMPLE: 2^3 (Read aloud as "two cubed.")

$2^3 = 2 \times 2 \times 2 = 8$

The opposite of cubing a number is to take a number's **CUBE ROOT**. The cube root of a number is indicated by putting it inside a radical sign with a 3 on top, or $\sqrt[3]{}$.

EXAMPLE: $\sqrt[3]{8} = 2$ (Read aloud as "cube root of 8," which equals $2 \times 2 \times 2$.)

EXAMPLE: $\sqrt[3]{27} = 3$ (Read aloud as "cube root of 27," which equals $3 \times 3 \times 3$.)

EXAMPLE: $\sqrt[3]{\dfrac{1}{125}} = \dfrac{1}{5}$ (Read aloud as "cube root of $\dfrac{1}{125}$," which equals $\dfrac{1}{5} \times \dfrac{1}{5} \times \dfrac{1}{5}$.)

> When simplifying a cube root, ask yourself, "What number to the third power equals the number under the radical sign?"

Perfect Cubes

Numbers like 8 and 27 are sometimes referred to as **PERFECT CUBES**. Perfect cubes can also be negative numbers.

EXAMPLE: $\sqrt[3]{-8} = -2$ (Read aloud as "cube root of negative 8," which equals $-2 \times -2 \times -2$.)

EXAMPLE: $\sqrt[3]{-1} = -1$ (Read aloud as "cube root of negative 1," which equals $-1 \times -1 \times -1$.)

EXAMPLE: $\sqrt[3]{-\dfrac{8}{27}} = -\dfrac{2}{3}$ (Read aloud as "cube root of negative $\dfrac{8}{27}$," which equals

$-\dfrac{2}{3} \times -\dfrac{2}{3} \times -\dfrac{2}{3}$.)

PERFECT!

16

PERFECTER!

8

IS THAT A WORD?

27

CHECK YOUR KNOWLEDGE

1. Fill in each missing value:

PERFECT SQUARE	SQUARE ROOT
1	
	±2
9	
	±4
25	
	±6
49	
	±8
81	
	±10

PERFECT CUBE	CUBE ROOT
1	
8	
27	

List the cube root of each of the following numbers.

2. -27

3. 64

4. -1

5. -125

6. 0

7. $\frac{1}{8}$

8. $\frac{8}{125}$

CHECK YOUR ANSWERS

1.

PERFECT SQUARE	SQUARE ROOT
1	±1
4	±2
9	±3
16	±4
25	±5
36	±6
49	±7
64	±8
81	±9
100	±10

PERFECT CUBE	CUBE ROOT
1	1
8	2
27	3

2. -3

3. 4

4. -1

5. -5

6. 0

7. $\dfrac{1}{2}$

8. $\dfrac{2}{5}$

Chapter 34

COMPARING IRRATIONAL NUMBERS

If we want to compare irrational numbers, it's easiest to use approximation. ←
AND STILL ACCURATE ENOUGH!

> There is a special irrational number called **π**. It is the Greek letter *pi* and is read like "pie." The value of pi is 3.14159265... but is commonly rounded to 3.14.

EXAMPLE: Which is larger? 6 or 2π?

Because π is approximately 3.14, it means that 2π is approximately $2 \times 3.14 = 6.28$.
$2\pi > 6$ ←

The square root of a perfect square is easy to find, like $\sqrt{9} = 3$. But we can also find the approximate values of numbers like $\sqrt{2}$ or $\sqrt{10}$ by "working backward."

EXAMPLE: Which is larger, $\sqrt{5}$ or 2.1?

First, we need to find out what is the approximate value of $\sqrt{5}$ to the tenth decimal place.

We know that $1^2 = 1$, $2^2 = 4$, $3^2 = 9$
or $\sqrt{1} = 1$, $\sqrt{4} = 2$, $\sqrt{9} = 3$.

≈ MEANS APPROXIMATELY EQUAL

So, $\sqrt{5}$ must be between 2 and 3...therefore, $\sqrt{5} \approx 2$.

The question asks us to compare the approximate value with a number that has a value in the tenth place, so we can then try:

$2.0^2 = 4$, $2.1^2 = 4.41$, $2.2^2 = 4.84$, $2.3^2 = 5.29$.

So, $\sqrt{5}$ must be between 2.2 and 2.3, but it's closer to 2.2...therefore, $\sqrt{5} \approx 2.2$.

Therefore $\sqrt{5}$ is larger than 2.1.

If you needed to find out what is the approximate value of $\sqrt{5}$ to the hundredth decimal place, you would just repeat the process of "working backward," and try:

$2.21^2 = 4.8841$, $2.22^2 = 4.9284$... and so on until you found the closest approximation.

CHECK YOUR KNOWLEDGE

1. Calculate 2π.

2. Calculate 5π.

3. Calculate -3π.

4. Calculate $\frac{1}{2}\pi$.

5. What is the approximate value of $\sqrt{3}$ to the tenth decimal place?

6. What is the approximate value of $\sqrt{6}$ to the tenth decimal place?

7. What is the approximate value of $\sqrt{2}$ to the hundredth decimal place?

8. What is the approximate value of $\sqrt{5}$ to the hundredth decimal place?

9. Which is the largest number: $\sqrt{10}$, π, or 3?

10. Draw a number line and place the following numbers in the correct location: $-3, 0, 1, \pi, \sqrt{5}$

ANSWERS

CHECK YOUR ANSWERS

1. 6.28

2. 15.7

3. -9.42

4. 1.57

5. $\sqrt{3} \approx 1.7$

6. $\sqrt{6} \approx 2.4$

7. $\sqrt{2} \approx 1.42$

8. $\sqrt{5} \approx 2.24$

9. The largest number is $\sqrt{10}$.

10.

◈ Chapter 35 ◎

EQUATIONS

○ ◇ ▢ ◿ ▢ ○ ◇ ▽ ▢ ◣ ○

An **EQUATION** is a mathematical sentence with an equal sign. To solve an equation, we find the missing number, or variable, that makes the sentence true. This number is called the **SOLUTION**.

EXAMPLE: Is $x = 8$ the solution for $x + 12 = 20$?

$8 + 12 = 20$ (Rewrite the equation and substitute 8 for x.)

$20 = 20$

Both sides are the same, so the solution ($x = 8$) makes the sentence true.

EXAMPLE: Is -6 the solution to $3x = 18$?

$3(-6) = 18$

$-18 \neq 18$

Both sides are NOT the same, so -6 is NOT the solution!

EVALUATION is the process of simplifying a mathematical expression by first **SUBSTITUTING** (replacing) a variable with a number, and then solving the expression using order of operations—kind of like when you have a substitute teacher. Your teacher is replaced by somebody else who does the same function.

HI! I'M YOUR SUBSTITUTE FOR THIS EQUATION!

GREAT! I REALLY NEED A DAY OFF!

EXAMPLE: Evaluate $x + 1$ when $x = 3$.

$3 + 1 = 4$ (Because we know $x = 3$, we can take the x out and replace it with 3.)

EXAMPLE: Evaluate $3y - 6$ when $y = 8$.

$3 \cdot 8 - 6$ (Because we know $y = 8$, we substitute y with 8. Then, we follow order of operations: In this case, we multiply first.)

$= 24 - 6$

$= 18$

If there are two or more variables, we follow the same steps: substitute and solve!

EXAMPLE: Evaluate $4x - 7m$ when $x = 6$ and $m = 4$.

$4 \cdot 6 - 7 \cdot 4$
$= 24 - 28$
$= -4$

EXAMPLE: Evaluate $\dfrac{8y + z}{6 - x}$ when $y = 3$; $z = -2$; $x = -5$.

$\dfrac{8 \cdot 3 + (-2)}{6 - (-5)}$

$= \dfrac{24 + (-2)}{6 - (-5)}$

$= \dfrac{22}{11}$

$= 2$

> **HINT:** When variables are in a numerator or denominator, first simplify the entire top, then simplify the entire bottom, then you can divide the numerator by the denominator. Think about the fraction bar like a grouping symbol.

Independent and Dependent Variables

There are different types of variables that can appear in an equation:

> The variable you are substituting for is called the
> **INDEPENDENT VARIABLE**.

> The other variable (that you solve for) is called the
> **DEPENDENT VARIABLE**.

Just remember: The dependent variable depends on the independent variable!

EXAMPLE: Solve for y in the expression $y = 5x + 3$ when $x = 4$.

$y = 5 \cdot 4 + 3$ (The variable x is the independent variable, and y is the dependent variable.)

$y = 20 + 3$

$y = 23$

CHECK YOUR WORK

$y = 5x + 3$

$23 = 5(4) + 3$

$23 = 20 + 3$

$23 = 23$ ✓

If you're unsure of your answer, go back to the original equation and insert both values for the variables, making sure both sides are equal.

The answer is correct!

CHECK YOUR KNOWLEDGE

1. Evaluate $x + 6$ when $x = 7$.

2. Evaluate $3m - 5$ when $m = 9$.

3. Evaluate $7b - b$ when $b = 4$.

4. Evaluate $9x - y$ when $x = 6$ and $y = 3$.

5. Evaluate $-5m - 2n$ when $m = 6$ and $n = -2$.

For **6** through **10**, solve for y in each expression.

6. $y = 7 - x$ when $x = -1$

7. $y = 19x$ when $x = 2$

8. $y = -77t^2$ when $t = 5$

9. $y = \dfrac{175}{x + z}$ when $x = 17$ and $z = 8$

10. $y = j(11 + k)^2$ when $j = -4$ and $k = 1$

ANSWERS

1. 13

2. 22

3. 24

4. 51

5. -26

6. $y = 8$

7. $y = 38$

8. $y = -550$

9. $y = 7$

10. $y = -576$

Chapter 36

SOLVING FOR VARIABLES

Often, we are not given a number to substitute for the variable. This is when we must "solve for the unknown," or "solve for x."

> Solving an equation is like asking, "Which value makes this equation true?"

In order to do so, we must ISOLATE THE VARIABLE on one side of the equal sign.

EXAMPLE: $x + 7 = 13$

In order to isolate the variable (x) on one side of the equal sign, we must:

1. Think of an equation as a scale, with the = sign as the middle. You *must* keep the scale balanced at all times.

2. Ask yourself, "What is happening to this variable?"
In this case, 7 is being added to the variable.

3. So, how do we get the variable alone? We use
INVERSE OPERATIONS on both sides of the equation.
What is the inverse of adding 7? Subtracting 7.

WHEN YOU SEE THE WORD **INVERSE**, *THINK ABOUT OPPOSITES!*

$x + 7 = 13$
$x + \cancel{7} - \cancel{7} = 13 - 7$ (We subtract 7 from both sides
$x = 6$ to keep the equation balanced.)

CHECK YOUR WORK

$x + 7 = 13$ Check your work by
$6 + 7 = 13$ plugging your answer into
$13 = 13$ ✓   the original equation.

Inverse is just another word for *opposite*. Here's a quick
rundown of all the operations and their inverse operations:

OPERATION	INVERSE
Addition	Subtraction
Subtraction	Addition
Multiplication	Division
Division	Multiplication
Squaring (exponent of 2)	Square root ($\sqrt{}$)
Cubing (exponent of 3)	Cube root $\sqrt[3]{}$

EXAMPLE: Solve for m: $m - 9 = -13$.

$m - 9 = -13$ (What is happening to the m? The 9 is being subtracted from m. What is the inverse of subtraction? Addition!)

$m - \cancel{9} + \cancel{9} = -13 + 9$
$m = -4$

CHECK YOUR WORK

$m - 9 = -13$ Plug your answer
$-4 - 9 = -13$ ($m = -4$) into the
$-13 = -13$ ✓   original equation.

EXAMPLE: Solve for t: $-3t = 39$.

$-3t = 39$ (What is the inverse of multiplication? Division.)

$t = -13$

Don't forget that in order to keep the equation balanced, whatever you do to one side, you MUST also do to the other side.

CHECK YOUR WORK

$3t = 39$
$-3(-13) = 39$
$39 = 39$ ✓

EXAMPLE: Solve for y: $\frac{y}{4} = -19$.

$\frac{y}{4} = -19$ (What is the inverse of division? Multiplication.)

$\frac{4}{1} \times \frac{y}{4} = -19 \times 4$

$y = -76$

CHECK YOUR WORK

$\frac{y}{4} = -19$

$\frac{-76}{4} = -19$

$-19 = -19$ ✓

EXAMPLE: Solve for g: $g^2 = 121$.

$g^2 = 121$ (What is the inverse of squaring?
$\sqrt{g^2} = \sqrt{121}$ Finding the square root.)
$g = \pm 11$

CHECK YOUR WORK

$g^2 = 121$
$11^2 = 121$ and
$121 = 121$ ✓

$g^2 = 121$
$(-11)^2 = 121$
$121 = 121$ ✓

Solve for each variable.

1. $x + 14 = 22$

2. $7x = -35$

3. $y + 19 = 24$

4. $x - 11 = 8$

5. $-7 + m = -15$

6. $-6r = 72$

7. $-74 = -2w$

8. $\dfrac{v}{7} = -6$

9. $\dfrac{x}{-12} = -14$

10. $h^2 = 169$

CHECK YOUR ANSWERS

1. $x = 8$

2. $x = -5$

3. $y = 5$

4. $x = 19$

5. $m = -8$

6. $r = -12$

7. $w = 37$

8. $v = -42$

9. $x = 168$

10. $h = \pm13$

Chapter 37

SOLVING MULTISTEP

◢ ○ ◇ ▽ ▢ ○ ◇ ▢ ◢ ○ ◇ ▢ ○ ◁

EQUATIONS

Isolating the variable is the goal of solving equations, because on the other side of the equal sign will be the answer!

I LIKE MY ALONE TIME.

Here are the ways to isolate a variable:

1. Use inverse operations (as many times as necessary):

EXAMPLE: Solve for x: $3x + 7 = 28$.

$3x + 7 = 28$ (What is the inverse of
$3x + 7 - 7 = 28 - 7$ addition? Subtraction.)

$3x = 21$ (What is the inverse of
$\dfrac{3x}{3} = \dfrac{21}{3}$ multiplication? Division.)

$x = 7$

2. Use the distributive property, then use inverse operations.

EXAMPLE: Solve for m: $3(m - 6) = -12$.

$3(m - 6) = -12$ (We can distribute the 3 across the terms in the parentheses like so: $3(m - 6) = 3m - 3 \cdot 6$.)

$3m - 18 = -12$ (Add 18 to both sides.)

$3m = 6$ (Divide both sides by 3.)

$m = 2$

3. Combine **LIKE TERMS**, then use inverse operations.

EXAMPLE: Solve for y: $4y + 5y = 90$.

$4y + 5y = 90$ (4y and 5y are like terms. So, we can combine them: $4y + 5y = 9y$.)

$9y = 90$ (Divide both sides by 9.)

$y = 10$

EXAMPLE: Solve for y: $6y + 5 = 2y - 3$.

$6y + 5 = 2y - 3$

$6y - 2y + 5 = 2y - 2y - 3$

($6y$ and $2y$ are like terms but they are on different sides of the equal sign. We can combine them only by doing the inverse operation on both sides of the equation—the opposite of $2y$ is $-2y$.)

$4y + 5 = -3$

IT'S USUALLY EASIER TO DO THE INVERSE OPERATION OF THE SMALLER TERM—IN THIS CASE $2y$ IS SMALLER THAN $6y$.

$4y + 5 - 5 = -3 - 5$

(Next, subtract 5 from both sides.)

$$\frac{4y}{4} = \frac{-8}{4}$$

(Last, divide both sides by 4 to get y alone.)

$y = -2$

Sometimes, several steps are necessary in order to isolate a variable on one side of the equal sign. This example uses all three of the previous tools!

EXAMPLE:

Solve for w: $-3(w-3)-9w-9 = 4(w+2)-12$.

$-3(w-3)-9w-9 = 4(w+2)-12$ (First, use the distributive property to simplify.)

$-3w+9-9w-9 = 4w+8-12$ (Now, combine like terms on each side of the equal sign.)

$-12w = 4w-4$ (Last, use inverse operations to get the variable alone on one side of the equation like so: $-12w-4w = 4\cancel{w}-4-4\cancel{w}$.)

$-16w = -4$ (Use inverse operations again.)

$w = \dfrac{1}{4}$ (Don't forget to always simplify fractions!)

Plug your answer into the original equation to check your work.

234

CHECK YOUR KNOWLEDGE

Solve for the unknown variable.

1. $6x + 10 = 28$

2. $-2m - 4 = 8$

3. $x + x + 2x = 48$

4. $3y + 4 + 3y - 6 = 34$

5. $9(w - 6) = -36$

6. $-5(t + 3) = -30$

7. $5z + 2 = 3z - 10$

8. $11 + 3x + x = 2x - 11$

9. $-5(n - 1) = 7(n + 3)$

10. $-3(c - 4) - 2c - 8 = 9(c + 2) + 1$

ANSWERS

CHECK YOUR ANSWERS

1. $x = 3$

2. $m = -6$

3. $x = 12$

4. $y = 6$

5. $w = 2$

6. $t = 3$

7. $z = -6$

8. $x = -11$

9. $n = -\dfrac{4}{3}$ or $-1\dfrac{1}{3}$

10. $c = -\dfrac{15}{14}$ or $-1\dfrac{1}{14}$

⬦ Chapter 38 ⌒

SOLVING AND GRAPHING INEQUALITIES

SOLVING INEQUALITIES

While an equation is a mathematical sentence that contains an equal sign, an **INEQUALITY** is a mathematical sentence that contains a sign indicating that the values on each side of it are NOT equal.

EXAMPLES: $x > 4$ $x < 4$ $x \leq 4$ $x \geq 4$

To SOLVE AN INEQUALITY, just follow the same steps as solving an equation.

> Solving an inequality is like asking, "Which set of values makes this equation true?"

EXAMPLE: $5x + 6 < 21$

$5x + 6 - 6 < 21 - 6$ (Subtract 6 from both sides.)

$\dfrac{5x}{5} < \dfrac{15}{5}$ (Divide to get the variable alone.)

$x < 3$

There's only one difference: Any time you multiply or divide by a negative number, you must reverse the direction of the inequality sign. (Some kids call this **THE FLIPPIN' INEQUALITY RULE!**)

EXAMPLE: Solve for x: $-4x \geq 24$.

(Divide to get the variable alone, but ALSO, when dividing with a negative number, reverse the inequality sign.)

$x \leq -6$

CHECK YOUR ANSWER!

Because our answer says that x is less than or equal to -6, we can test this by picking any number that is less than or equal to -6.

Test $x = -6$. $-4(-6) \geq 24$
This is true! $24 \geq 24$ ✓

Test $x = -10$. $-4(-10) \geq 24$
This is true! $40 \geq 24$ ✓

Therefore, our answer is correct.

The answer to any inequality is an infinite set of numbers. (The answer $x \le -6$ literally means ANY number less than or equal to -6, which can go on forever!) But we can still represent this set of numbers with inequality symbols.

GRAPHING INEQUALITIES

In addition to writing inequalities using symbols, we can **GRAPH INEQUALITIES** on a number line as well. Here are the different ways to graph inequalities:

1. If the sentence uses a $<$ or $>$ sign, we indicate that the number is not included with an open circle.

EXAMPLE: Graph $x < 8$.

The number represented by x is less than 8, so 8 is NOT included in the possible numbers. Therefore, the circle is open.

2. If the sentence uses a $\le$ or $\ge$ sign, we indicate this with a "closed circle" to indicate that the solutions could equal the number itself.

EXAMPLE: Graph $x \geq 0$.

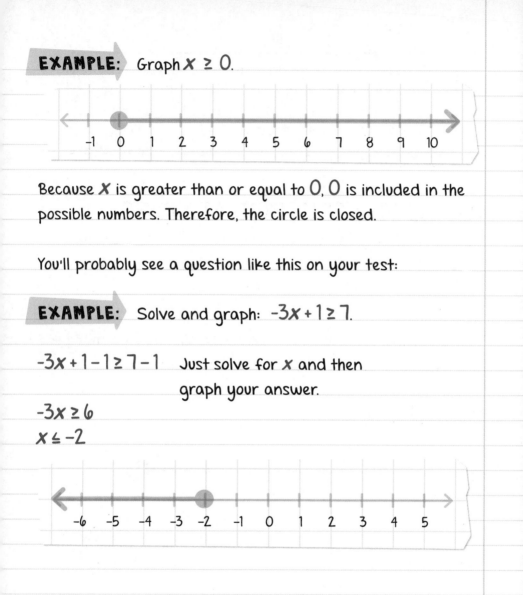

Because x is greater than or equal to 0, 0 is included in the possible numbers. Therefore, the circle is closed.

You'll probably see a question like this on your test:

EXAMPLE: Solve and graph: $-3x + 1 \geq 7$.

$-3x + 1 - 1 \geq 7 - 1$ Just solve for x and then
graph your answer.

$-3x \geq 6$

$x \leq -2$

CHECK YOUR KNOWLEDGE

1. Graph $x > 3$ on a number line.
2. Graph $y < -3$ on a number line.
3. Graph $m \leq -7$ on a number line.
4. Write the inequality that this number line represents using x as your variable:

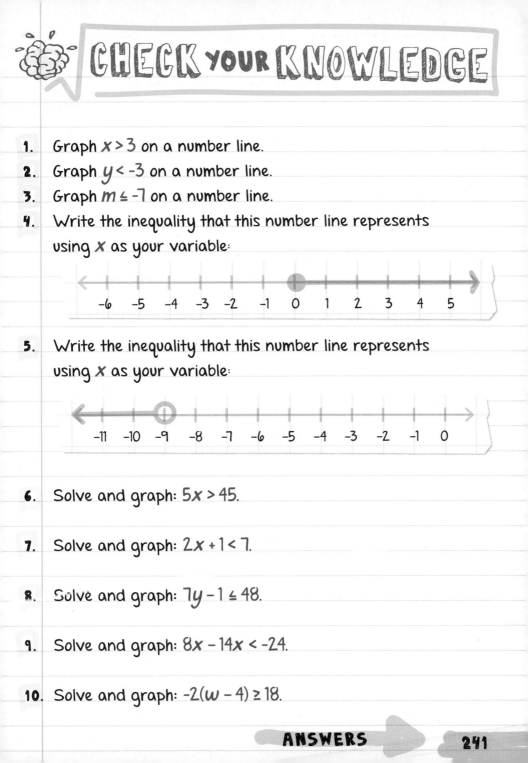

5. Write the inequality that this number line represents using x as your variable:

6. Solve and graph: $5x > 45$.

7. Solve and graph: $2x + 1 < 7$.

8. Solve and graph: $7y - 1 \leq 48$.

9. Solve and graph: $8x - 14x < -24$.

10. Solve and graph: $-2(w - 4) \geq 18$.

ANSWERS ➤

CHECK YOUR ANSWERS

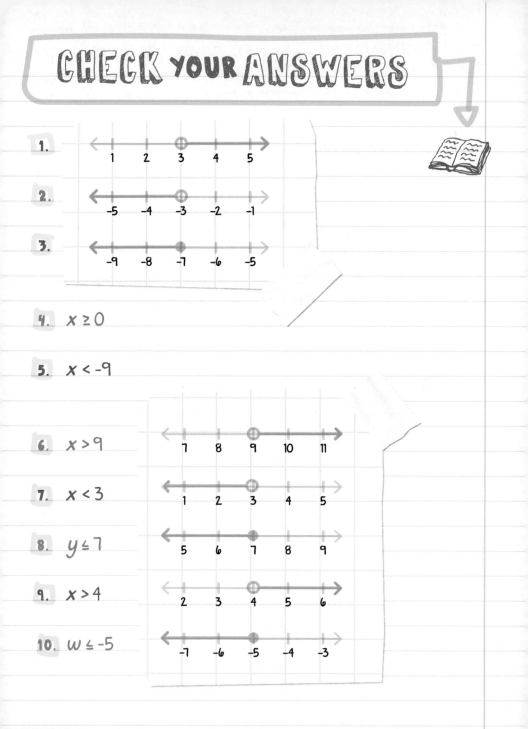

1. number line with open circle at 3 (1, 2, 3, 4, 5)

2. number line with open circle at −3 (−5, −4, −3, −2, −1)

3. number line with closed circle at −7 (−9, −8, −7, −6, −5)

4. $x \geq 0$

5. $x < -9$

6. $x > 9$ — number line with open circle at 9, shaded right (7, 8, 9, 10, 11)

7. $x < 3$ — number line with open circle at 3, shaded left (1, 2, 3, 4, 5)

8. $y \leq 7$ — number line with closed circle at 7, shaded left (5, 6, 7, 8, 9)

9. $x > 4$ — number line with open circle at 4, shaded right (2, 3, 4, 5, 6)

10. $w \leq -5$ — number line with closed circle at −5, shaded left (−7, −6, −5, −4, −3)

⬛ Chapter 39 ⊜

WORD PROBLEMS WITH EQUATIONS ◁ ○ ◇ ▽ AND INEQUALITIES

Often, we encounter real-life situations that we can solve with an equation or inequality.

EXAMPLE: Josh is trying to weigh his dog. Because the dog keeps running away, he decides to hold the dog and step on the scale. The total weight is 175 pounds. Josh knows that he weighs 151 pounds. How much does his dog weigh?

> To solve, we must translate the given situation into a mathematical equation or inequality:

1. Determine what operations are occurring. ← THINK: WHAT INFO DO I KNOW?

Josh's weight + dog's weight = total weight

2. What is your unknown quantity? This becomes your variable. ← THINK: WHAT INFO **DON'T** I KNOW?

The unknown quantity is the dog's weight, which we'll call "d."

3. Write your equation or inequality.

$151 + d = 175$

4. Now, solve your equation or inequality.

$151 + d = 175$
$151 - 151 + d = 175 - 151$
$d = 24$

DON'T FORGET TO CHECK YOUR WORK BY PLUGGING YOUR ANSWER INTO THE ORIGINAL EQUATION.

The dog weighs 24 pounds.

In word problems, look for key words:
"is" usually means =
"is greater than" usually means >
"is less than" usually means <
"at least" usually means ≥
"at most" usually means ≤

244

EXAMPLE: A clothing salesperson earns a base salary of $800 per month, plus a commission of 20% on sales. How much must the salesperson sell each month if she wants to earn at least $1,200 per month?

1. What info do I know? The base salary of $800 + 20% commission on sales must be greater than or equal to $1,200.

2. What is the unknown? The sales, which we'll call "S."

3. $800 + 0.2s \geq 1,200$

4. $800 - 800 + 0.2s \geq 1,200 - 800$

$$\frac{0.2s}{0.2} \geq \frac{400}{0.2}$$

$s \geq 2,000$

The salesperson must sell at least $2,000 to earn at least $1,200 per month.

EXAMPLE: Julian needs an average of at least 90 points in order to earn an "A" in his history class. So far, his test scores are 92, 86, and 88. What is the lowest grade Julian can score on his next test in order to earn an "A"?

Here's what we know: In order to find an average, you must add up all of the numbers and then divide by how many numbers there are (in this case, there are four numbers). Also, 90 is the lowest that we need the average to be, so the inequality sign must be "greater than or equal to." Additionally, we know the first three test scores, but not the fourth, so we'll call that one "t."

$$\frac{92 + 86 + 88 + t}{4} \geq 90$$

$$(4)\frac{266 + t}{4} \geq 90 \, (4) \qquad \text{(Multiply both sides by 4.)}$$

$$266 - 266 + t \geq 360 - 266 \qquad \text{Subtract 266 from each side.}$$

$t \geq 94$ Julian needs to score a 94 or higher on his next test in order to earn an "A" in the class.

Don't forget to check your work and ask: Is this reasonable? In this case, yes! Because he got two scores in the 80s, he'll need two scores in the 90s to keep the average at 90 (or higher).

OH BOY...

CHECK YOUR KNOWLEDGE

1. Jeremy spends $84 on a bat and a skateboard. The bat costs $33. How much does the skateboard cost?

2. Lucy goes to a department store and spends $90 on clothing. She buys a dress for $30, a hat for $12, and also buys a jacket. How much does the jacket cost?

3. Delilah wants to purchase a used car that costs $7,200. She has $900 and can save $450 per month. How many months will it take her to save $7,200?

4. Robert tutors two students, Andy and Sue. Andy pays Robert $70 per month. Sue pays Robert $50 per month. How many months will Robert have to tutor until he earns $600?

5. A car salesperson earns a base salary of $1,400 per month plus a commission of 5% on sales. How much must the salesperson sell in order to earn at least $4,500 per month?

6. Ling makes a base salary of $800 per month plus a commission of 15% on sales. How much must Ling sell in order to earn $5,000 per month?

7. Latrell wants to keep his test average in his science class at 85 or higher. So far, he has earned scores of 85, 76, 94, and 81 on his tests. What score must he get on his next test to keep his average at 85 or higher?

8. A construction team is building several buildings. They want the average time spent on each building to be 15 hours or less. So far, they have spent the following times for the first 4 buildings: 17 hours, 10 hours, 19 hours, 13 hours. How many hours should they spend building the fifth building in order to match their goal of an average of 15 hours or less?

9. In order to lose weight, Gerry calculates that he can consume at most 2,300 calories per day. For breakfast, he eats 550 calories. For a snack, he eats 220 calories, and for lunch, he eats 600 calories. How many calories can he eat for the rest of the day and not exceed his limit?

10. Larry is giving interviews to different news reporters and can spend up to 2 hours doing all of the interviews. He spends 35 minutes with Channel 1 News and then spends 45 minutes with Channel 7 News. If Channel 5 wants to interview him, how much time can Larry spend with them and not go over his time limit?

ANSWERS

CHECK YOUR ANSWERS

1. The skateboard costs $51.

2. $48

3. It will take Delilah 14 months (or 1 year and 2 months) to save $7,200.

4. 5 months

5. The salesperson must sell at least $62,000.

6. Ling must sell at least $28,000.

7. Latrell must score at least 89.

8. They need to spend 16 hours or less.

9. Gerry can eat less than or equal to 930 calories.

10. Larry can spend less than or equal to 40 minutes.

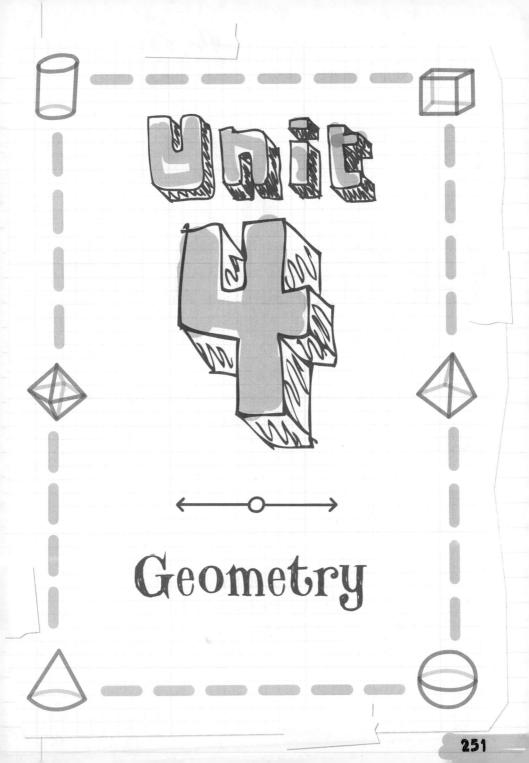

Unit 4

Geometry

Chapter 40

INTRODUCTION TO GEOMETRY

○ △ □ ○ ◁ △ □ ○ □ ◁

GEOMETRY is the branch of mathematics that deals with lines, shapes, and space. Here are some key concepts in geometry:

Term and Definition	Symbol	Example
LINE SEGMENT: a part of a line that has two endpoints	A horizontal bar above the two endpoints $\overline{AB}$	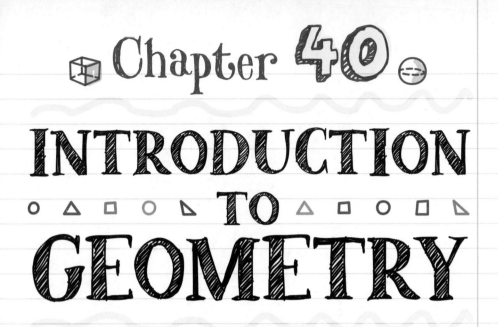

Term and Definition	Symbol	Example
LINE: a line that continues forever in both directions	A horizontal arrow above two points on the line $\overleftrightarrow{AB}$	
RAY: A line with only one endpoint	A horizontal arrow that extends in one direction. The endpoint must be named first $\overrightarrow{CD}$	
POINT	The name of the point A	A.
PARALLEL LINES: lines that are always the same distance apart. They NEVER intersect.	Two vertical bars $m\|n$	
ANGLE: formed by two rays with the same endpoint	$\angle A$	

Term and Definition	Symbol	Example
VERTEX: the point of intersection of rays or lines that form an angle	The name of the angle that forms the vertex $\angle A$ Or the point that forms the angle $\angle BAC$	
RIGHT ANGLE: a 90-degree angle		
PERPENDICULAR LINES: two lines that form a right angle	$P \perp Q$	
CONGRUENT LENGTHS or **CONGRUENT ANGLES:** the shapes, lines, or angles are equal in size	$\cong$	

GEOMETRIC SHAPES

Plane geometry deals with "flat" shapes such as squares and circles. "Flat" shapes are **TWO-DIMENSIONAL**, or **2-D**. A **POLYGON** is a closed plane figure (so it's two-dimensional) with at least three straight sides.

EXAMPLES:

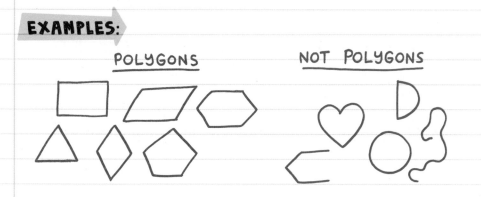

POLYGONS

NOT POLYGONS

Solid geometry deals with "solid" shapes such as cubes and spheres. Solid shapes are **THREE-DIMENSIONAL**, or **3-D**. A **POLYHEDRON** is a 3-D figure.

EXAMPLES:

SORRY, I THOUGHT THIS WAS CHEESE. CARRY ON!

TOOLS for GEOMETRY

Here are some tools that can help us with geometry problems. These tools provide clearly marked intervals to help us determine the length of a line or the measurement of an angle, etc., on a diagram.

RULER
ACTUAL SIZE!

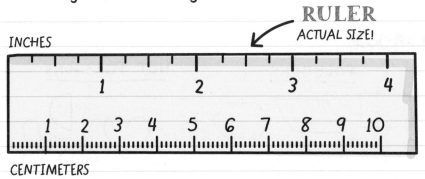

INCHES

1   2   3   4

1 2 3 4 5 6 7 8 9 10

CENTIMETERS

A **RULER** is a tool that we use to measure distances as well as draw straight lines on diagrams. Most rulers measure lengths in two different units: One side measures inches and feet, and the other side measures centimeters and meters.

EXAMPLE: Measure the length of the line in centimeters.

CM 1   2   3   4   5   6   7   8   9   10

We place the ruler over the line to see what length the line is: Therefore, we see that the line is 6 cm long.

PROTRACTOR

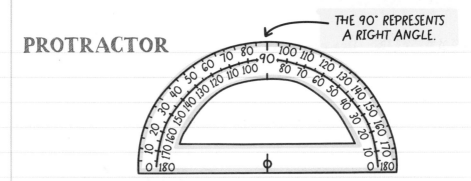

THE 90° REPRESENTS A RIGHT ANGLE.

A **PROTRACTOR** helps us calculate the measurement of an angle, as well as draw an accurate angle. There are several types of protractors, but most protractors are in the shape of a half circle with measurements on the protractor that show the size of any angle.

MEASURING ANGLES

EXAMPLE: Use a protractor to analyze the measurement of:

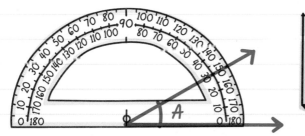

We place the protractor over the angle to see what degree it is:

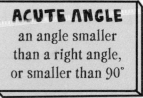

> **ACUTE ANGLE**
> an angle smaller than a right angle, or smaller than 90°

The protractor tells us that the angle is either 30° or 150°. But because we can see that ∠A is an **ACUTE ANGLE**, we know that the correct answer is 30°.

257

EXAMPLE: Use a protractor to analyze the measurement of $\angle B$:

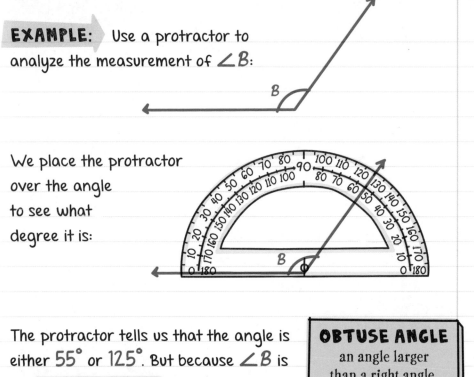

We place the protractor over the angle to see what degree it is:

The protractor tells us that the angle is either 55° or 125°. But because $\angle B$ is an **OBTUSE ANGLE**, we know that the correct answer is 125°.

> **OBTUSE ANGLE**
> an angle larger than a right angle, or larger than 90°

DRAWING ANGLES

EXAMPLE: Use a protractor to draw an angle that is 20°.

←————————————• VERTEX

First, we draw a horizontal line for the base. We place a dot on one end of the arm—this will be the vertex. Then we place the center of the protractor at this dot and align the 0° line on the protractor with the horizontal line we drew.

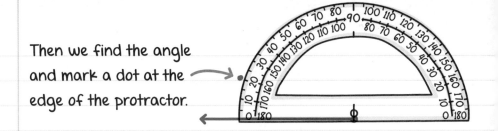

Then we find the angle and mark a dot at the edge of the protractor.

Lastly, we remove the protractor and use a ruler to draw a straight line from the vertex to the angle's dot.

EXAMPLE: Use a protractor and a ruler to draw a triangle that has the following angles of measurements: 95°, 20°, and 65°.

We first use the protractor and ruler to draw an angle that is 95°:

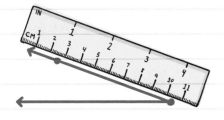

We then use the protractor and ruler to draw the 20° angle and to complete the triangle:

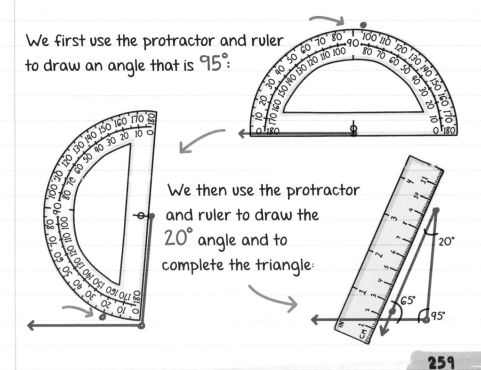

20°

65° 95°

259

Set Square

A **SET SQUARE** (also known as a **TRIANGLE**) is another tool that we can use to draw geometric shapes and angles. A set square is also known as a triangle because it is in the shape of a triangle. There are two types of set squares: a 60-30 **SET SQUARE** and a 45 **SET SQUARE**.

A 60-30 set square has the same angles as a 30-60-90 triangle and a 45 set square has the same angles as a 45-45-90 triangle.

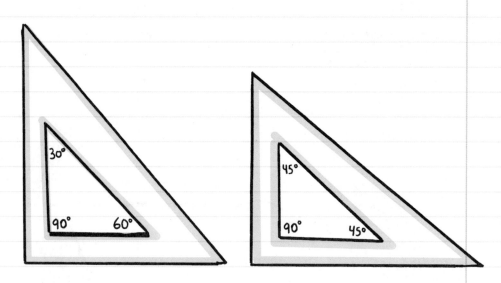

Because each of the set squares are in the shape of a right triangle, we can easily draw perpendicular lines by using the set square and a ruler. We can even use set squares to draw parallel lines!

EXAMPLE: Draw perpendicular lines using a set square and a ruler.

The set square already is in the shape of a right triangle, so all we need to do is use a ruler to draw out the rest of the line:

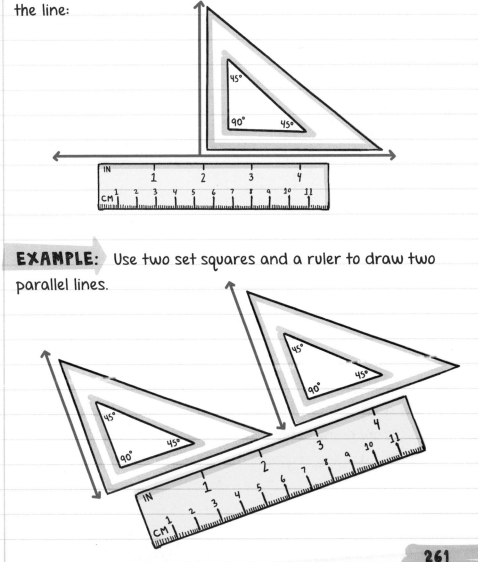

EXAMPLE: Use two set squares and a ruler to draw two parallel lines.

CHECK YOUR KNOWLEDGE

Fill in the missing parts of the table.

YOU CAN USE THE LETTERS **A** AND **B** THROUGHOUT YOUR ANSWERS.

	TERM	DEFINITION	SYMBOLS USED
1.	Parallel Lines		
2.	Perpendicular Lines		
3.	Line Segment		
4.	Line		
5.	Ray		

6. Use a ruler to complete each of the following exercises:

    (a) Draw a line segment that is 4 inches long.

    (b) Draw a line segment that is 12 centimeters long.

7. Use a protractor to complete each of the following exercises:
(a) Draw an angle that is 63°.
(b) Draw an angle that is 150°.

8. Use a set square to draw a line perpendicular to the one below:

9. Use two set squares and a ruler to draw a parallel line to the one below:

ANSWERS

CHECK YOUR ANSWERS

TERM	DEFINITION	SYMBOLS USED
1. Parallel Lines	Lines that are always the same distance apart and that never intersect	$a \| b$
2. Perpendicular Lines	Two lines that form a 90-degree angle (also known as a right angle)	$a \perp b$
3. Line Segment	A part of a line that has two endpoints	$\overline{AB}$
4. Line	A straight line that continues forever in both directions	$\overleftrightarrow{AB}$
5. Ray	A line with only one endpoint	$\overrightarrow{AB}$

6. (a)

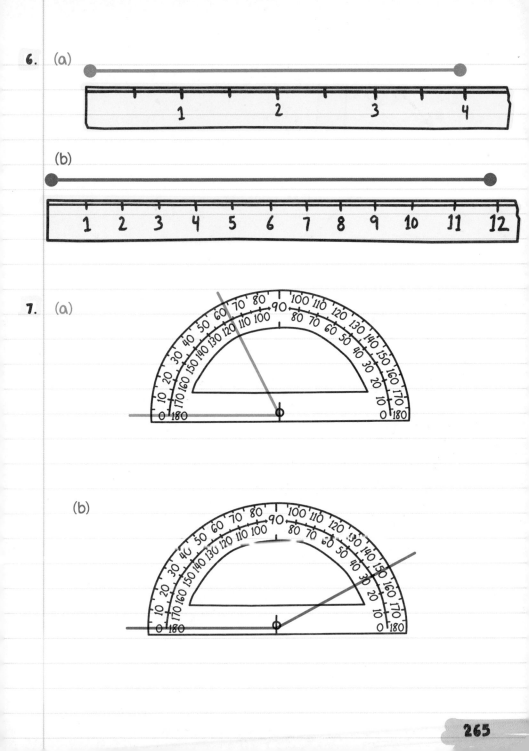

(b)

7. (a)

(b)

8.

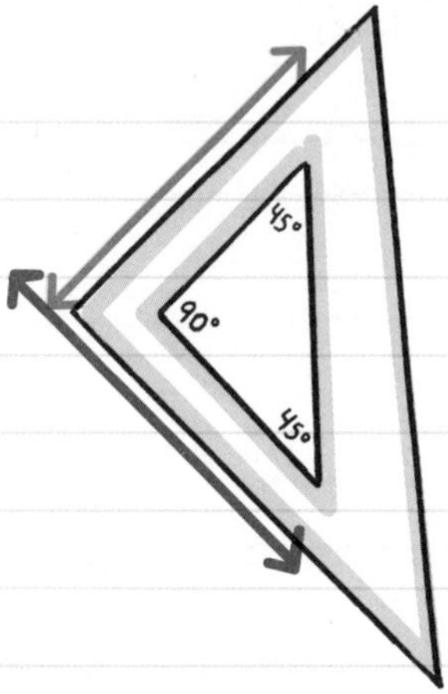

9.

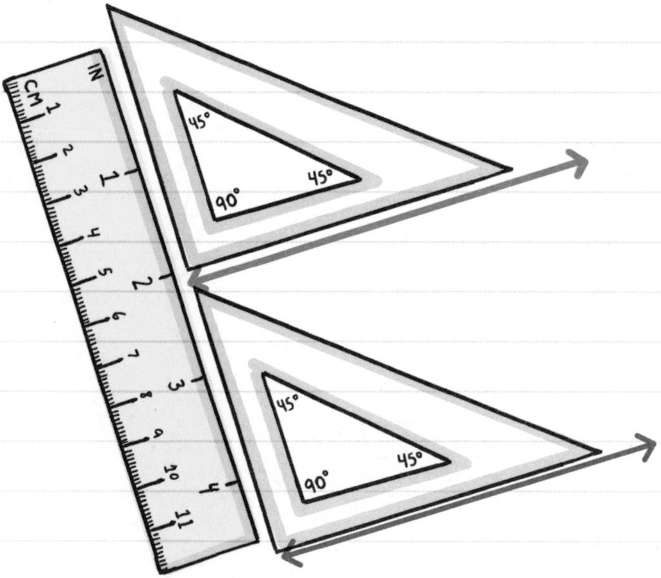

#8 and #9 have more than one correct answer.

Chapter 41

ANGLES

◿ ○ ◇ ▽ ▢ ○ ◇ ▢ ◿ ○ ◇ ▢ ○ ◺

An **ANGLE** (∠) is formed by two rays with a common endpoint. We use **DEGREES** (°) to measure the size of an angle.

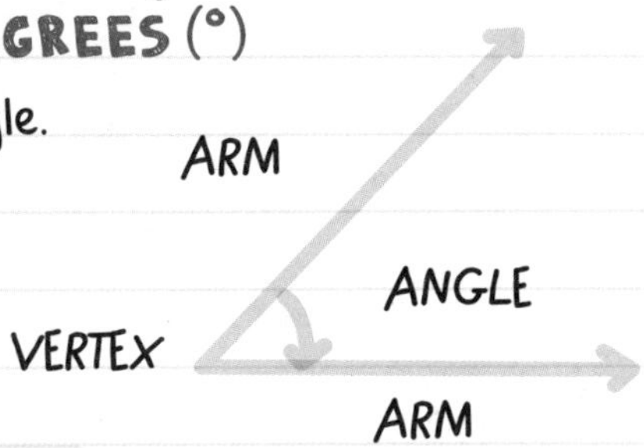

ARM

ANGLE

VERTEX

ARM

The three most "famous" angles:

➤ A **90°** angle is a quarter of a rotation. It is also known as a **RIGHT ANGLE**.

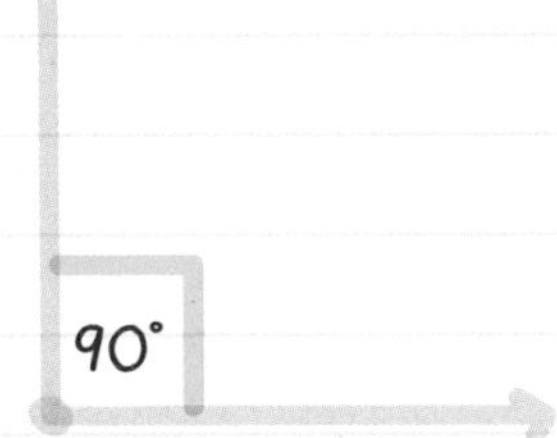

90°

A 180° angle is half of a rotation. It forms a straight line.

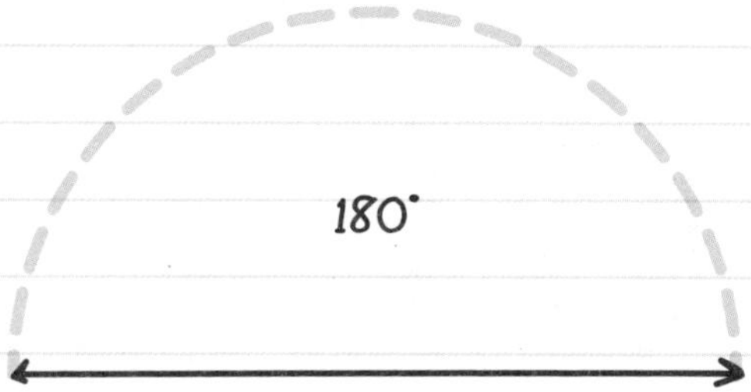

180°

A 360° angle is a complete rotation.

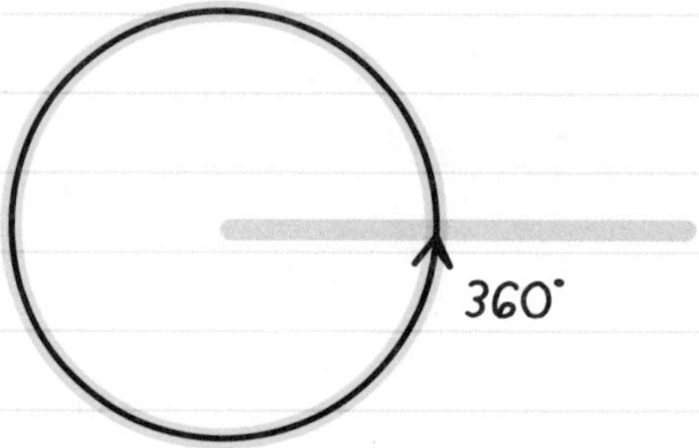

360°

Here's a quick breakdown of the different types of angles:

TYPE OF ANGLE(S)	DEFINITION	EXAMPLE
ACUTE ANGLE	Measures less than 90°	54°
OBTUSE ANGLE	Measures greater than 90°	 130°

TYPE OF ANGLE(S)	DEFINITION	EXAMPLE
RIGHT ANGLE	Measures exactly $90°$	
COMPLEMENTARY ANGLE	Two angles whose sum is $90°$ $\angle a$ and $\angle b$ are complementary. Likewise, a $25°$ angle and a $65°$ angle are complementary.	
SUPPLEMENTARY ANGLE	Two angles whose sum is $180°$ $\angle A$ and $\angle B$ are supplementary. Likewise, a $45°$ angle and a $135°$ angle are supplementary.	

TYPE OF ANGLE(S)	DEFINITION	EXAMPLE
ADJACENT ANGLES	Angles that share a vertex and a common side. $\angle AOB$ and $\angle BOD$ are adjacent angles.	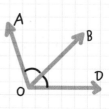
VERTICAL ANGLES	Angles formed by two intersecting lines that are opposite each other; they have equal measures. $\angle a$ and $\angle b$ are vertical angles.	 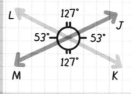
CONGRUENT ANGLES	Angles that are related because they have the same measure. We can use the $\cong$ sign to note congruent angles: $\angle a \cong \angle b$	

We can use the various properties of angles to find the measure of unknown angles.

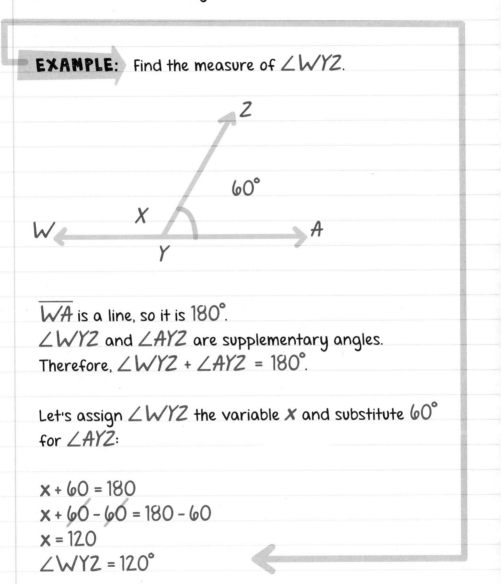

EXAMPLE: Find the measure of ∠WYZ.

$\overline{WA}$ is a line, so it is 180°.
∠WYZ and ∠AYZ are supplementary angles.
Therefore, ∠WYZ + ∠AYZ = 180°.

Let's assign ∠WYZ the variable **x** and substitute 60° for ∠AYZ:

x + 60 = 180
x + ̶6̶0̶ - ̶6̶0̶ = 180 - 60
x = 120
∠WYZ = 120°

Find the measure of $\angle B$, $\angle C$, and $\angle D$:

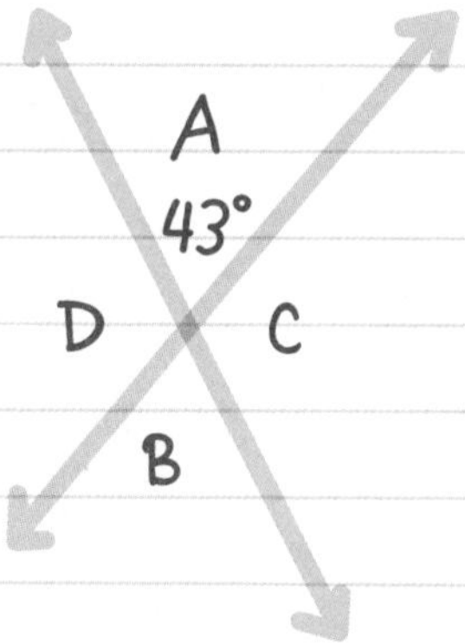

$\angle A$ and $\angle B$ are vertical (opposite) angles.

Therefore, $\angle A = 43°$, $\angle B = 43°$.

Also, $\angle A$ and $\angle C$ are supplementary angles, so

$\angle C + 43° = 180°$

$\angle C + 43° - 43° = 180° - 43°$

$\angle C = 137°$

$\angle C$ and $\angle D$ are vertical, so $\angle D$ also equals $137°$.

CHECK YOUR WORK

Do all the angles add up to $360°$?

$43° + 43° + 137° + 137° = 360°$ ✓

CHECK YOUR KNOWLEDGE

Fill in the blanks:

1. An _ _ _ _ _ angle is less than 90°.

2. _ _ _ _ _ _ _ _ _ _ _ _ _ angles add up to 180°.

3. ∠a and ∠b are
   _ _ _ _ _ _ _ _ angles.

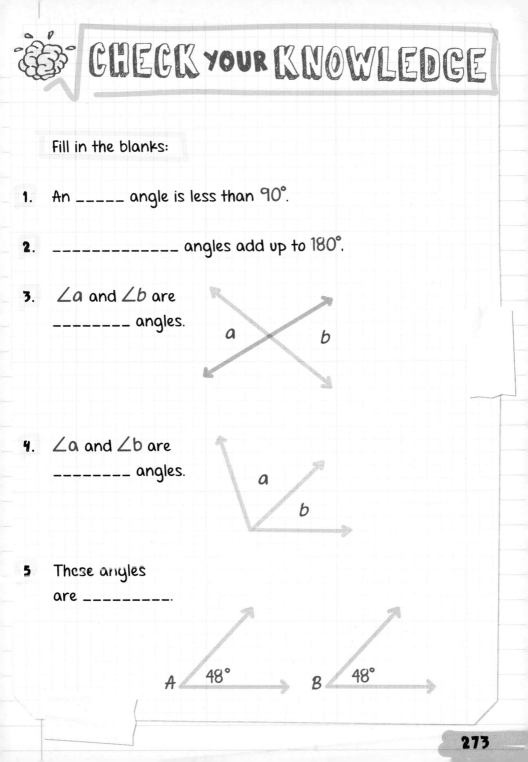

4. ∠a and ∠b are
   _ _ _ _ _ _ _ _ angles.

5 These angles
  are _ _ _ _ _ _ _ _ _.

A 48°   B 48°

6. In the diagram below, $\angle X$ and $\angle Y$ are complementary. If $\angle X$ is 40°, what is $\angle Y$?

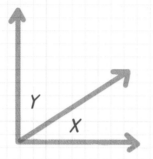

7. In the diagram below, $\angle G$ and $\angle H$ are supplementary. If $\angle G$ is 137°, what is $\angle H$?

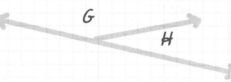

8. If $\angle S$ is 100° and $\angle S$ is congruent to $\angle T$, what is $\angle T$?

9. In the diagram below, ∠A is 50°. What is ∠B?

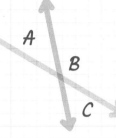

10. In the diagram above, what is ∠C?

1. Acute

2. Supplementary

3. Vertical

4. Adjacent

5. Congruent

6. 50°

7. 43°

8. 100°

9. 130°

10. 50°

⬡ Chapter 42 ⊜

QUADRILATERALS AND AREA

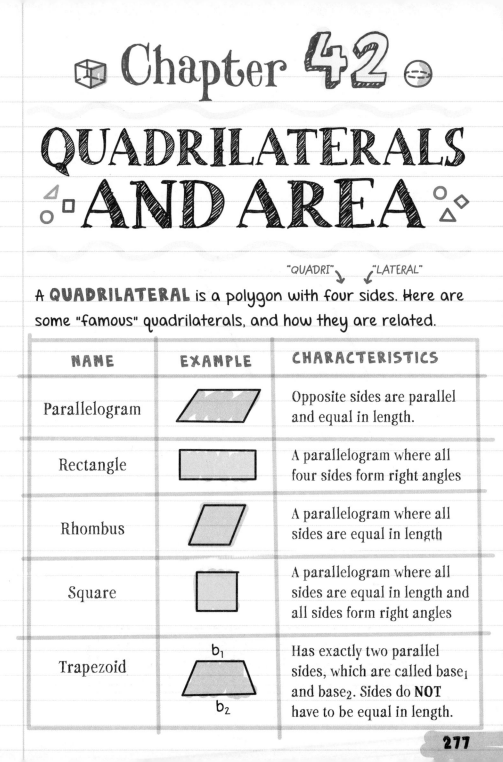

"QUADRI" ↘ ↙ "LATERAL"

A **QUADRILATERAL** is a polygon with four sides. Here are some "famous" quadrilaterals, and how they are related.

NAME	EXAMPLE	CHARACTERISTICS
Parallelogram		Opposite sides are parallel and equal in length.
Rectangle		A parallelogram where all four sides form right angles
Rhombus		A parallelogram where all sides are equal in length
Square		A parallelogram where all sides are equal in length and all sides form right angles
Trapezoid	b_1 b_2	Has exactly two parallel sides, which are called $base_1$ and $base_2$. Sides do **NOT** have to be equal in length.

The **PERIMETER** is the distance around a two-dimensional object. To calculate the perimeter of an object, you add the length of all of its sides.

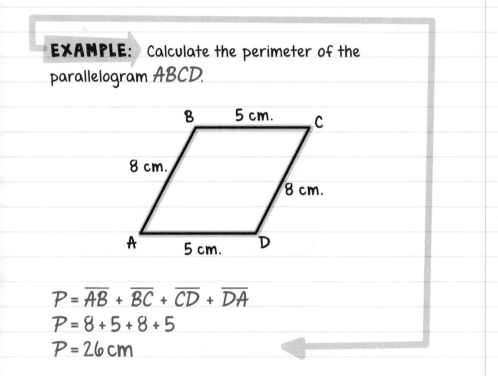

EXAMPLE: Calculate the perimeter of the parallelogram *ABCD*.

$$P = \overline{AB} + \overline{BC} + \overline{CD} + \overline{DA}$$
$$P = 8 + 5 + 8 + 5$$
$$P = 26 \, cm$$

The **AREA** is the size of a surface or is the amount of space inside a two-dimensional object. Area is written in "units squared," or *units²*.

Finding the area is like asking,
"How many squares can we fit inside the object?"

In order to calculate the **AREA OF A PARALLELOGRAM**, multiply the base by the height. (This formula applies to rectangles, rhombuses, and squares, too.)

A = base × height
or A = *bh*

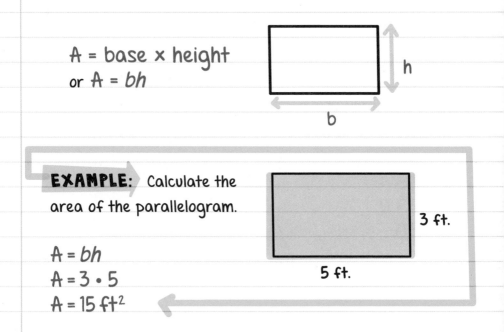

EXAMPLE: Calculate the area of the parallelogram.

A = *bh*
A = 3 • 5
A = 15 ft²

5 ft.

3 ft.

An area of 15 ft² means that 15 squares with an area of 1 foot² each can fit inside, so we say "fifteen feet squared," or "fifteen square feet.")

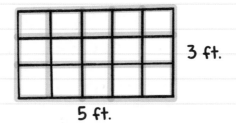

3 ft.

5 ft.

A parallelogram has the same formula as a rectangle because it is made up of the same parts, so it must have the same area. If we cut apart a parallelogram and rearrange its parts, you can make it into a rectangle.

height { = = = { [rectangle]

base

EXAMPLE: Calculate the area of the rhombus.

5cm.

$A = b \cdot h$

$A = 5 \cdot 6$

$A = 30$

6cm.

$A = 30 \text{ cm}^2$

In order to calculate the **AREA OF A TRAPEZOID**, use the formula:

b_1

$$A = \frac{base_1 + base_2}{2} \cdot h$$

h

b_2

YOU MAY ALSO SEE THIS FORMULA FORMATTED LIKE THIS:

$$A = \frac{1}{2} h (b_1 + b_2)$$

YOU CAN CALCULATE THE AREA EITHER WAY.

In actuality, we calculate a trapezoid much like a rectangle or square. If we cut a trapezoid in half horizontally, the height of each part is now half of what it was. Then we flip one part over, and now it looks like a parallelogram. We've cut the height in half and put the bases together to get the full length, which is how we end up with this formula:

$$A = \frac{1}{2}h(b_1 + b_2)$$

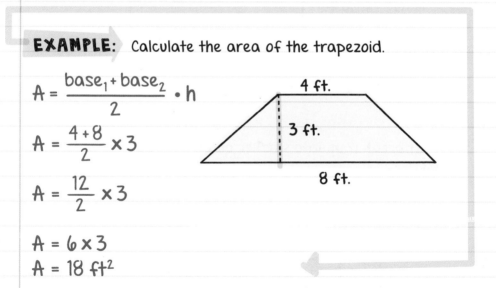

EXAMPLE: Calculate the area of the trapezoid.

$$A = \frac{base_1 + base_2}{2} \cdot h$$

$$A = \frac{4 + 8}{2} \times 3$$

$$A = \frac{12}{2} \times 3$$

$$A = 6 \times 3$$

$$A = 18 \text{ ft}^2$$

4 ft.

3 ft.

8 ft.

We can also calculate the area of a **COMPOUND SHAPE** (a shape made up of two or more other shapes) that is made up of quadrilaterals.

We do this by first breaking up the compound shapes into separate quadrilaterals. Then we find the area of each of the quadrilaterals, and then add all the areas together to find the area of the entire compound shape.

EXAMPLE: Find the area of the following compound shape.

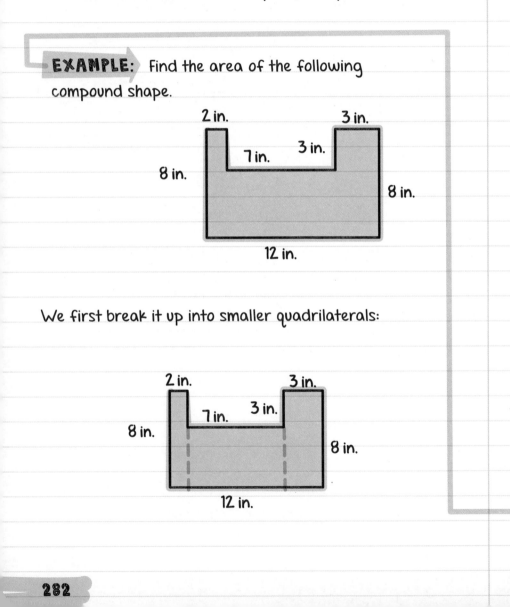

We first break it up into smaller quadrilaterals:

In other words, we have three smaller quadrilaterals that look like:

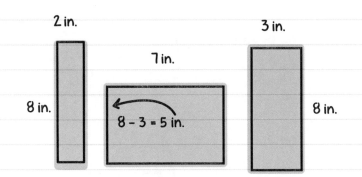

Calculating the area of each of the quadrilaterals and adding them all up looks like this:

Area = 2 x 8 + 7 x 5 + 3 x 8
A = 16 + 35 + 24
A = 75 in²

CHECK YOUR KNOWLEDGE

1. Calculate the area of the following rectangle.

7 in.

5 in.

2. Calculate the area of the following trapezoid.

14 cm.

16 cm.

20 cm.

3. Calculate the area of the following trapezoid.

5 in.

7 in.

9 in.

4. Calculate the area of the following rhombus.

8 m.

8 m.

10 m.

8 m.

8 m.

5. Calculate the area of the following rhombus.

9 cm.

12 cm.

6. Roxie is coloring a rectangular sheet of paper. If the base of the rectangle is 8 inches and the height is 11 inches, what is the area that Roxie colors?

7. Max wants to buy a carpet that covers his entire floor, which is in the shape of a square. If each of the 4 sides is 25 feet long, what is the area of the carpet?

8. Linda sees a rhombus someone drew in chalk on the playground. She measures one base and finds out that it is 6 feet long. She measures the height and finds out that it is 12 feet long. Calculate the area of the rhombus.

9. Sammy draws 3 identical rectangles on his paper. If each rectangle has a base of 15 cm and a height of 12 cm, what is the total area of all 3 rectangles added together?

10. Mr. Lee draws a diagram of his property. His house is shaped like a rectangle, with a base of 100 feet and a height of 75 feet. Next to this house is his garage, which is shaped like a square. Each of the sides of the garage is 25 feet. Calculate the area of the entire property belonging to Mr. Lee.

ANSWERS

CHECK YOUR ANSWERS

1. 35 in²

2. 272 cm²

3. 49 in²

4. 80 m²

5. 108 cm²

6. 88 in²

7. 625 ft²

8. 72 ft²

9. A = 15 × 12 + 15 × 12 + 15 × 12 = 540 cm²

10. A = 100 × 75 + 25 × 25 = 8,125 ft²

Chapter 43

TRIANGLES AND AREA

A **TRIANGLE** has three sides and three angles. The symbol for a triangle is △. We can classify triangles by their sides:

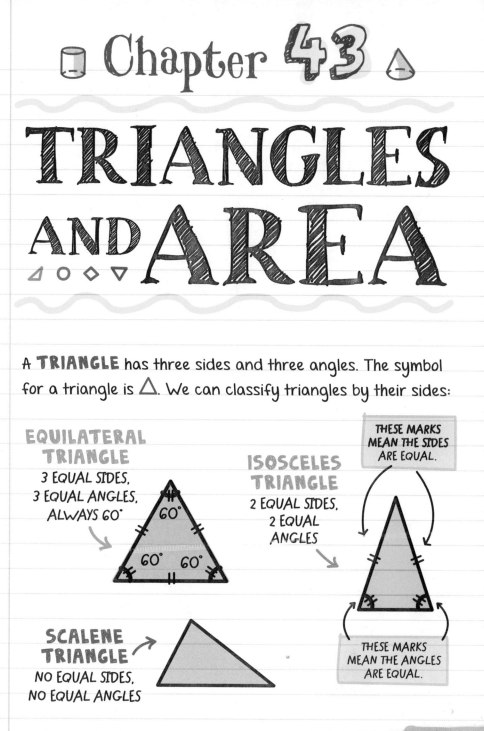

EQUILATERAL TRIANGLE
3 EQUAL SIDES,
3 EQUAL ANGLES,
ALWAYS 60°

60°
60° 60°

ISOSCELES TRIANGLE
2 EQUAL SIDES,
2 EQUAL ANGLES

THESE MARKS MEAN THE SIDES ARE EQUAL.

THESE MARKS MEAN THE ANGLES ARE EQUAL.

SCALENE TRIANGLE
NO EQUAL SIDES,
NO EQUAL ANGLES

We can also classify triangles
by their angles:

RIGHT TRIANGLE
HAS A RIGHT
ANGLE (90°)

90°

OBTUSE TRIANGLE
HAS AN ANGLE
MORE THAN 90°

>90°

ACUTE TRIANGLE
ALL ANGLES
ARE LESS
THAN 90°

<90°

We can even combine both systems of classification
to describe a triangle more precisely by using this
TRIANGLE TREE!

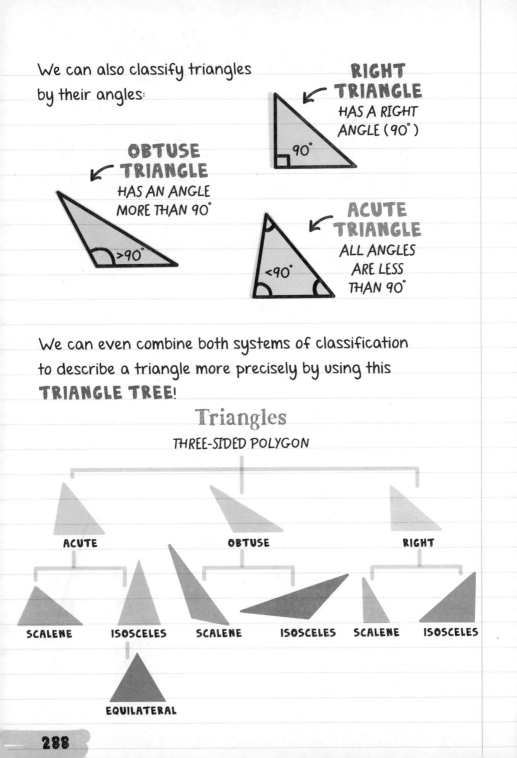

Triangles
THREE-SIDED POLYGON

ACUTE   OBTUSE   RIGHT

SCALENE   ISOSCELES   SCALENE   ISOSCELES   SCALENE   ISOSCELES

EQUILATERAL

EXAMPLE:

ANGLES: There is an angle greater than 90°, so it's obtuse.

SIDES: It has two equal sides.

TYPE: This is an obtuse isosceles triangle.

110°

EXAMPLE:

ANGLES: There is a right angle.

SIDES: None of the sides are equal in length.

TYPE: This is a right scalene triangle.

In order to calculate the **AREA OF A TRIANGLE**, multiply the base times the height, then multiply that amount by half. The base and the height must always form a right angle.

Area of a triangle $A = \dfrac{1}{2} \cdot \text{base} \cdot \text{height}$

or $A = \dfrac{1}{2} bh$

If you cut a rectangle in half, the area formed by the remaining triangle is only half as large as the area of the original rectangle—that's why the formula for the area of a triangle is:

$A = \dfrac{1}{2} bh$

h

b

EXAMPLE: Find the area of the triangle.

$A = \frac{1}{2} bh$

$A = \frac{1}{2} (14)(9)$

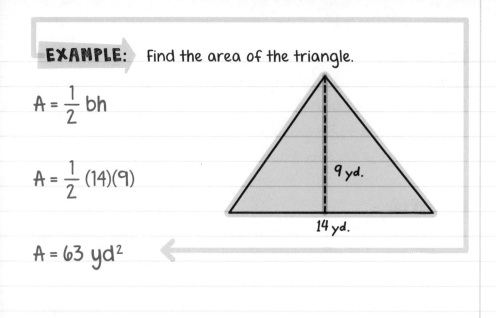

9 yd.

14 yd.

$A = 63 \text{ yd}^2$

EXAMPLE: Find the area of the triangle. We know that the base and the height must form a right angle. So, the height and the base are 3 inches and 7 inches.

3 in.

4 in.

7 in.

$A = \frac{1}{2} bh$

$A = \frac{1}{2} \cdot 3 \cdot 7$

$A = \frac{21}{2}$

$A = 10\frac{1}{2} \text{ in}^2$

We can also calculate the area of a triangle that is a compound shape.

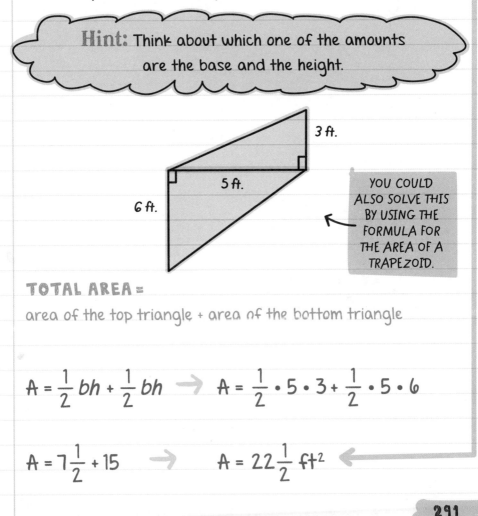

EXAMPLE: An artist draws a shape on the ground and wants to color inside his shape with paint. What is the total area of space that he will paint?

Hint: Think about which one of the amounts are the base and the height.

3 ft.

5 ft.

6 ft.

YOU COULD ALSO SOLVE THIS BY USING THE FORMULA FOR THE AREA OF A TRAPEZOID.

TOTAL AREA =
area of the top triangle + area of the bottom triangle

$$A = \frac{1}{2}bh + \frac{1}{2}bh \rightarrow A = \frac{1}{2} \cdot 5 \cdot 3 + \frac{1}{2} \cdot 5 \cdot 6$$

$$A = 7\frac{1}{2} + 15 \rightarrow A = 22\frac{1}{2} \text{ ft}^2 \leftarrow$$

Find the area of the triangles below.

1.

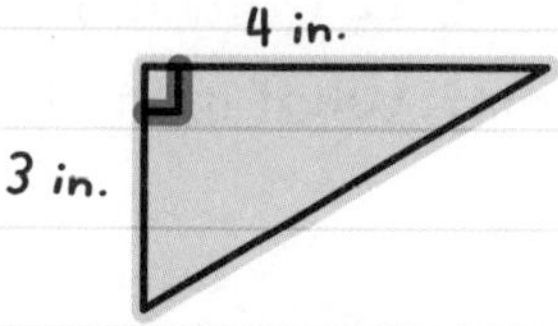

4 in.

3 in.

2.

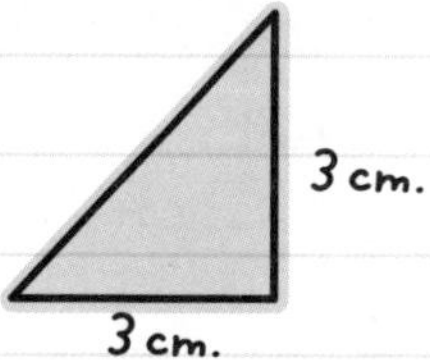

3 cm.

3 cm.

3.

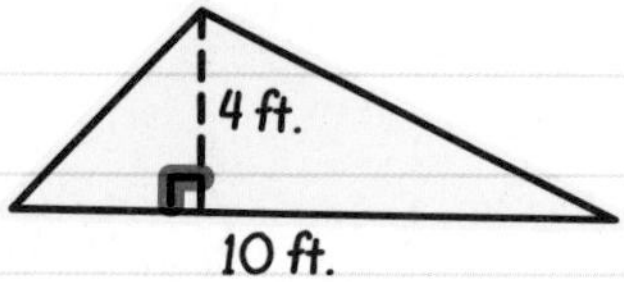

4 ft.

10 ft.

4.

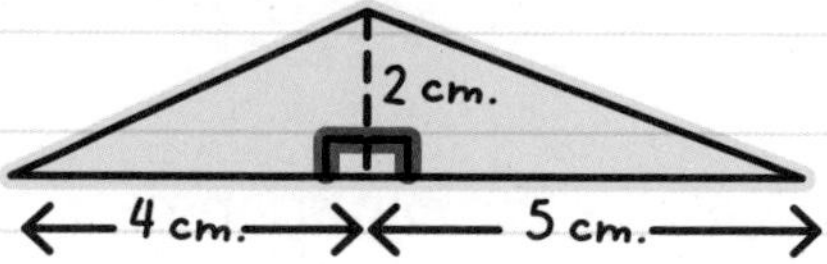

2 cm.

← 4 cm. → ← 5 cm. →

5. Find the area of this shape.

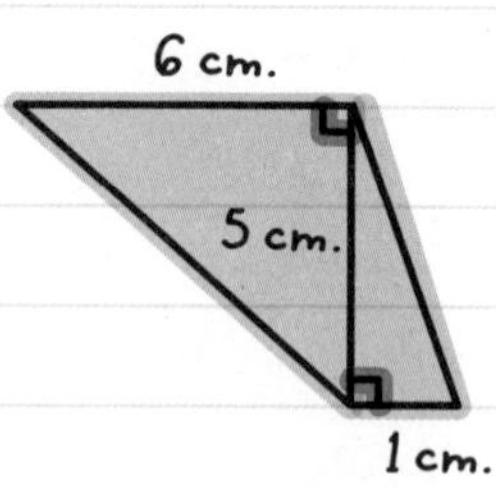

6 cm.

5 cm.

1 cm.

6. Linda has one side of a pyramid to paint for the scenery of her school play. The side has a base of 30 feet and a height of 10 feet. How much area will she paint?

7. Bruno is designing a flag with a height of 8 inches and a base of 5 inches. He draws a line along the diagonal and paints the area above the line red. How much area did he paint?

8. The area of a triangular-shaped sail on a boat is 62 ft². The height is 8 ft. What is the base?

9. Josh, Alice, and Henry stand at the same point. Josh walks north 25 feet while Alice walks west 12 feet. What is the area of the shape that Josh, Alice, and Henry make?

10. Mr. Lee paints a picture of a house. The wall has the shape of a rectangle, which has a height of 5 inches and a base of 8 inches. The roof has the shape of a triangle, which has a height of 3 inches and a base of 10 inches. What is the total area that Mr. Lee paints?

ANSWERS

CHECK YOUR ANSWERS

1. 6 in²

2. $4\frac{1}{2}$ cm²

3. 20 ft²

4. $A = 9$ cm²

5. $A = 17\frac{1}{2}$ cm²

6. 150 ft²

7. 20 in²

8. $15\frac{1}{2}$ ft

9. 150 ft²

10. Total area = area of the rectangle + area of the triangle = 55 in²

Chapter 44

THE PYTHAGOREAN THEOREM

A right triangle has two "legs" and a
HYPOTENUSE—the longest side of a
right-angled triangle, which is always
the side opposite the right angle. The
two legs are connected at the right
angle. a and b are the length of the
legs (it doesn't matter which is a and

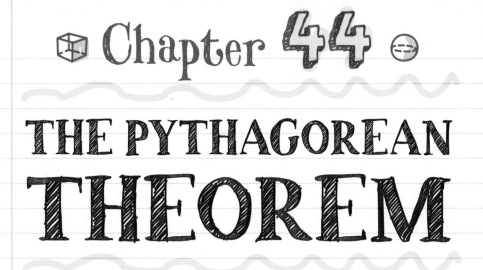

which is b). The length of the hypotenuse, c, is always longer
than the length of leg a or the length of leg b.

The **PYTHAGOREAN THEOREM** is used to
find the length of a side of a right triangle.

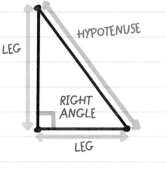

$$a^2 + b^2 = c^2$$

In a right triangle, the sum of the squares of the lengths of
the legs is equal to the square of the length of the hypotenuse.

EXAMPLE: Use the Pythagorean theorem to find the length of the hypotenuse of this triangle.

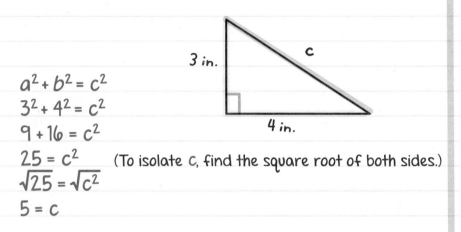

$a^2 + b^2 = c^2$
$3^2 + 4^2 = c^2$
$9 + 16 = c^2$
$25 = c^2$ (To isolate c, find the square root of both sides.)
$\sqrt{25} = \sqrt{c^2}$
$5 = c$

The length of the hypotenuse is 5 inches.

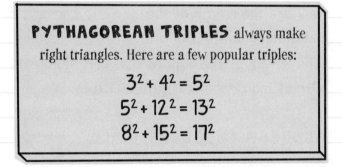

PYTHAGOREAN TRIPLES always make right triangles. Here are a few popular triples:

$$3^2 + 4^2 = 5^2$$
$$5^2 + 12^2 = 13^2$$
$$8^2 + 15^2 = 17^2$$

We can also use the Pythagorean theorem to find the missing length of a leg—solve it just like an equation.

EXAMPLE: Find the length of b.

$a^2 + b^2 = c^2$
$6^2 + b^2 = 10^2$
$36 + b^2 = 100$
$36 - 36 + b^2 = 100 - 36$
$b^2 = 64$
$\sqrt{b^2} = \sqrt{64}$
$b = 8$

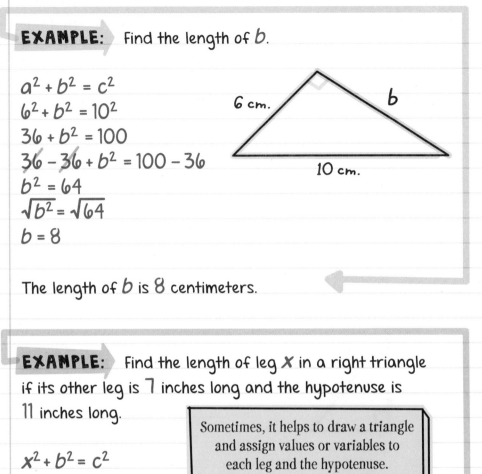

6 cm.

b

10 cm.

The length of b is 8 centimeters.

EXAMPLE: Find the length of leg x in a right triangle if its other leg is 7 inches long and the hypotenuse is 11 inches long.

Sometimes, it helps to draw a triangle and assign values or variables to each leg and the hypotenuse.

$x^2 + b^2 = c^2$
$x^2 + 7^2 = 11^2$
$x^2 + 49 = 121$
$x^2 + 49 - 49 = 121 - 49$
$\sqrt{x^2} = \sqrt{72}$
$x = \sqrt{72}$

← BECAUSE $\sqrt{72}$ IS NOT A PERFECT SQUARE, WE CAN LEAVE IT AS IS.

I MAY NOT BE PERFECT, BUT I CAN **DANCE**!

The length of leg x is $\sqrt{72}$ inches.

297

CHECK YOUR KNOWLEDGE

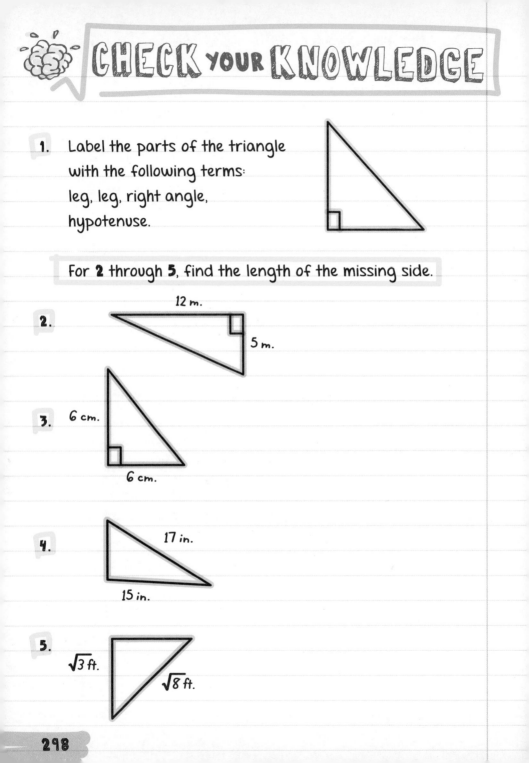

1. Label the parts of the triangle with the following terms: leg, leg, right angle, hypotenuse.

For **2** through **5**, find the length of the missing side.

2. 12 m.
   5 m.

3. 6 cm.
   6 cm.

4. 17 in.
   15 in.

5. $\sqrt{3}$ ft.
   $\sqrt{8}$ ft.

6. Adam and Betty start at the same point. Adam walks 3 feet north while Betty walks 4 feet west. If a straight line were to be drawn between Adam and Betty, how long would the line be?

7. A carpenter has a rectangular piece of wood that is 8 meters long and 3 meters wide. He cuts the piece of wood into two triangular pieces by cutting it from one corner to the other corner. How long is the diagonal that he cuts?

8. Johnny starts at the base of a slide. He walks 10 feet to a ladder. He then climbs up the ladder that is 7 feet tall before sitting down on the slide. How long is the slide?

9. Beth takes different measurements of her door. The diagonal length is 12 feet, and the base is 4 feet. What is the height of her door?

10. An artist makes a sculpture that is a right triangle. The height and the base are both 7 feet long. What is the length of the hypotenuse?

7 ft.

7 ft.

ANSWERS

CHECK YOUR ANSWERS

1.

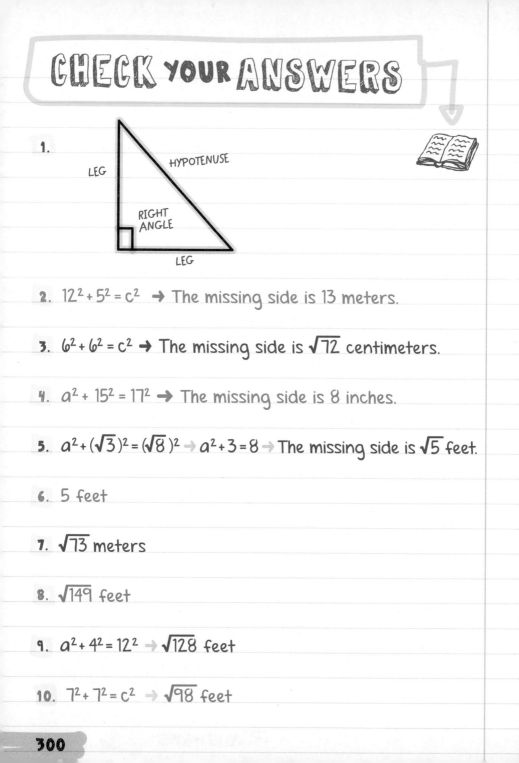

LEG

HYPOTENUSE

RIGHT ANGLE

LEG

2. $12^2 + 5^2 = c^2$ → The missing side is 13 meters.

3. $6^2 + 6^2 = c^2$ → The missing side is $\sqrt{72}$ centimeters.

4. $a^2 + 15^2 = 17^2$ → The missing side is 8 inches.

5. $a^2 + (\sqrt{3})^2 = (\sqrt{8})^2$ → $a^2 + 3 = 8$ → The missing side is $\sqrt{5}$ feet.

6. 5 feet

7. $\sqrt{73}$ meters

8. $\sqrt{149}$ feet

9. $a^2 + 4^2 = 12^2$ → $\sqrt{128}$ feet

10. $7^2 + 7^2 = c^2$ → $\sqrt{98}$ feet

Chapter 45

CIRCLES, CIRCUMFERENCE, AND AREA

A **CIRCLE** is the set of all points that are equal distance from a point that is called the **CENTER**.

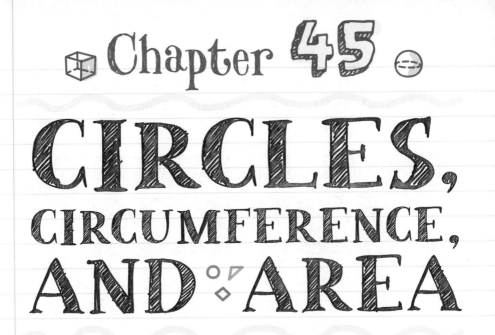

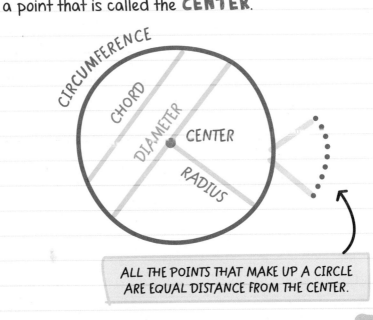

ALL THE POINTS THAT MAKE UP A CIRCLE ARE EQUAL DISTANCE FROM THE CENTER.

These are the important parts of a circle:

Circumference (c): The distance around the circle
(the perimeter of the circle)

Chord: A line segment whose endpoints are on the circle

Diameter (d): A chord that passes
through the center of the circle

Radius (r): A line segment that has one endpoint at
the center and the other on the circle. The diameter is
twice the length of the radius, or

$$2r = d.$$

Therefore, the radius is half the length of the diameter, or

$$r = \frac{1}{2}d.$$

Pi (π): The ratio of a circle's circumference to its diameter:

$$\pi = \frac{\text{circumference}}{\text{diameter}} \quad \text{or} \quad \pi = \frac{c}{d}$$

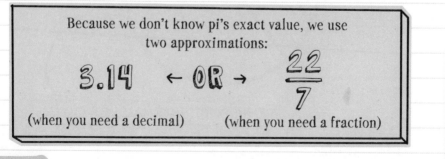

Because we don't know pi's exact value, we use
two approximations:

3.14   ← OR → $\frac{22}{7}$

(when you need a decimal)   (when you need a fraction)

To **FIND THE CIRCUMFERENCE OF A CIRCLE**, we rearrange the equation for pi in order to solve for c:

$$\pi = \frac{c}{d}$$ To get c by itself, multiply both sides by d:

$$\pi(d) = \frac{c}{d}(d)$$

$$\pi(d) = c$$

Thus, the formula for finding the circumference of a circle is:

$$\Big\{ \text{ circumference } = \pi \bullet \text{ diameter } \Big\}$$

And because the diameter is twice the length of the radius, you can also find the circumference with this formula:

$$\Big\{ C = 2\pi r \Big\}$$

EXAMPLE: Find the circumference of the circle. (Use 3.14 as the approximation of π.)

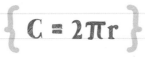

6 cm.

$C = \pi d$
$C = 3.14\ (6)$
$C = 18.84$ cm

The circumference is 18.84 centimeters.

To find the **AREA OF A CIRCLE**, use the following formula:

$$\text{area} = \pi \cdot \text{radius}^2$$

or

$$A = \pi r^2$$

(ANSWER IS IN UNITS²)

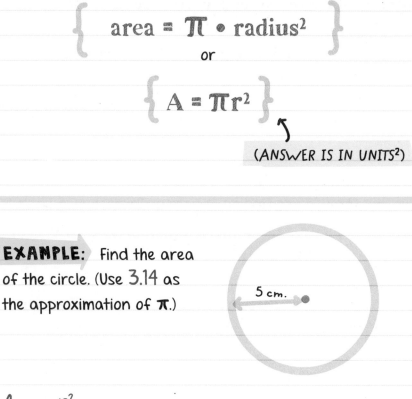

EXAMPLE: Find the area of the circle. (Use 3.14 as the approximation of π.)

5 cm.

$A = \pi \cdot r^2$
$A = 3.14 \cdot 5^2$ (Don't forget order of operations!)
$A = 3.14 \cdot 25$

$A = 78.5 \text{ cm}^2$

EXAMPLE: Find the area of the circle. (Use $\dfrac{22}{7}$ as the approximation of π.)

Because we know only the diameter, we need to divide it in half to get the radius: $14 \div 2 = 7$ inches. Now, we can use the formula for area.

14 in.

$A = \pi r^2$

$A = \pi 7^2$

$A = \dfrac{22}{7} \cdot 7^2$

$A = \dfrac{22}{7} \cdot \dfrac{\cancel{49}^{7}}{1}$

$A = 154 \text{ in}^2$

CHECK YOUR KNOWLEDGE

1. Label the parts of a circle with the following terms: chord, center, diameter, radius, circumference.

2. The radius of a circle is 9 cm. Find the area of the circle. (Use 3.14 as the approximation of π.)

3. The radius of a circle is 2 feet. Find the area of the circle. (Use 3.14 as the approximation of π.)

4. The diameter of a circle is 21 inches. Find the area of the circle. (Use $\frac{22}{7}$ as the approximation of π.)

5. The diameter of a circle is 6 inches. Find the area of the circle. (Use 3.14 as the approximation of π.)

6. A builder wants to make a window that is shaped as a circle. The radius of the circle is 8 feet. How much glass should he buy to cover the area of the window? (Use 3.14 as the approximation of π.)

7. A baker makes a circular cake that has a radius of 7 inches. If the baker wants to cover the top of the cake with frosting, how much frosting should the baker use? (Use $\frac{22}{7}$ as the approximation of π.)

8. An architect wants to build a flat roof for a circular building. The diameter of the circular roof is 20 feet. What is the area of the roof? (Use 3.14 as the approximation of π.)

9. A furniture maker builds a round table that has a diameter of 12 feet and wants to order a glass tabletop to go with it. How large must the glass tabletop be to cover the entire top of the table? (Use 3.14 as the approximation of π.)

10. A painter is painting a circular sculpture. The sculpture has a radius of 5 meters. How much paint should she use to paint the sculpture? (Use 3.14 as the approximation of π.)

HMM...

5m.

ANSWERS

1. 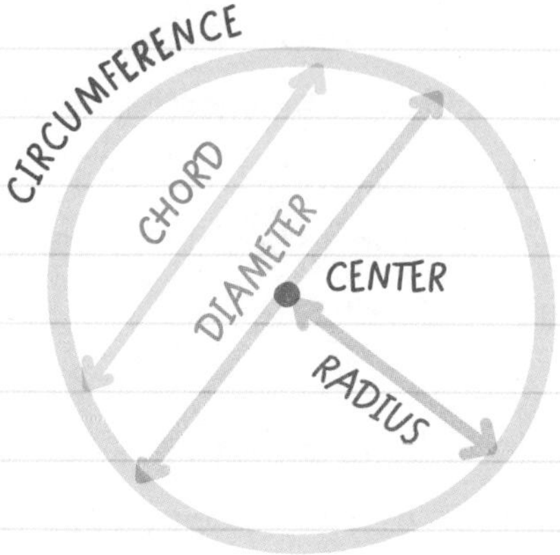 ⟶

CIRCUMFERENCE

CHORD

DIAMETER

CENTER

RADIUS

2. 254.34 cm²

3. 12.56 ft²

4. 346.5 in²

5. 28.26 in²

6. 200.96 ft²

7. 154 in²

8. 314 ft²

9. 113.04 ft²

10. 78.5 m²

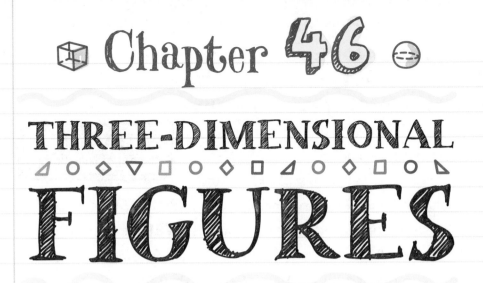

Chapter 46

THREE-DIMENSIONAL
FIGURES

A three-dimensional figure (3-D figure) is a shape that has length, width, and height. It is also called a **"SPACE FIGURE"** or a "solid."

EXAMPLES:

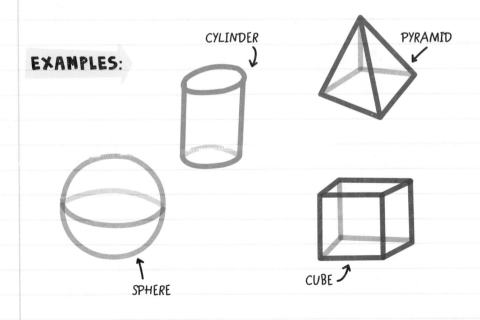

CYLINDER

PYRAMID

SPHERE

CUBE

A **POLYHEDRON** is a 3-D figure that is made up of regions that are in the shape of polygons. The regions share a side. (The plural of polyhedron is **POLYHEDRA**.)

One type of polyhedron is a **PRISM**.
A prism is a 3-D figure that has two

LATERAL
side(s) of something

polygon bases that are parallel and **CONGRUENT** (exactly the same shape and size), as well as **LATERAL** faces (the sides next to each other) that are parallelograms. Prisms are categorized by the type of bases they have.

A **RECTANGULAR PRISM** has all right angles, the bases are parallel, and the lateral faces are parallelograms.

RECTANGULAR PRISM

CUBE

A **TRIANGULAR PRISM** has bases that are parallel triangles and lateral faces that are parallelograms.

HEXAGONAL PRISM

And other types:
PENTAGONAL PRISM

There are other types of polyhedra:

A **CYLINDER** has two parallel bases that are congruent circles.

A **CONE** has one circular base and one vertex (or point).

A **SPHERE** is a set of points in a space that are a given distance from a center point (it looks just like a ball).

A **PYRAMID** has a polygon (not a circle) at its base. All of its lateral faces are triangles. Similarly, pyramids are named by their bases:

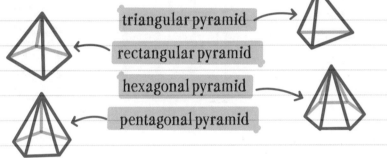

triangular pyramid

rectangular pyramid

hexagonal pyramid

pentagonal pyramid

There is a special type of polyhedron called a **REGULAR POLYHEDRON**. A regular polyhedron is a polyhedron where all the faces are identical polygons, such as:

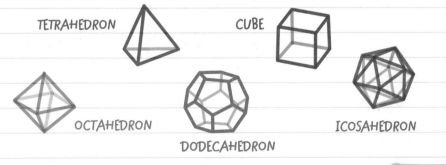

TETRAHEDRON

CUBE

OCTAHEDRON

DODECAHEDRON

ICOSAHEDRON

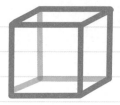

Imagine that we are slicing a 3-D polyhedron open—you can get different 2-D shapes depending on how you slice it. These are known as **CROSS SECTIONS**.

If we slice a cube open with a plane, what are the possible cross sections that we can get?

If we cut the cube like this, we end up with a square (the shaded 2-D shape).

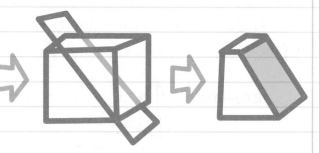

OH NO! YOU CAN SEE MY CROSS SECTION. HOW EMBARRASSING!

If we cut the cube in a diagonal direction like this, we end up with a rectangle (as the shaded 2-D shape).

If you slice a cylinder with a plane, there are a few possible cross sections that can result.

If we slice the cylinder horizontally, the resulting 2-D cross section is a circle (the shaded region).

If we slice the cylinder vertically, the resulting 2-D cross section is a rectangle (the shaded region).

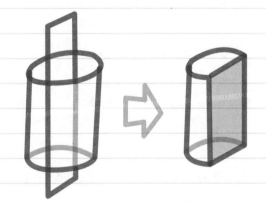

CHECK YOUR KNOWLEDGE

For **1** through **8**, match each shape to its name.

1. Rectangular prism

2. Cube

3. Pyramid

4. Cone

5. Cylinder

6. Rectangular pyramid

7. Octagonal pyramid

8. Triangular pyramid

9. State the definition of a regular polyhedron and draw a sample of a regular polyhedron.

For **10** through **13**, what is the shape of each cross section?

10.

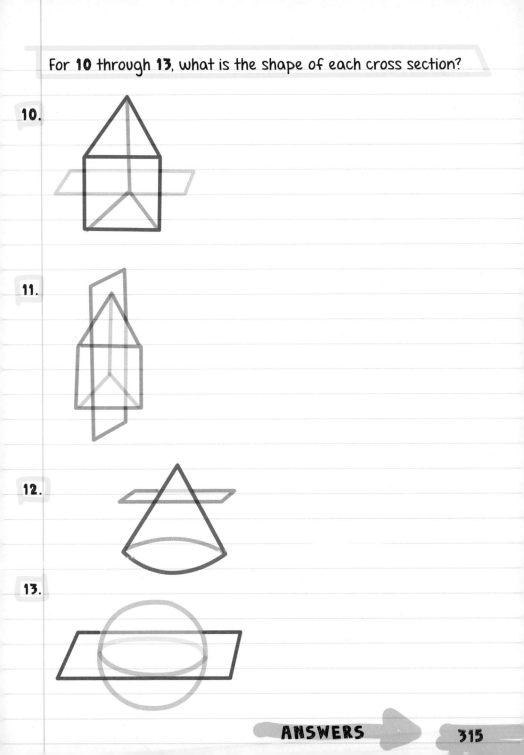

11.

12.

13.

CHECK YOUR ANSWERS

1. Rectangular prism

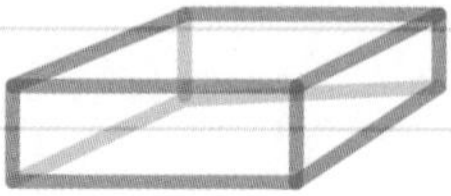

2. Cube

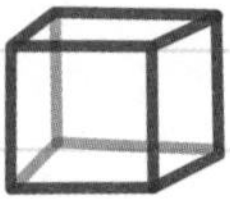

3. Pyramid

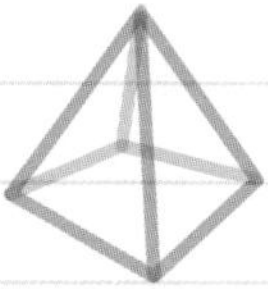

4. Cone

5. Cylinder

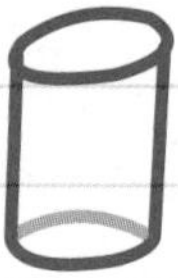

6. Rectangular pyramid

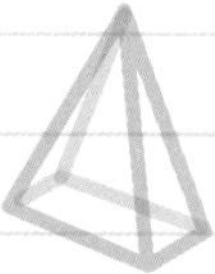

7. Octagonal pyramid

8. Triangular pyramid

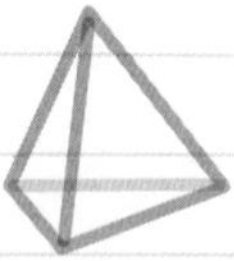

9. A regular polyhedron is a polyhedron where all the faces are identical polygons. Possible regular polyhedra are:

TETRAHEDRON   CUBE   OCTAHEDRON

DODECAHEDRON   ICOSAHEDRON

10. The shape is a triangle.

11. The shape is a rectangle.

12. The shape is a circle.

13. The shape is a circle.

Chapter 47

VOLUME

The **VOLUME** of a 3-D figure refers to the number of cubic units needed to fill the figure. Or, put more simply, "How much will fit in here?" The answer is the volume.

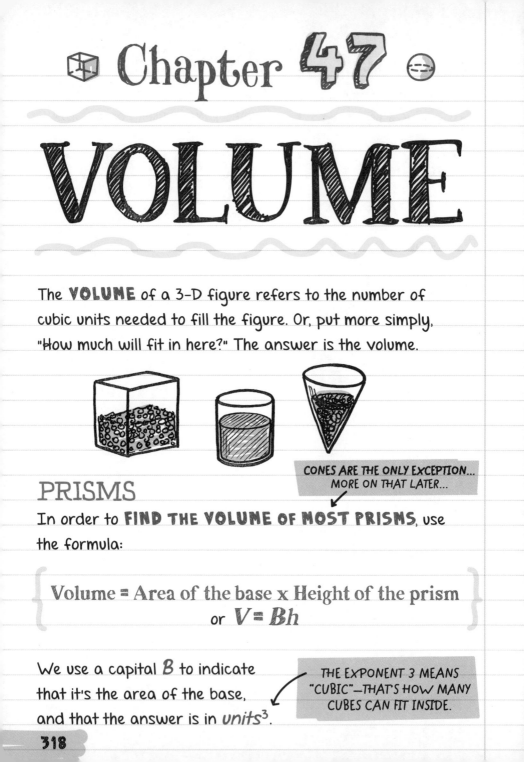

CONES ARE THE ONLY EXCEPTION... MORE ON THAT LATER...

PRISMS

In order to **FIND THE VOLUME OF MOST PRISMS**, use the formula:

$$\{ \text{Volume} = \text{Area of the base} \times \text{Height of the prism} \}$$
$$\text{or } V = Bh$$

We use a capital B to indicate that it's the area of the base, and that the answer is in $units^3$.

THE EXPONENT 3 MEANS "CUBIC"—THAT'S HOW MANY CUBES CAN FIT INSIDE.

Rectangular Prisms

To find the **VOLUME OF A RECTANGULAR PRISM**, we can use

$$V = Bh \text{ or}$$
$$V = \text{length} \times \text{width} \times \text{height } (V = lwh)$$

because in actuality, those are exactly the same equations.

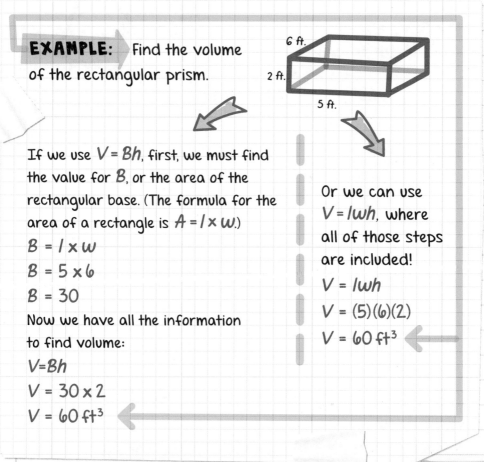

EXAMPLE: Find the volume of the rectangular prism.

6 ft.

2 ft.

5 ft.

If we use $V = Bh$, first, we must find the value for B, or the area of the rectangular base. (The formula for the area of a rectangle is $A = l \times w$.)

$B = l \times w$

$B = 5 \times 6$

$B = 30$

Now we have all the information to find volume:

$V = Bh$

$V = 30 \times 2$

$V = 60 \text{ ft}^3$

Or we can use $V = lwh$, where all of those steps are included!

$V = lwh$

$V = (5)(6)(2)$

$V = 60 \text{ ft}^3$

Triangular Prisms

For the same reasons, in order to find the **VOLUME OF A TRIANGULAR PRISM**, we can use

$$V = Bh_p \text{ or}$$
$$V = \frac{1}{2} \times \text{base} \times \text{height of the triangle} \times \text{height of the prism}$$

$$\left(V = \frac{1}{2} bh_t h_p\right)$$ where h_t represents the height of the triangle and h_p represents the height of the prism.

EXAMPLE: Find the volume of the triangular prism.

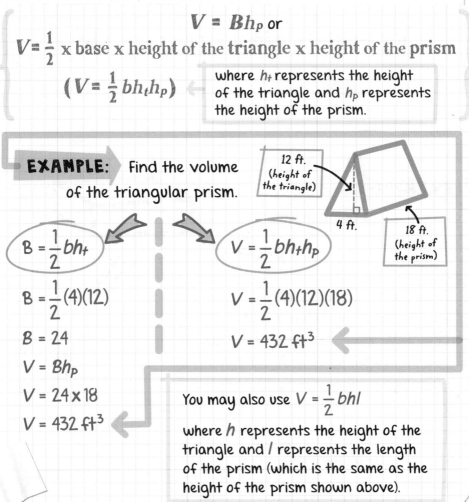

12 ft. (height of the triangle)

4 ft.

18 ft. (height of the prism)

$$B = \frac{1}{2} bh_t$$

$$B = \frac{1}{2}(4)(12)$$

$$B = 24$$

$$V = Bh_p$$

$$V = 24 \times 18$$

$$V = 432 \text{ ft}^3$$

$$V = \frac{1}{2} bh_t h_p$$

$$V = \frac{1}{2}(4)(12)(18)$$

$$V = 432 \text{ ft}^3$$

You may also use $V = \frac{1}{2} bhl$

where h represents the height of the triangle and l represents the length of the prism (which is the same as the height of the prism shown above).

3-D FIGURES THAT ARE NOT PRISMS

Cylinders

To find the **VOLUME OF A CYLINDER**, we can use

$$\left\{ \begin{array}{c} V = Bh \text{ or} \\ V = \pi \times \text{radius}^2 \times \text{height} \ (V = \pi r^2 h) \end{array} \right\}$$

In a cylinder, the base is a circle, so we use the formula for the area of a circle ($A = \pi r^2$) to find the area of the base.

EXAMPLE: Find the volume of the cylinder.

$V = \pi r^2 h$

$V = (3.14)(3^2)(5)$

$V = 141.3$ in^3

3 ft.

5 ft.

Cones

Cones are a little different from other 3-D figures—
to calculate the **VOLUME OF A CONE**, use the formula:

$$\left\{ \begin{array}{c} V = \dfrac{1}{3} \times \text{area of the base} \times \text{height} \ \left(V = \dfrac{1}{3} Bh\right) \\ \text{or} \\ V = \dfrac{1}{3} \times \pi \times \text{radius}^2 \times \text{height} \ \left(V = \dfrac{1}{3}\pi r^2 h\right) \end{array} \right\}$$

The volume of three cones added together amounts to a cylinder, so that's why the volume of a cone is $\dfrac{1}{3}$ of the area of the base x height!

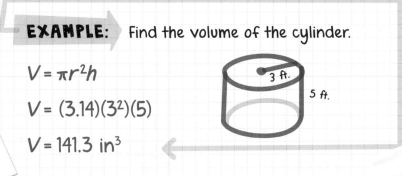

Like a cylinder, the base of a cone is a circle, so we can use the formula for the area of a circle ($A = \pi r^2$) to find the area of the base. So, if we combine the formulas, we get: $V = \frac{1}{3}\pi r^2 h$.

EXAMPLE: Find the volume of the cone. Round to the nearest hundredth.

$V = \frac{1}{3}\pi r^3 h$

$V = \frac{1}{3}(\pi)(6^2)(8)$

$V = \frac{1}{3}(3.14)(36)(8)$

$V = 301.44 \text{ in}^3$

8 in.

6 in.

Pyramids

Similarly, to calculate the **VOLUME OF A PYRAMID**, we can use

$$\left\{ V = \frac{1}{3}Bh \right\}$$

(like the cylinder, the volume of three pyramids put together amounts to a prism). This base is a rectangle, so we can calculate it with the formula $A = bh$—just be careful not to confuse the height of the pyramid with the height of the base.

EXAMPLE: Find the volume of the pyramid.

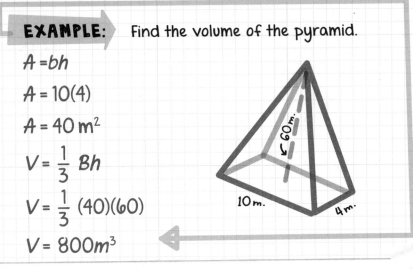

$A = bh$

$A = 10(4)$

$A = 40 \, m^2$

$V = \dfrac{1}{3} \, Bh$

$V = \dfrac{1}{3} \, (40)(60)$

$V = 800 \, m^3$

Spheres

To calculate the **VOLUME OF A SPHERE**, we use the formula

$$\left\{ \; V = \dfrac{4}{3} \, \pi r^3 \; \right\}$$

All you need is the radius and then you can solve. And in a sphere, every line from the center to the edge is a radius!

EXAMPLE: Find the volume of the sphere.

$V = \dfrac{4}{3} \, \pi r^3$

$V = \dfrac{4}{3} \, (3.14)(6^3)$

$V = \dfrac{4}{3} \, (3.14)(216)$

$V = 904.32 \, in^3$

CHECK YOUR KNOWLEDGE

For **1** through **5**, match each figure with its formula for volume. (Each figure may match more than one formula, and more than one figure may match each formula.)

1. **RECTANGULAR PRISM**

2. **CONE**

3. **PYRAMID**

4. **CYLINDER**

5. **SPHERE**

$V = lwh$

$V = \dfrac{1}{3}Bh$

$V = \pi r^2 h$

$V = \dfrac{4}{3}\pi r^3$

$V = \dfrac{1}{3}\pi r^2 h$

6. Find the volume of the rectangular prism.

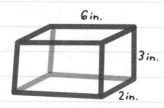

6 in.

3 in.

2 in.

7. Find the volume of the cone.

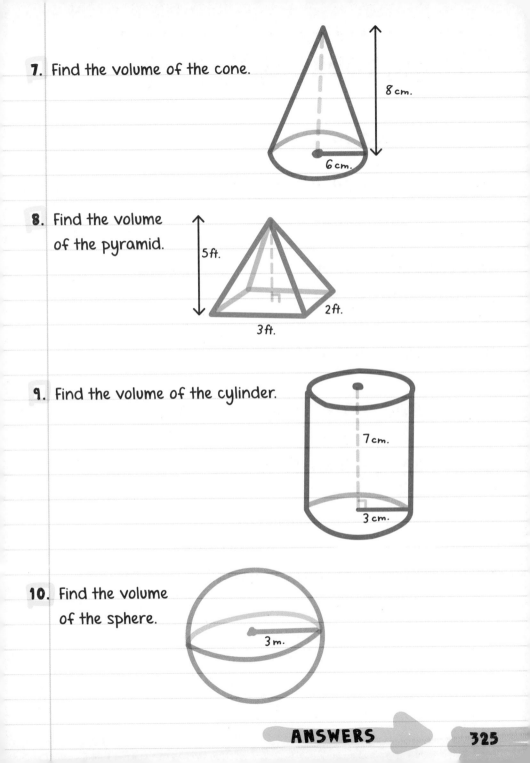

8 cm.

6 cm.

8. Find the volume of the pyramid.

5 ft.

2 ft.

3 ft.

9. Find the volume of the cylinder.

7 cm.

3 cm.

10. Find the volume of the sphere.

3 m.

ANSWERS

CHECK YOUR ANSWERS

1. **RECTANGULAR PRISM** $V = lwh$

2. **CONE** $V = \frac{1}{3}\pi r^2 h$ or $V = \frac{1}{3}Bh$

3. **PYRAMID** $V = \frac{1}{3}Bh$

4. **CYLINDER** $V = \pi r^2 h$

5. **SPHERE** $V = \frac{4}{3}\pi r^3$

6. $V = lwh = 6 \cdot 3 \cdot 2 = 36 \text{ in}^3$

7. $V = \frac{1}{3}Bh = \frac{1}{3} \cdot (3.14) \cdot 6^2 \cdot 8 = 301.44 \text{ cm}^3$

8. $V = \frac{1}{3}Bh = \frac{1}{3} \cdot (3 \cdot 2) \cdot 5 = 10 \text{ ft}^3$

9. $V = \pi r^2 h = (3.14) \cdot (3)^2 \cdot 7 = 197.82 \text{ cm}^3$

10. $V = \frac{4}{3}\pi r^3 = \frac{4}{3} \cdot (3.14) \cdot (3)^3 = 113.04 \text{ m}^3$

Chapter 48

SURFACE AREA

SURFACE AREA is exactly what it sounds like—the area of a shape's surfaces. We can calculate the surface area of a prism by adding together the area of the base(s) and the lateral faces. To find the surface area, it is often easiest to find the surface area of the **NET**—the net is what you have when you unfold a figure:

SURFACE AREA of PRISMS

To find the **SURFACE AREA OF A CUBE**, calculate the area of each side of the cube and add them together. Each side is a square, so use the formula $A = lw$. Or because we know that each side has equal dimensions, we can simply calculate the area of one side and multiply it by 6 because there are six sides to a cube.

EXAMPLE: Find the surface area of the cube.

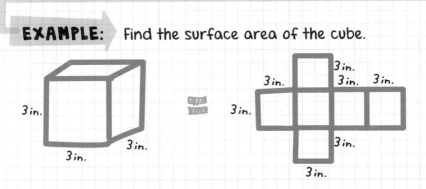

You can unfold the cube to see the surface area more clearly. Because each side of a cube is the same, the area of each surface is length x width, or in this example, $3 \cdot 3 = 9 \text{ in}^2$.

If we add up all the areas of each surface:

Top: 9 in^2 Left: 9 in^2 Front: 9 in^2

Bottom: 9 in^2 Right: 9 in^2 Back: 9 in^2

Surface area of the cube: $9+9+9+9+9+9 = 54 \text{ in}^2$

We can also calculate this by taking the area of one side (9 in^2) and multiplying it by the number of sides (6).

$9 \text{ in}^2 \times 6 \text{ sides} = 54 \text{ in}^2$

To find the **SURFACE AREA OF A RECTANGULAR PRISM**, calculate the area of each side and add them together. Each side is a rectangle, so we use the formula $A = lw$ for all sides.

EXAMPLE: Find the surface area of the rectangular prism.

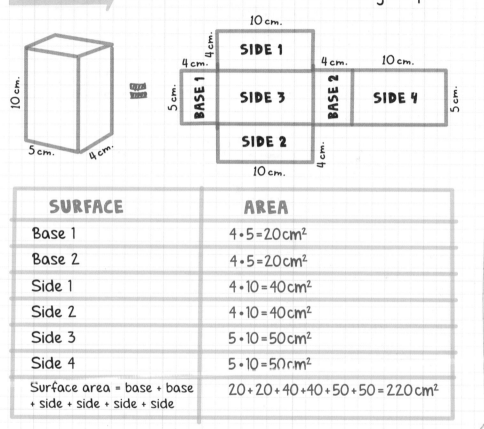

SURFACE	AREA
Base 1	$4 \cdot 5 = 20 \, cm^2$
Base 2	$4 \cdot 5 = 20 \, cm^2$
Side 1	$4 \cdot 10 = 40 \, cm^2$
Side 2	$4 \cdot 10 = 40 \, cm^2$
Side 3	$5 \cdot 10 = 50 \, cm^2$
Side 4	$5 \cdot 10 = 50 \, cm^2$
Surface area = base + base + side + side + side + side	$20 + 20 + 40 + 40 + 50 + 50 = 220 \, cm^2$

To find the **SURFACE AREA OF A TRIANGULAR PRISM**, again, simply calculate the area of each side and add them together. When you "unfold" a triangular prism, the lateral areas are shaped like rectangles, so use the formula for the area of a rectangle ($A = lw$). The bases are triangles, so use the formula for the area of a triangle ($A = \frac{1}{2}bh$). Lastly, add all of the areas together.

EXAMPLE: Find the surface area of the triangular prism.

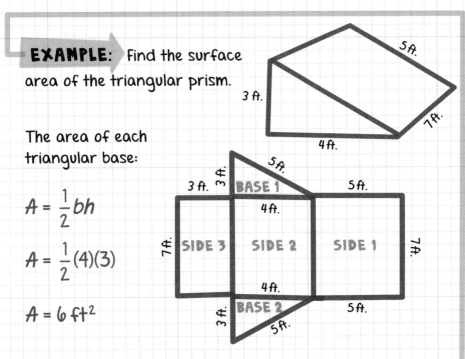

The area of each triangular base:

$$A = \frac{1}{2}bh$$

$$A = \frac{1}{2}(4)(3)$$

$$A = 6 \text{ ft}^2$$

The area of each rectangular side:

SIDE 1:	SIDE 2:	SIDE 3:
$A = lw$	$A = lw$	$A = lw$
$A = 5 \times 7$	$A = 4 \times 7$	$A = 3 \times 7$
$A = 35$	$A = 28$	$A = 21$

Surface area = base + base + side + side + side

Surface area = $6 + 6 + 35 + 28 + 21 = 96 \text{ ft}^2$

SURFACE AREA of FIGURES THAT ARE NOT PRISMS

To find the **SURFACE AREA OF A CYLINDER**, calculate the area of each side and add them together. When you "unfold" a cylinder, the lateral area is shaped like a rectangle, so you use the formula for the area of a rectangle ($A = lw$). The bases are circles, so you use the formula for the area of a circle ($A = \pi r^2$). Lastly, add all the areas together, like so:

$$\text{surface area =}$$
area of rectangle + area of top circle + area of bottom circle

EXAMPLE: Rex wants to find the surface area of a cylinder. He already knows that the area of the rectangle is 36 in². If the radius of each of the bases is 2 in, what is the surface area of the cylinder?

2 in.

4 in.

9 in.

2 in.

$A = 36 + \pi r^2 + \pi r^2$

$A = 36 + (3.14) \cdot 2^2 + (3.14) \cdot 2^2$

$A = 61.12 \text{ in}^2$

Sometimes, we are not given all the measurements we need. But that's no problem—we can **DERIVE** (extract) all the measurements we need from the cylinder's diameter and height.

EXAMPLE: Find the surface area of the cylinder.

First, let's calculate the area of the rectangular lateral area with $A = l \times w$. The width of the rectangular lateral area isn't given, but the width is equal to the circumference of the base, which we can find out by using the formula for circumference ($C = \pi d$).

C = WIDTH OF THE LATERAL AREA

$C = \pi d$
$C = (3.14)(6)$
$C = 18.84$ inches

Now we can find the area of the rectangular lateral area:

$A = l \times w$
$A = 8 \times 18.84$
$A = 150.72$ in^2

8 in.

6 in.

Next, we find the area of the bases (simply halve the diameter to get the radius: half of 6 inches is 3 inches).

$A = \pi r^2$
$A = 3.14(3^2)$
$A = 3.14(9)$
$A = 28.26$ in^2

Finally, add up the surface areas of both bases and lateral area:

Surface area = $28.26 + 28.26 + 150.72 = 207.24$ in^2

The **SURFACE AREA OF A SPHERE** is easy to calculate. If we know what the length of the radius is, the surface area is

$$A = 4\pi r^2$$

EXAMPLE: Find the surface area of the sphere:

$A = 4\pi r^2$

$A = 4\,(3.14)\,(2)^2$

$A = 50.24 \text{ in}^2$

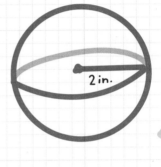

2 in.

CHECK YOUR KNOWLEDGE

Find the surface area of each figure.

1.

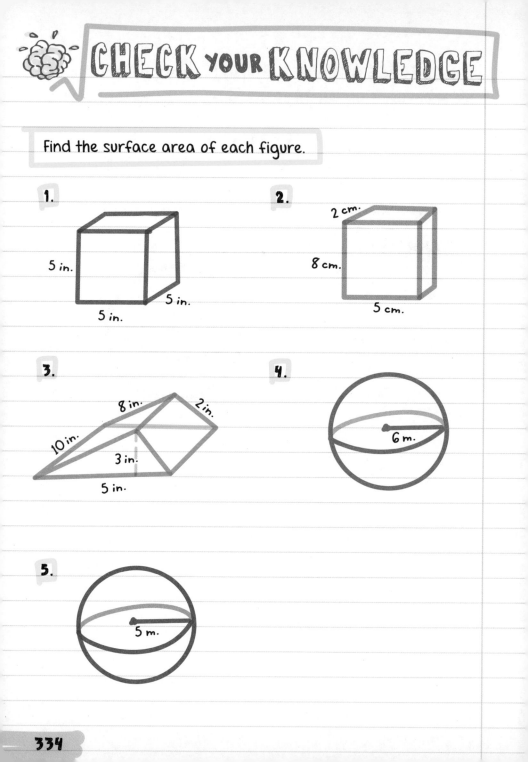

5 in.

5 in.

5 in.

2.

2 cm.

8 cm.

5 cm.

3.

8 in.

2 in.

10 in.

3 in.

5 in.

4.

6 m.

5.

5 m.

6. Susie has a small rubber ball that has a radius of 3 inches. If she wants to paint the entire surface of the ball, how much paint will she use?

7. Susie pumps some air into the ball and increases the radius by 1 more inch. If she wants to paint the entire surface of the ball a different color, how much paint will she use?

8. Myles has a cardboard box and wants to figure out the surface area. The length is 6 inches, the height is 4 inches, and the width is 8 inches. What is the surface area of the box?

9. Sarah wants to make a can of soup that is shaped as a cylinder. If the can is 7 inches tall and has a radius of 3 inches, how much material should she use to make the can?

10. Lance has a wedge of cheese and knows the measurements of certain parts of the cheese wedge. What is the surface area of the wedge?

NOTE: You might need to use the Pythagorean theorem to find the missing side!

6 cm.

2 cm.

8 cm.

ANSWERS

CHECK YOUR ANSWERS

1. $A = 6 \times 5^2 = 150 \text{ ft}^2$

2. $A = 2(2 \cdot 5) + 2(2 \cdot 8) + 2(8 \cdot 5) = 132 \text{ cm}^2$

3. $A = 2(\frac{1}{2}Bh) + Bh + Bh + Bh$

   $= 2(\frac{1}{2} \cdot 5 \cdot 3) + 2 \cdot 10 + 8 \cdot 10 + 5 \cdot 10 = 165 \text{ in}^2$

4. $A = 4\pi r^2 = 4 \cdot (3.14) \cdot 36 = 452.16 \text{ m}^2$

5. $A = 4\pi r^2 = 4 \cdot (3.14) \cdot 25 = 314 \text{ m}^2$

6. 113.04 in^2

7. 200.96 in^2

8. 208 in^2

9. 188.4 in^2

10. The missing side is 10 cm. Therefore, the surface area is 96 cm².

WAIT, DID I MISS THE CHEESE? RATS!

☐ Chapter 49 ⊜

ANGLES, TRIANGLES, AND TRANSVERSAL LINES

△ ◇ ○ ◿ ▢   ◿ ◇ ○ △ ▢

INTERIOR ANGLES

We know that a triangle has three sides and three angles.
One of the special properties of a triangle is that the sum of
all three interior angles is always equal to 180°. Always!

EXAMPLE: In △ABC, ∠A is 30° and ∠B is 70°.
What is ∠C?

Because we know that the angles
of a triangle always total 180°,

$A + B + C = 180$
$30 + 70 + C = 180$
$100 + C = 180$
$C = 80$

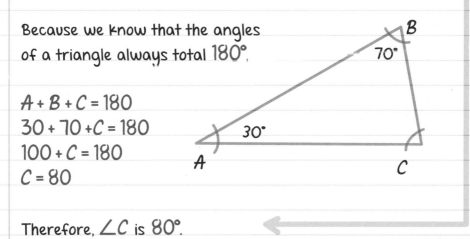

Therefore, ∠C is 80°.

EXAMPLE: In $\triangle JKL$, $\angle J$ is $45°$ and $\angle L$ is $45°$. What is $\angle K$?

Because we know that the angles of a triangle total $180°$,

$$J + K + L = 180$$
$$45 + K + 45 = 180$$
$$K = 90$$

Therefore, $\angle K$ is $90°$.

EXTERIOR ANGLES

We know that a triangle has three interior angles. But triangles also have **EXTERIOR ANGLES**—angles on the outside of the triangle. In $\triangle ABC$ below, $\angle S$ is one of the exterior angles.

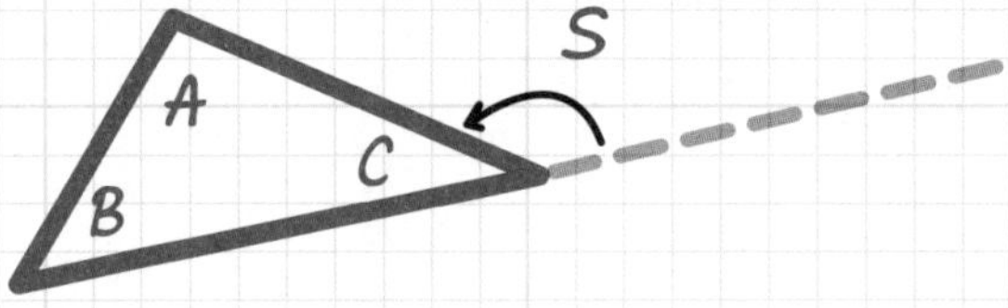

Angles C and S are supplementary to each other, therefore $C + S = 180°$.

EXAMPLE: In the diagram below, $\angle X$ is $100°$ and $\angle Y$ is $50°$. What is $\angle W$?

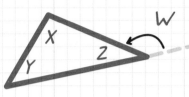

We must first find the value of $\angle Z$.

Because all three interior angles add up to $180°$,

$X + Y + Z = 180$
$100 + 50 + Z = 180$
$Z = 30$

$\angle W$ is an exterior angle to $\angle Z$, therefore Angles Z and W are supplementary,

$Z + W = 180°$
$30 + W = 180°$
$W - 150°$

Notice anything about the previous problem? The measurement of an exterior angle is the same value as the sum of the other two interior angles!

EXAMPLE: In the diagram below, $\angle A$ is 55° and $\angle B$ is 43°. What is $\angle D$?

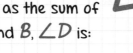

Because $\angle D$ is the same value as the sum of Angles A and B, $\angle D$ is:

$55 + 43 = 98°$.

TRANSVERSAL LINES

A transversal line is a line that cuts through two parallel lines, such as:

OR

As we can see, a transversal line creates 8 angles. But by studying the angles, we can see that many of the angles are congruent!

In the diagram below, Line R is a transversal that cuts through Lines P and Q, which are parallel to each other.

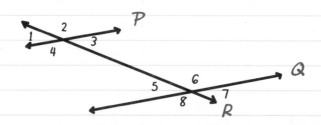

We know that ∠1 is congruent to ∠3 because they are vertical angles. For the same reason, we know that the following angles are also congruent:

∠2 = ∠4
∠5 = ∠7
∠6 = ∠8

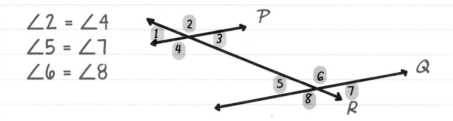

But what else do we know? Because P and Q are parallel, the transversal forms **CORRESPONDING ANGLES—** angles that are in the same position in relation to the tranversal and therefore congruent. Thus, the following corresponding angles are congruent:

∠1 = ∠5
∠2 = ∠6
∠3 = ∠7
∠4 = ∠8

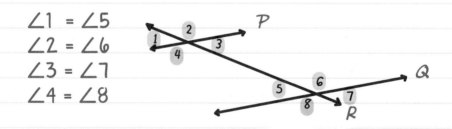

Furthermore, because P and Q are parallel and cut by a transversal, it means that ∠1 is congruent to ∠7 because they are **ALTERNATE EXTERIOR ANGLES**. Alternate exterior angles are on opposite sides of a transversal and outside the parallel line. Thus, the following alternate exterior angles are congruent:

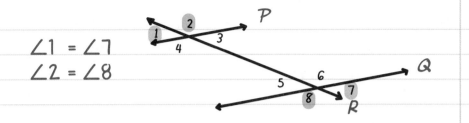

$\angle 1 = \angle 7$
$\angle 2 = \angle 8$

Similarly, because Lines P and Q are parallel, it means that $\angle 3$ is congruent to $\angle 5$ because they are **ALTERNATE INTERIOR ANGLES**—angles that are on opposite sides of a transversal and inside the parallel line. For the same reason, $\angle 4$ is congruent to $\angle 6$.

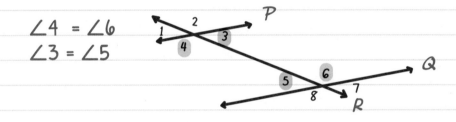

$\angle 4 = \angle 6$
$\angle 3 = \angle 5$

So, putting all of this information together:

$\angle 1, 3, 5,$ and 7 are congruent.
$\angle 2, 4, 6,$ and 8 are congruent.

> The opposite of all of this is also true:
> If you don't know if two lines are parallel—
> look at the alternate interior or exterior angles.
> If they are congruent, the lines are parallel.

CHECK YOUR KNOWLEDGE

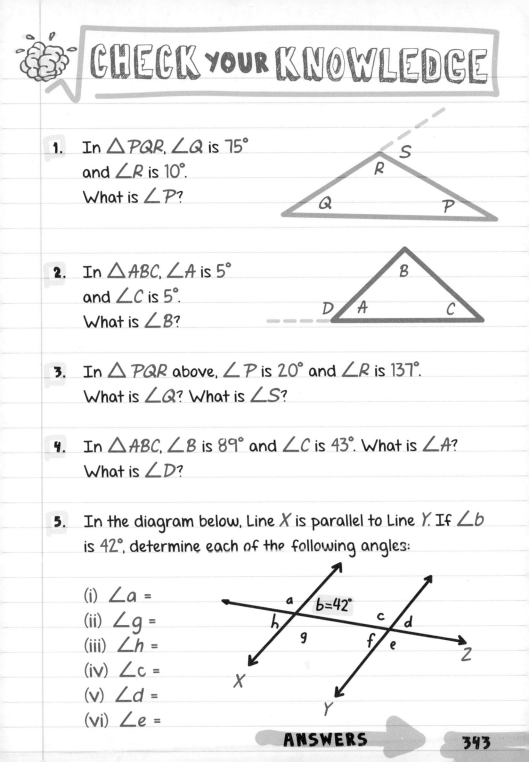

1. In △PQR, ∠Q is 75°
   and ∠R is 10°.
   What is ∠P?

2. In △ABC, ∠A is 5°
   and ∠C is 5°.
   What is ∠B?

3. In △PQR above, ∠P is 20° and ∠R is 137°.
   What is ∠Q? What is ∠S?

4. In △ABC, ∠B is 89° and ∠C is 43°. What is ∠A?
   What is ∠D?

5. In the diagram below, Line X is parallel to Line Y. If ∠b
   is 42°, determine each of the following angles:

   (i) ∠a =
   (ii) ∠g =
   (iii) ∠h =
   (iv) ∠c =
   (v) ∠d =
   (vi) ∠e =

ANSWERS   343

CHECK YOUR ANSWERS

1. 95°

2. 170°

3. $\angle Q = 23°$, $\angle S = 43°$

4. $\angle A = 48°$, $\angle D = 132°$

5. (i) $\angle a = 138°$
   (ii) $\angle g = 138°$
   (iii) $\angle h = 42°$
   (iv) $\angle c = 138°$
   (v) $\angle d = 42°$
   (vi) $\angle e = 138°$

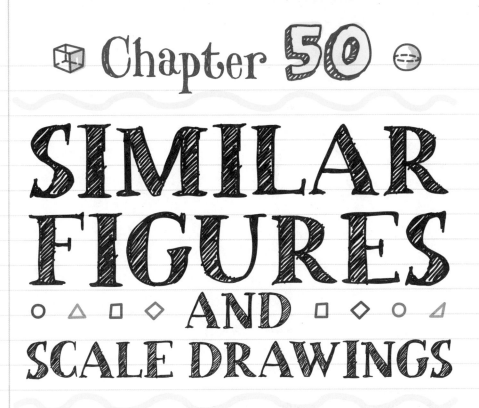

Chapter 50

SIMILAR FIGURES

○ △ □ ◇ AND □ ◇ ○ ◁

SCALE DRAWINGS

SIMILAR FIGURES are figures that have the same shape, but not necessarily the same size. Similar figures have corresponding angles (angles that are in the same relative position on each figure) that are congruent (equal in size). Similar figures also have corresponding sides (sides that are in the same relative position on each figure) that are proportional in size (when one part of the shape changes, all parts of the shape change).

> The symbol for similar figures is ~.

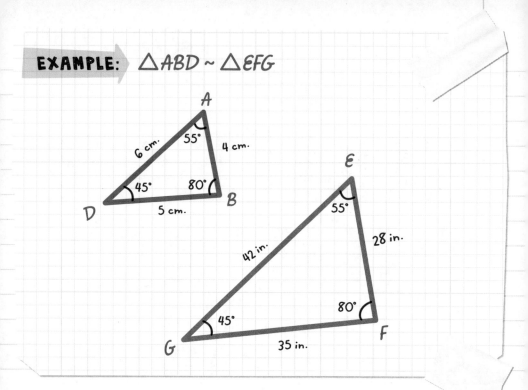

The triangles are similar because they have congruent angles...

$\angle A \cong \angle E$
$\angle B \cong \angle F$
$\angle D \cong \angle G$

...and their corresponding sides are proportional in size!

$EF = 7 \cdot AB$
$EG = 7 \cdot AD$
$FG = 7 \cdot BD$

If we know two figures are similar figures, we can use their proportionality to find missing measurements.

EXAMPLE: $\triangle ABC \sim \triangle GHI$. Find the missing lengths x and y.

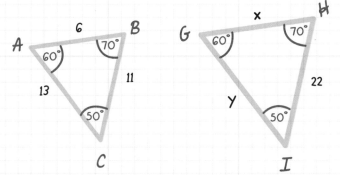

Because the triangles are similar, the corresponding sides are proportional in size. Start with a complete set of sides, and find the missing proportional size in the other triangle.

$$\frac{BC}{AB} = \frac{HI}{GH}$$

$$\frac{11}{6} \diagup\!\!\!\!\diagup \frac{22}{x}$$

$$11x = 132$$

$$x = 12$$

$$\frac{BC}{AC} = \frac{HI}{GI}$$

$$\frac{11}{13} \diagup\!\!\!\!\diagup \frac{22}{y}$$

$$11y = 286$$

$$y = 26$$

USE CROSS PRODUCTS TO FIND THE MISSING NUMBER

If we know two figures are similar figures, then we can
also use their proportionality to find missing measurements
in BOTH figures.

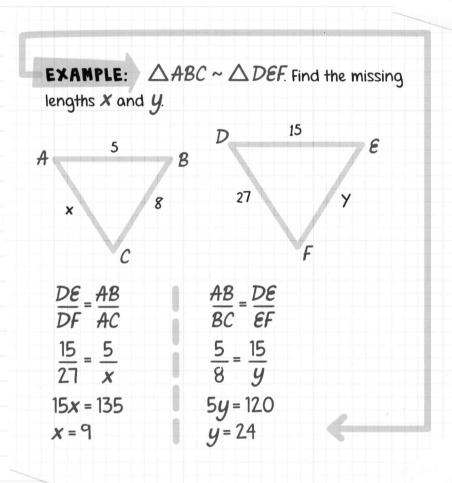

EXAMPLE: $\triangle ABC \sim \triangle DEF.$ Find the missing
lengths x and y.

$$\frac{DE}{DF} = \frac{AB}{AC}$$

$$\frac{15}{27} = \frac{5}{x}$$

$$15x = 135$$

$$x = 9$$

$$\frac{AB}{BC} = \frac{DE}{EF}$$

$$\frac{5}{8} = \frac{15}{y}$$

$$5y = 120$$

$$y = 24$$

We can also use the proportionality of similar figures
to find missing angles.

$\triangle MNO \sim \triangle PQR$. Find the missing $\angle M$.

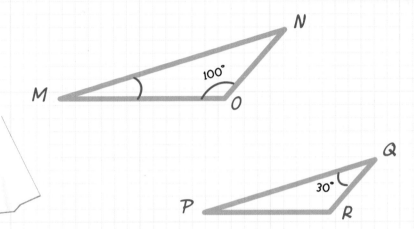

Because the triangles are similar, the corresponding angles are congruent.

Therefore: $\angle N \cong \angle Q = 30°$ and $\angle O \cong \angle R = 100°$.

Because all the angles of a triangle add up to $180°$:

$\angle M + \angle N + \angle O = 180°$

$\angle M + 30° + 100° = 180°$

$\angle M = 50°$

A **SCALE DRAWING** is a drawing that is similar to an actual object (or place)—just made bigger or smaller. The **SCALE** is the ratio of the length in the drawing to the actual length.

EXAMPLE: In this scale drawing, 1 inch equals 3 feet of floor. What is the actual perimeter and area of the room?

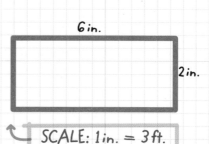

6 in.

2 in.

SCALE: 1 in. = 3 ft.

Because 1 inch equals 3 feet of floor, the length is:

$$\frac{1 \text{ inch}}{3 \text{ feet}} = \frac{6 \text{ inches}}{x \text{ feet}}$$

The length is 18 feet.

Because 1 inch equals 3 feet of floor, the width is:

$$\frac{1 \text{ inch}}{3 \text{ feet}} = \frac{2 \text{ inches}}{x \text{ feet}}$$

The width is 6 feet.

The actual perimeter is: 18 + 6 + 18 + 6 = 48 feet.

The actual area is: 18 × 6 = 108 ft².

Where do you often see scale drawings? **MAPS!**
They are one of the most common places that scale is used!

EXAMPLE: A map shows the road between the cities of Springton and Fogsville. The legend of the map says that 2 inches represents 5 miles. If the distance on the map between Springton and Fogsville is 7 inches, what is the real distance?

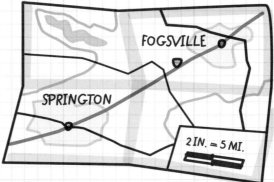

Set up a proportion:

$$\frac{2 \text{ inches}}{5 \text{ miles}} = \frac{7 \text{ inches}}{x \text{ miles}}$$

Therefore, the real distance is 17.5 miles.

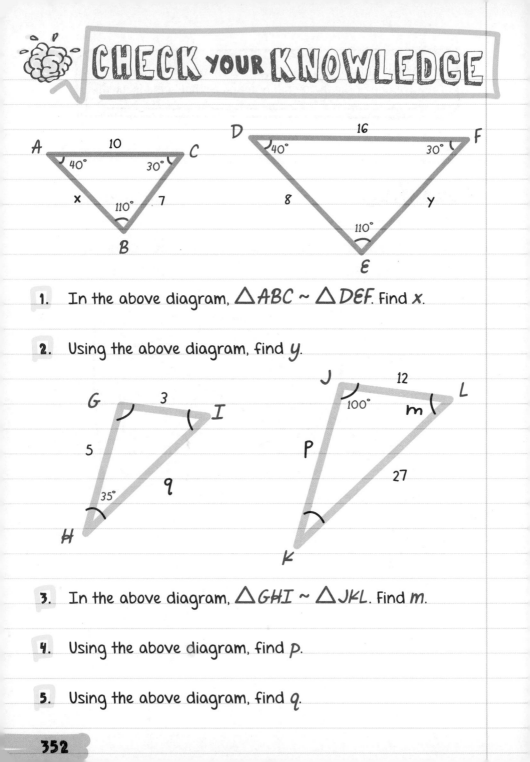

1. In the above diagram, $\triangle ABC \sim \triangle DEF$. Find x.

2. Using the above diagram, find y.

3. In the above diagram, $\triangle GHI \sim \triangle JKL$. Find m.

4. Using the above diagram, find p.

5. Using the above diagram, find q.

6. Paul reads on a map that 1 inch represents 7 miles. He measures the distance between two spots to be 8.5 inches. What is the real distance?

7. A map says that 4 centimeters represents 10 kilometers. What is the real distance that 18 centimeters represents?

8. Mark is drawing a map of his room. His room is 15 feet long. He wants to let 1 inch represent 5 feet. What is the length of his room on the map?

9. The distance between Appleville and Tanwood is 350 miles. Joe wants to draw a map where 1 centimeter represents 7 miles. What is the length between Appleville and Tanwood on the map?

10. A map says that 4 inches represents 10 feet. A barn on the map has a length of 6 inches and a width of 12 inches. What is the real perimeter of the barn?

ANSWERS ➤

CHECK YOUR ANSWERS

1. 5

2. 11.2

3. 45°

4. 20

5. 6.75

6. 59.5 miles

7. 45 kilometers

8. 3 inches

9. 50 centimeters

10. 15 + 30 + 15 + 30 = 90 feet

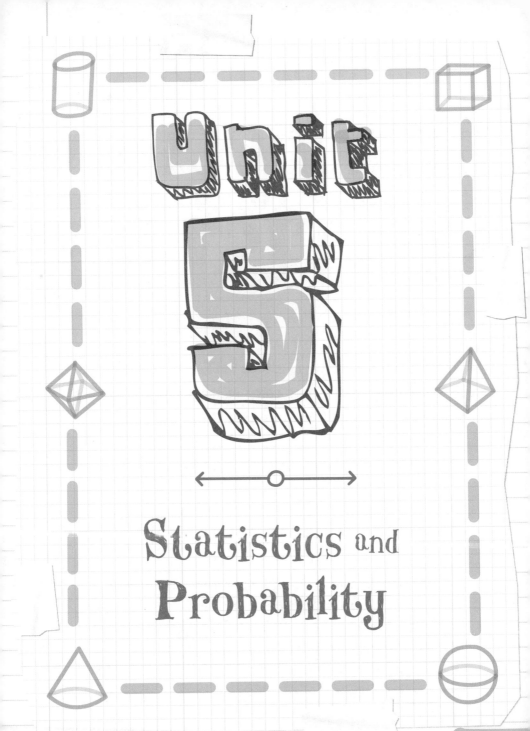

Unit 5

Statistics and Probability

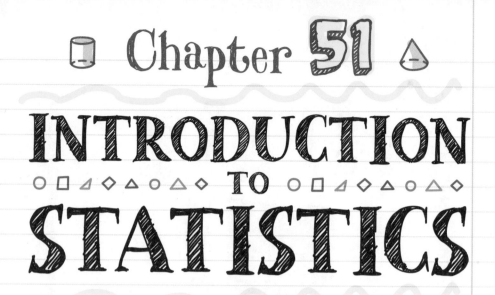

Chapter 51

INTRODUCTION TO STATISTICS

○□◿◇△○△◇ **TO** ○□◿◇△○△◇

STATISTICS is the study of data. **DATA** is a collection of facts—sometimes these facts come in the form of numbers, words, or descriptions. There are two types of data:

QUANTITATIVE DATA
information given in numbers. Usually this is information that you can count or measure.

QUALITATIVE DATA
information given that describes something. Usually this is information that you can observe, such as appearances, textures, smells, tastes, etc.

Quantitative Data	
The # of students in your class	1 2 3 4 5 6 7
The # of boys in your class	1 2 3 4
The # of girls in your class	1 2 3
How many students are getting A's	ME! ME! ME!
How many students are out sick	UH OH.

Qualitative Data	
Do students like the class?	YAY! YAY! YAY!
Are the students friendly?	GRR! GRR!
Are the students paying attention?	↓ ↓ ↓ ↓ ↓
Are the students awake?	Z.

Statistics help us collect, interpret, summarize, and present data.

COLLECTING DATA

What is a statistical question? A **STATISTICAL QUESTION** is a question that anticipates many different responses. Answers that differ have **VARIABILITY**—variability describes how spread out or closely clustered a set of data is.

THINK: "How many answers are possible?"
If only 1, then it's not a statistical question.
If more than 1, then it is a statistical question.

CONSIDER THESE 2 QUESTIONS:

1. **How old am I?** This question has only one answer. It is not a statistical question because the answer cannot vary (there is no variability).

2. **How old are the students at my school?** This question is a statistical question because there can be different answers. Not every student is the same age, so the answers will vary (there is variability).

EXAMPLES: Is each question a statistical question?

What is your phone number? **NO**—there is no variability.

How many televisions does each family on your street own? **YES**—answers will vary.

How much did you pay for your last hamburger? **NO**—there is only one answer.

How many brothers and sisters does each student in your school have? **YES**—answers will vary.

The answers to a statistical question are "spread out" and can be quite different—so there can be **HIGH VARIABILITY** or **LOW VARIABILITY**.

EXAMPLES:

How old are the people shopping at the mall? The answers will vary greatly, so this question has high variability.

How old are the students in the 7th grade? The answers will all generally be within one or two years of one another. Because the answers won't differ much, this question has low variability.

Why are data and statistics important?

1. They help us identify problems in the world.

2. They provide evidence if we are trying to make a point in presentations or discussions.

3. They help us make informed decisions for our future.

EXAMPLE: Should I go to college?

Statistics tell me that in 2012, the average salary for college graduates was $46,900 per year, while the average salary for high school graduates was $29,960. So, I better go to college!

SAMPLING

SAMPLING is when we take a small part of a larger group to estimate characteristics about the whole group. For example, there is a group of a thousand people, and we want to find out how many of them love math. It would take a **VERY** long time to ask all one thousand of them! Instead, we interview only a portion of that group and use our findings about that portion to draw approximate conclusions about the entire group. In other words, we take a sample! A sample represents the entire group.

Of course, it is important to make sure that your sample is a good representation of the entire group. For example, you know that at your school of 100 students, there are a lot of boys and also a lot of girls. You randomly choose 20 people and discover that in your sample, there are 19 girls and only 1 boy. Most likely, this is not a good sample because your sample is not a true representation of the entire school.

EXAMPLE: A thousand people work at a factory. You want to find out how many people are left-handed, so you ask 20 people if they are left- or right-handed. Out of the 20 people, only 3 are left-handed. (Approximately how many left-handed people work at the factory?)

Because there are 3 left-handed people out of the 20,

it means that $\frac{3}{20}$ of the sample is left-handed.

So, we can apply this number to our entire population of 1,000 people:

$$1,000 \times \frac{3}{20} = 150$$

YOU COULD ALSO SET UP A PROPORTION TO SOLVE THIS:

$$\frac{3}{20} = \frac{L}{1,000}$$

Approximately 150 people are left-handed.

EXAMPLE: There are 520 students in Jimmy's school. Jimmy wants to know how many students play soccer. He asks 60 classmates and finds out that 8 students play soccer. Approximately how many students at his school play soccer?

Because 8 out of 60 students play soccer, it means that

$\frac{8}{60} = \frac{2}{15}$ of the sample play soccer.

To apply this number to our entire population of 520 students:

$$520 \times \frac{2}{15} = 69.33$$

So, we can estimate approximately 69 students play soccer.

CHECK YOUR KNOWLEDGE

1. State whether each of the following questions asks about quantitative or qualitative data.

   (A) How many boys are there in a school?

   (B) What is your favorite ice cream flavor?

   (C) What color shirt are people wearing?

   (D) How many students are excited about the game?

2. State whether each of the following questions is a statistical question.

   (A) How many cars does your family have?

   (B) How long does it take you to do your homework each night?

   (C) Did you watch TV last night?

   (D) What is the average height of the students in your grade?

3. State whether each of the following situations has high variability or low variability.

   (A) How much do people spend on their food at a restaurant?

   (B) How many cell phones do you use?

   (C) What grade did each student in your class get on the last math test?

   (D) How many bathrooms are in your home?

4. Janet has 30 classmates in her classroom. 18 of those classmates are girls. If there are a total of 500 students in her school, approximately how many students are girls?

5. John swims 2.5 miles and sees a total of 12 fish. If John swims for a total of 8 miles, approximately how many fish will John see?

6. Susan plays basketball for 8 minutes and makes 14 points. If she plays for a total of 21 minutes, approximately how many points will Susan make?

7. Larry wants to guess how many marbles are in a box that has a height of 18 inches. He calculates that there are 32 marbles in a height of 5 inches. Approximately how many marbles are in the box?

8. There are 140 cars in a parking lot. Bob looks at 15 cars and finds out that 2 of those cars are gray-colored. Approximately how many cars in the parking lot are gray-colored?

ANSWERS

CHECK YOUR ANSWERS

1. **(A)** Quantitative
   (B) Qualitative
   (C) Qualitative
   (D) Quantitative

2. **(A)** Not a statistical question
   (B) Is a statistical question
   (C) Not a statistical question
   (D) Is a statistical question

3. **(A)** High variability
   (B) Low variability
   (C) High variability
   (D) Low variability

4. approximately 300 girls

5. approximately 38.4 (or 38) fish

6. approximately 36.75 (or 37) points

7. approximately 115.2 (or 115) marbles

8. approximately 18.66 (or 19) cars

Chapter 52

MEASURES OF CENTRAL TENDENCY AND VARIATION

After a statistical question is asked, we collect all the data. All the numbers in the data are called a **SET**. Once we have our set, we then have to describe and analyze the data.

MEASURES of CENTRAL TENDENCY

One tool we can use with our data set is **MEASURES OF CENTRAL TENDENCY**. A measure of central tendency is a single number that is a summary of all of a data set's values. This is much easier to understand than trying to present all of the data.

EXAMPLE: My grade point average (GPA) is a measure of central tendency for all of my grades.

The three measures of central tendency most used are:

1. The **MEAN** (also called the **ARITHMETIC AVERAGE**) is a calculated central value of a set of numbers. To calculate the mean, add all of the numbers, then divide the sum by how many items there are.

EXAMPLE: We surveyed five city blocks to see how many buildings are on each. Our data set was: 5, 10, 12, 13, 15. What is the mean?

5 + 10 + 12 + 13 + 15 = 55   Add all the items.

55 ÷ 5 = 11   Next, divide the total by the number of items (there are 5).

The mean is 11. This means that there is an average of 11 buildings on each city block.

The mean might or might not be one of the items that you started with—it doesn't have to be!

2. The **MEDIAN** is the middle number of a data set when all of the items are written in order, from least to greatest.

EXAMPLE: I tracked how many leaves fell from the tree outside our classroom window each day in October. My data set was 52, 84, 26, 61, 73. What is the median?

26, 52, 61, 73, 84 First, write the items in order from least to greatest.

The median is 61, because 61 is the number that falls in the middle of the ordered data set.

The greatest value in a data set is called the **MAXIMUM**. The lowest value is called the **MINIMUM**. And of course, the middle number is called the median.

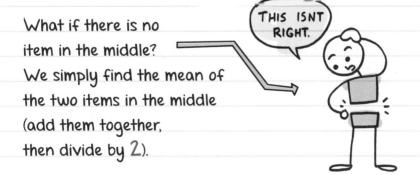

What if there is no item in the middle? We simply find the mean of the two items in the middle (add them together, then divide by 2).

THIS ISNT RIGHT.

EXAMPLE: Our school held a car wash fundraiser for a class trip. During one hour, I received six donations in my bucket. I received $13, $15, $34, $28, $25, $20. What was the median donation?

13, 15, 20, 25, 28, 34   First, write the items in order from least to greatest.

The middle numbers are 20, 25.

20 + 25 = 45

45 ÷ 2 = 22.5

The median is 22.5. ←

> The median might or might not be one of the items that you started with—it doesn't have to be!

This means that median is equally between the two numbers in the middle of the ordered data set.

---

3. The **MODE** is the item in a data set that occurs most often. It's OK to have just one mode, more than one mode, or no mode!

EXAMPLE: Ten students took a math test, and their scores were:

75, 80, 90, 68, 95, 100, 78, 90, 55, 75. What was the mode?

55, 68, 75, 75, 78, 80,   Put the items in order to
90, 90, 95, 100.   see if any items repeat.

Both 75 and 90 occur twice.
So there are two modes: 75 and 90.

This means that the numbers 75 and 90 occur most often in the data set.

EXAMPLE: I asked six people how many pencils they have in their bag. The amounts were: 1, 4, 8, 8, 1, 4. What was the mode?

1, 1, 4, 4, 8, 8. Put the items in order to see if any items repeat.

Because ALL the items occur the same amount of times (two times), there is no mode.

This means all the numbers appear in the data set the same amount of times.

MEASURES of VARIATION

Another tool we can use to describe and analyze our data set is **MEASURES OF VARIATION**, which describes how the values of a data set vary. The main measure of variation is **RANGE**; range is the difference between the minimum and maximum unit in a data set. The range shows how "spread out" a data set is.

EXAMPLE: When asked how much money they had in their pockets, students in Mrs. Philler's class gave the following answers:
$6, $11, $20, $4, $1, $15, $10, $8, $5, $1, $2, $12, $4.

What is the range of the data set?

OR THINK
✓ RANGE = HIGH − LOW

20 − 1 = 19   (Range = maximum unit − minimum unit)
So, the range of answers is $19.

This means the money each student has can range up to $19 in difference.

A data value that is significantly lower or higher than the other values is called an **OUTLIER**. An outlier can throw off the mean of a data set and give a skewed portrayal of the data.

EXAMPLE: At Carlitos' Taco Shop, five students ate the following number of tacos:

JED: 3 tacos

DENISE: 2 tacos

VERONICA: 3 tacos

KATRINA: 4 tacos

MIKE: 9 tacos

Which person seems to be the outlier? **MIKE**

If we calculate the mean, we can see clearly that Mike skews the data:

$3 + 2 + 3 + 4 + 9 = 21$

$21 \div 5 = 4.2$

THINK CRITICALLY!
ASK, "DO THESE NUMBERS MAKE SENSE GIVEN THE DATA?"

Most students ate 4 or fewer tacos, but Mike's amount skews the average to above 4.

CHECK YOUR KNOWLEDGE

1. When asked how many hours they spend on a computer each day, students gave the following answers (in hours): 2, 5, 4, 1, 17, 5, 4, 5, 2.

   (A) Find the mean.

   (B) Find the median.

   (C) Find the mode.

   (D) Find the minimum and maximum.

   (E) Find the range.

   (F) Do there seem to be any outliers? If so, what are they?

2. On their last science test, ten students earned the following scores: 70, 71, 82, 100, 97, 87, 71, 91, 38, 81.

   (A) Find the mean.

   (B) Find the median.

   (C) Find the mode.

   (D) Find the minimum and maximum.

   (E) Find the range.

   (F) Do there seem to be any outliers? If so, what are they?

ANSWERS

CHECK YOUR ANSWERS

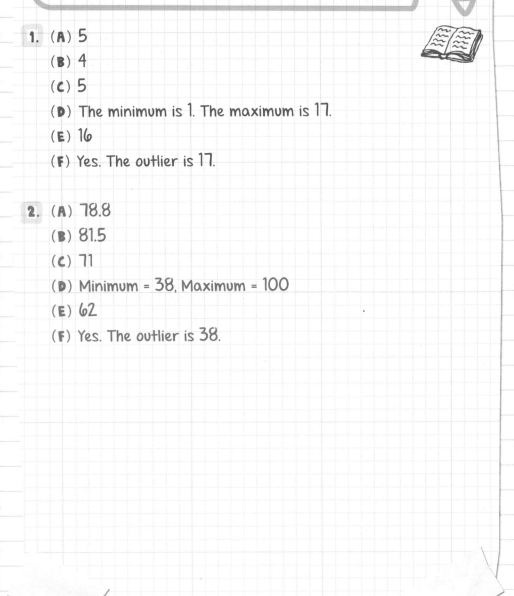

1. (A) 5
   (B) 4
   (C) 5
   (D) The minimum is 1. The maximum is 17.
   (E) 16
   (F) Yes. The outlier is 17.

2. (A) 78.8
   (B) 81.5
   (C) 71
   (D) Minimum = 38, Maximum = 100
   (E) 62
   (F) Yes. The outlier is 38.

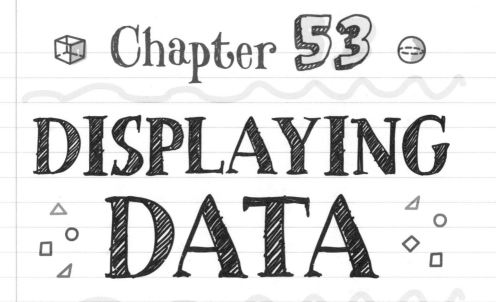

Chapter 53

DISPLAYING DATA

Once data has been collected and organized, it can be displayed with charts, graphs, or diagrams. For example, just by looking at a pie chart, a scientist can see what percentage of extinct animals were primates.

TWO-WAY TABLES

A **TWO-WAY TABLE** is a lot like a regular table, except that it shows two or more sets of data about the same subject. The data relates to two or more different categories or qualities. You use a two-way table to see if there is a relationship between the categories.

EXAMPLE: Mr. Nayeri collects data from the students in his class about whether they play sports after school and whether they complete all of their homework. Is there evidence that those who play sports after school also tend to complete their homework?

	PLAY SPORTS	DO NOT PLAY SPORTS	TOTAL
COMPLETE HOMEWORK	14	6	(14 + 6) = 20
DO NOT COMPLETE HOMEWORK	2	4	(2 + 4) = 6
TOTAL	(14 + 2) = 16	(6 + 4) = 10	26

From the totals, we can see that there are 26 students, and we can answer a lot of questions, like:

✳ How many students only play a sport after school? ☐2☐

✳ How many students only complete their homework? ☐6☐

✳ How many students do both? ☐14☐

✳ How many students do not play a sport and do not complete their homework? ☐4☐

The common subject is the students, and we can conclude that if you play sports after school, you are also likely to complete your homework.

READ TWO-WAY TABLES CAREFULLY! SOMETIMES, THE RELATIONSHIP THEY SHOW IS THAT THERE IS **NO** RELATIONSHIP AT ALL!

376

LINE PLOTS

A **LINE PLOT** displays data by placing an "X" above numbers on a number line.

EXAMPLE: This line plot displays the number of books bought by each of the 15 customers at the local bookstore last week.

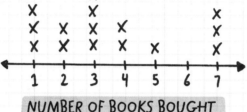

NUMBER OF BOOKS BOUGHT

EXAMPLE: Ten students were asked, "How many people (including yourself) live in your house?" Their answers were:

4, 6, 3, 2, 4, 5, 4, 7, 4, 5. Create a line plot to show this data.

2, 3, 4, 4, 4, 4, 5, 5, 6, 7. First, put the data in numerical order. Then write an "X" above each response on the number line.

What can you "read" from this line plot? The most common answer was 4 (the mode), followed by 5. The range is between 2 and 7, so the range is 5. The median is 4.

HISTOGRAMS

Like a line plot, a **HISTOGRAM** shows the frequency of data. Instead of marking the data items with Xs, however, a histogram shows them as a graph. Note that a histogram has two axes (sides) in order to show the different frequencies and characteristics.

EXAMPLE: This histogram shows the heights of trees on each street in my town. In this case, the frequency is the number of trees, and the characteristic is the height of the trees.

From the graph, we see:

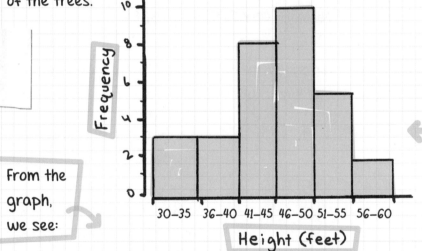

There are 3 trees whose heights are between 30 and 35 feet; there are 3 trees whose heights are between 36 and 40 feet; there are 8 trees whose heights are between 41 and 45 feet, etc.

> This is the same example as the earlier line plot. Compare the difference between line plots and histograms.

EXAMPLE: Ten students were asked, "How many people (including yourself) live in your house? Their answers were: 4, 6, 3, 2, 4, 5, 4, 7, 4, 5. Create a histogram to show this data. First, put the data in numerical order. Then, create a bar above each set of responses.

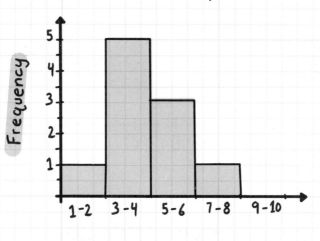

Number of People Living in Your Home

BOX PLOTS

A **BOX PLOT** (also known as a **BOX AND WHISKER PLOT**) displays data along a number line and splits the data into **QUARTILES** (quarters). The different boxes show the different quarters—25% of the data is in each of the four quarters. The size of each section indicates the variability of the data. The median splits the data into two halves.

The median of the lower half is known as the **LOWER QUARTILE** and is represented by "**Q1.**" The median of the upper half is known as the **UPPER QUARTILE** and is represented by "**Q3.**"

EXAMPLES:

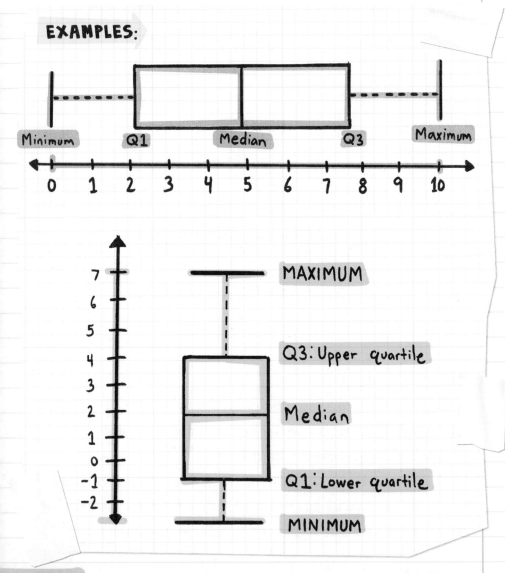

TO CREATE A BOX PLOT:

1. Arrange the data from least to greatest along a number line.
2. Identify the minimum, maximum, median, lower half, and upper half.
3. Identify the lower quartile (find the median of the lower half of the data).
4. Identify the upper quartile (find the median of the upper half of the data).
5. Mark these values on a number line and draw the boxes.

EXAMPLE: The students in Mr. Kruk's class earned the following scores on their test: 64, 82, 76, 68, 94, 96, 74, 76, 86, 70. Create a box plot of this data.

64, 68, 70, 74, 76, 76, 82, 86, 94, 96

↑ MINIMUM   ↑ MEDIAN   ↑ MAXIMUM

LOWER HALF   UPPER HALF

 First, arrange the data from least to greatest.

 Next, identify the minimum (64), maximum (96), median (76), the lower half, and the upper half.

 Next, calculate the lower quartile by finding the median of the lower half of the data.

Lower quartile = the median of 64, 68, 70, 74, and 76, which is 70. ← *THIS IS THE BEGINNING OF Q1.*

➡️ Next, calculate the upper quartile by finding the median of the upper half of the data:
Upper quartile = the median of: 76, 82, 86, 94, and 96, which is 86. ← THIS IS THE END OF Q3.

➡️ Last, put values above a number line, and draw the boxes.

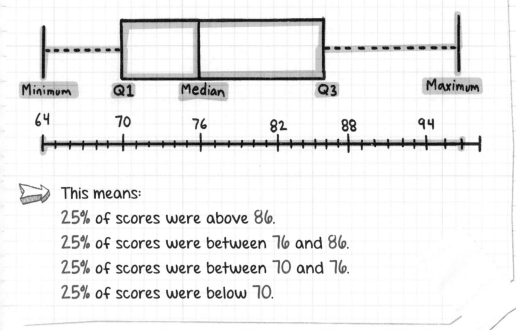

| Minimum | Q1 | Median | | Q3 | Maximum |

64   70   76   82   88   94

➡️ This means:
25% of scores were above 86.
25% of scores were between 76 and 86.
25% of scores were between 70 and 76.
25% of scores were below 70.

In the box plot above, the right-hand portion of the box appears wider than the left-hand portion of the box. When box graphs are not evenly divided in half, this is known as **SKEW**. If the box plot has a wider right side, the graph is described as being **SKEWED RIGHT**, as above. If the box plot has a wider left side, it is **SKEWED LEFT**. If the box plot is evenly divided into two equal sections, it is described as being **SYMMETRIC**.

SCATTER PLOTS

A **SCATTER PLOT** is a type of graph that shows the relationship between two sets of data. Scatter plots graph data as **ORDERED PAIRS** (this is simply a pair of numbers or mathematical objects—but the order in which they appear together matters).

EXAMPLE: After a test, Ms. Phinney asked her students how many hours they studied. She recorded their answers, along with their test scores. Create a scatter plot of hours studied and test scores.

NAME	NUMBER OF HOURS STUDIED	TEST SCORE
Tammy	4.5	90
Latril	1	60
Sophia	4	92
Michael	3.5	88
Monica	2	76
Davey	5	100
Eva	3	90
Lance	1.5	72
Becca	3	70
Sarina	4	86

To show Tammy's data, mark the point whose horizontal value is 4.5 and whose vertical value is 90.

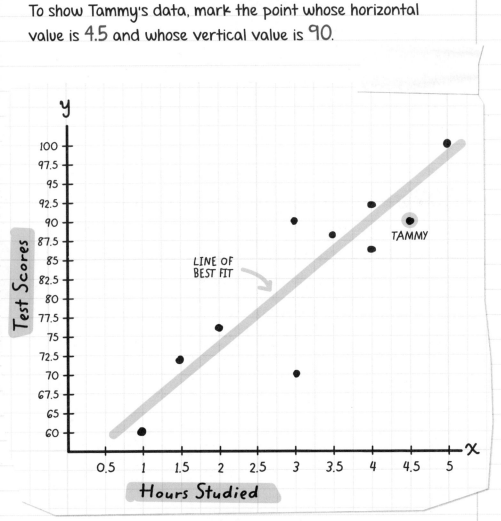

By graphing the data on a scatter plot, we can see if there is a relationship between the number of hours studied and test scores. The scores generally go up as the hours of studying go up, so this shows that there IS a relationship between test scores and studying.

We can draw a line on the graph that roughly describes the relationship between the number of hours studied and test scores. This line is known as the **LINE OF BEST FIT** because it is the best description of how the points are related to one another. As we can see, none of the points lie on the line of best fit, but that's okay! This is because the line of best fit is the best line that describes the relationship of ALL the points on the graph.

Eva studied only 3 hours, but still got a 90. Becca also studied for 3 hours, but got a 70. A scatter plot shows the overall relationship between the data, while individual ordered pairs (like Eva and Becca) don't show the general trend. Eva and Becca might be considered outliers in this situation because they don't follow the typical pattern.

Scatter plots show three types of relationships, called **CORRELATIONS**:

POSITIVE CORRELATION: As one set of values increases, the other set increases as well (but not necessarily every value).

EXAMPLE: As the population increases, so does the number of primary schools.

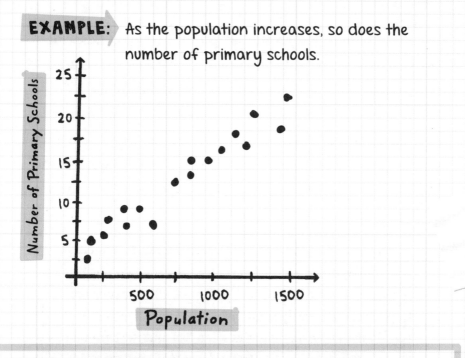

NEGATIVE CORRELATION: As one set of values increases, the other set decreases (but not necessarily every value).

EXAMPLE: As the price of peaches goes down, the number of peaches sold goes up.

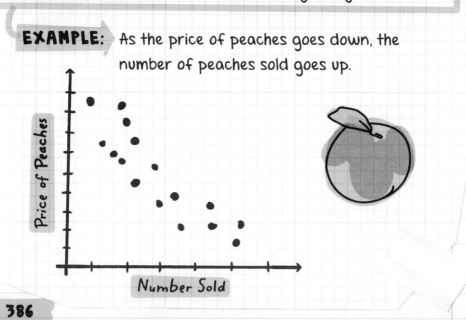

NO CORRELATION: The values have no relationship.

EXAMPLE: A person's IQ is not related to his or her shoe size, so there is no correlation.

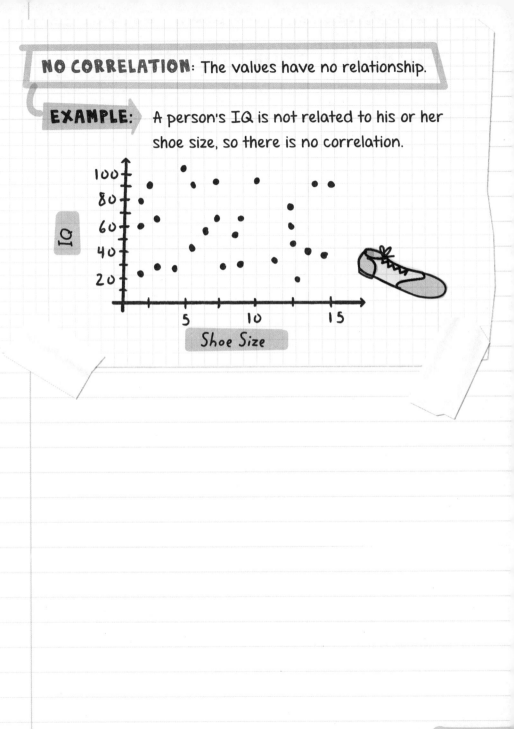

CHECK YOUR KNOWLEDGE

1. Answer the questions based on the two-way table below.

	CARPOOL	DO NOT CARPOOL	TOTAL
RECYCLE	44	54	98
DO NOT RECYCLE	16	27	43
TOTAL	60	60	60

a) How many people only recycle?

b) How many people only carpool?

c) How many people do both?

d) How many people do not recycle and do not carpool?

e) What conclusions can you make from this information?

2. A jewelry store keeps track of how many items each customer buys. Create a line plot of the data they find: 3, 7, 1, 2, 5, 4, 5, 1, 2, 8, 3, 5, 4, 1.

3. A store asks its customers how many plants they own. The answers were 3, 5, 7, 10, 12, 5, 8, 3, 1, 2, 9, 7, 4, 3, 2, 8, 9. Create a histogram of their responses (use a range of 2 for the horizontal scale).

4. The track team recorded the number of kilometers each runner ran for one week. The results were as follows: 14, 25, 40, 10, 14, 16, 25, 16, 23, 11, 18, 22, 34, 12, 16, 15. Find the median, the 1st quartile, and the 3rd quartile, and then create a box plot with this data.

5. A food delivery company calculates the distance that it drives to different customers in one night. The results are as follows: 11, 30, 27, 5, 9, 17, 7, 22, 4, 25. Find the median, the 1st quartile, and the 3rd quartile. Then create a box plot with data.

6. In each of the following scatter plots, state whether there is positive correlation, negative correlation, or no correlation.

(A)

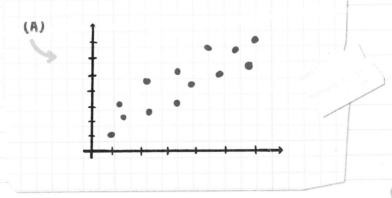

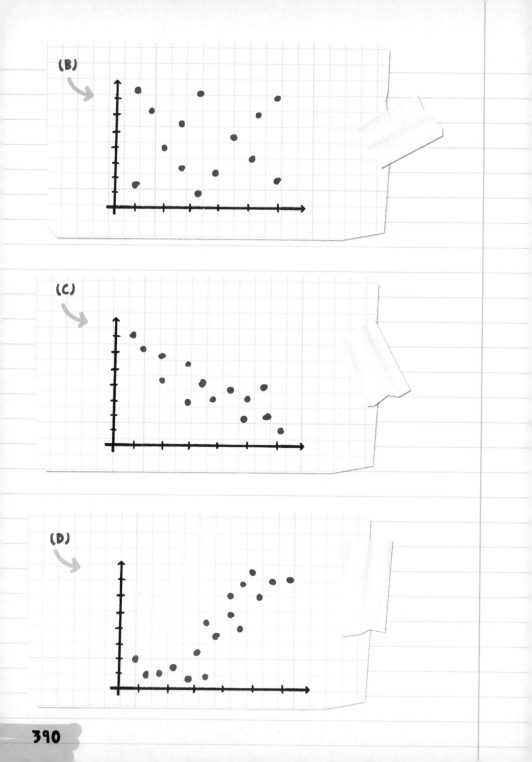

7. Twelve students were asked how many books they read last year, as well as their ELA final exam score. Create a scatter plot that displays their responses below. Conclude whether there is a positive, negative, or no correlation.

FINAL EXAM SCORE	NUMBER OF BOOKS READ
90	42
62	14
85	32
72	25
64	18
88	30
92	44
54	11
92	39
76	29
100	44
76	32

ANSWERS 391

CHECK YOUR ANSWERS

1. a) 54   b) 16   c) 44   d) 27
   e) There is not a strong relationship between recycling and carpooling.

2. Number of Items Bought:
   1, 1, 1, 2, 2, 3, 3, 4, 4,
   5, 5, 5, 7, 8

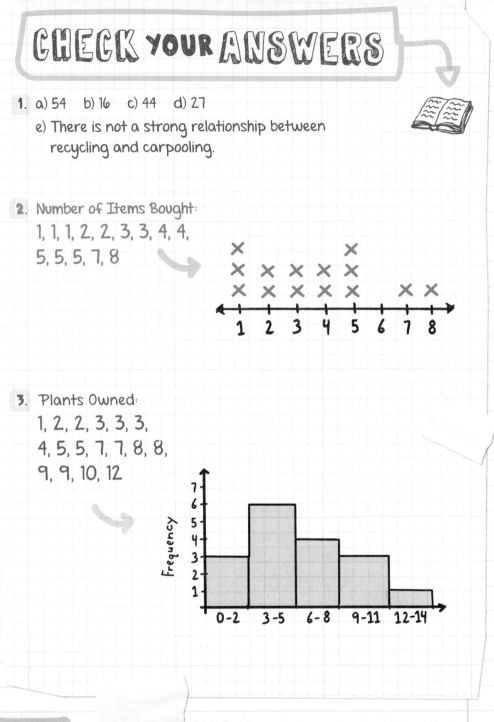

3. Plants Owned:
   1, 2, 2, 3, 3, 3,
   4, 5, 5, 7, 7, 8, 8,
   9, 9, 10, 12

4. Median = 16, 1st Quartile = 14, 3rd Quartile = 24

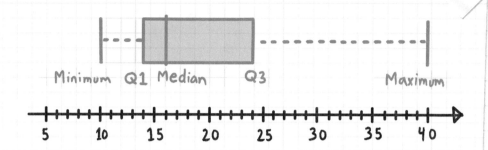

5. Median = 14, 1st Quartile = 7, 3rd Quartile = 25

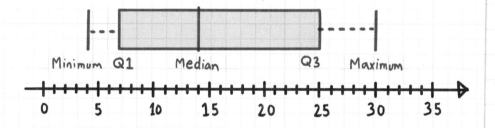

6. (A) Positive correlation   (B) No correlation
(C) Negative correlation   (D) Positive correlation

7.

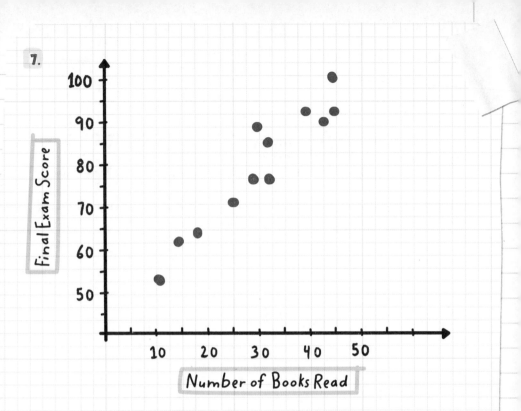

There is a positive correlation.

 Chapter 54

PROBABILITY

PROBABILITY is the likelihood that something will happen. It is a number between 0 and 1, and can be written as a percent. When you asked about something's probability, you are asking, "How likely is it?" A larger number means there is a greater likelihood that the event will happen.

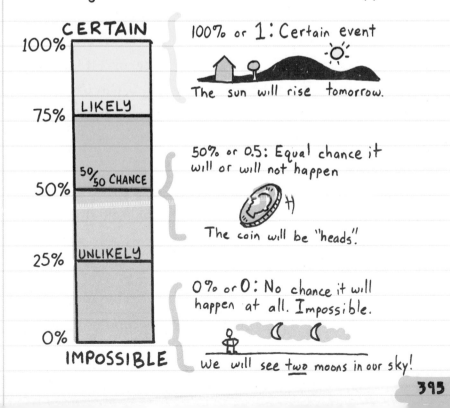

100% or 1: Certain event

The sun will rise tomorrow.

50% or 0.5: Equal chance it will or will not happen

The coin will be "heads".

0% or 0: No chance it will happen at all. Impossible.

We will see two moons in our sky!

Flipping a coin is a well-known probability question. When we flip, it could land on **HEADS** or **TAILS**:

HEADS

TAILS

The **ACTION** is what is happening. In this case, the action is flipping a coin. The **OUTCOMES** are all of the possible results of an action. In this case, there are exactly two outcomes: heads or tails. An **EVENT** is any outcome, or group of outcomes. In this case, if the coin lands on heads, the event is heads. If we flip the coin twice, and it lands on heads twice, the event is heads and heads. When we flip a coin, both outcomes are equally likely to occur—this feature is sometimes called **RANDOM**.

When we are trying to figure out the **PROBABILITY OF AN EVENT** (**P**), we use a ratio to find out how likely it is that an event will happen:

$$\left\{ \text{Probability(Event)} = \frac{\text{number of favorable outcomes}}{\text{number of possible outcomes}} \right\}$$

EXAMPLE: What is the probability of a coin landing on tails?

$$\text{Probability(Event)} = \frac{\text{number of favorable outcomes}}{\text{number of possible outcomes}}$$

The number of favorable outcomes (landing tails) is 1, and the number of possible outcomes (landing heads or landing tails) is 2.

$$P(\text{tails}) = \frac{1}{2} = 50\%$$

So, there is a 50% chance that the coin will land on tails.

EXAMPLE: What is the probability of the spinner landing on red?

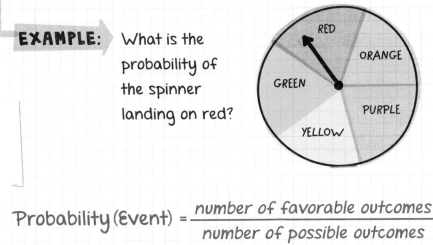

$$\text{Probability(Event)} = \frac{\text{number of favorable outcomes}}{\text{number of possible outcomes}}$$

$$P(\text{Red}) = \frac{1}{5} = 20\%$$

There is a 20% probability that the spinner will land on red.

EXAMPLE: What is the probability of the spinner landing on red or purple?

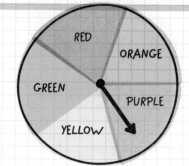

$$\text{Probability(Event)} = \frac{\text{number of favorable outcomes}}{\text{number of possible outcomes}}$$

$$P(\text{Red or Purple}) = \frac{2}{5} = 40\%$$

There is a 40% probability that the spinner will land on red or purple.

If a probability question is more complicated, we can make a table to help ourselves.

EXAMPLE: Bob flips a coin twice. What is the probability that he will flip heads twice?

Let's make a table that lists all the possible combinations Bob can have when he flips the coin twice:

OUTCOME OF THE 1ST FLIP	OUTCOME OF THE 2ND FLIP	COMBINATION OF THE 2 FLIPS
heads	heads	2 heads
heads	tails	1 head, 1 tail
tails	heads	1 tail, 1 head
tails	tails	2 tails

Then we plug this info into the probability formula:

$$\text{Probability(Event)} = \frac{number\ of\ favorable\ outcomes}{number\ of\ possible\ outcomes}$$

$$\text{Probability(2 heads)} = \frac{1}{4} = 25\% \leftarrow$$

In addition to using a chart, we could also draw a tree diagram.

EXAMPLE: Sue rolls a die twice. What is the probability that she rolls "double sixes" (she rolls 6 twice)?

Let's make a tree diagram that lists all of the different possible outcomes:

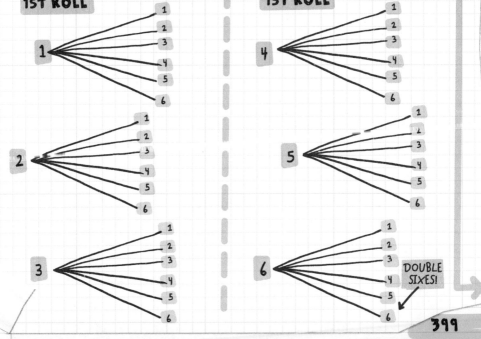

399

Then we use the probability formula:

$$\text{Probability(Event)} = \frac{\text{number of favorable outcomes}}{\text{number of possible outcomes}}$$

Therefore, out of the 36 possible outcomes, there is a total of 1 outcome that has double sixes.

$$\text{Probability(double sixes)} = \frac{1}{36} = 2.8\%$$

ROUNDED TO THE NEAREST TENTH OF A PERCENT

The **COMPLEMENT OF AN EVENT** is the opposite of the event happening.

EVENT	COMPLEMENT
win	lose
rain	no rain
heads	tails

The probability of an event plus the probability of its complement always equals 1. In other words, there is a 100% chance that either an event or its complement will happen.

Probability(event) + Probability(complement) = 1

OR

Probability(event) + Probability(complement) = 100%

If the chance of rain is 30%, then the chance of no rain (the complement) is 70%.

30% + 70% = 100%

EXAMPLE: The probability that a student at your school is left-handed is 10%. What is the complement of being left-handed, and what is the probability of the complement?

The complement of being left-handed is being right-handed.

If P(left-handed) is 10%, then...

$$P(\text{left-handed}) + P(\text{right-handed}) = 100\%$$
$$10\% + P(\text{right-handed}) = 100\%$$
$$P(\text{right-handed}) = 90\%$$

So, the probability that a student at school is right-handed is 90%.

CHECK YOUR WORK!

Does P(left-handed) + P(right-handed) = 100%?
Yes! 10% + 90% = 100%. ✓

EXAMPLE: A company has 12 male employees and 20 female employees. If one employee is chosen at random to receive a prize, find the probability that the person selected will be a female.

$$\text{Probability(Event)} = \frac{\text{number of favorable outcomes}}{\text{number of possible outcomes}}$$

The number of favorable outcomes is calculated as the number of female employees: 20. The number of possible outcomes is the same as the total number of employees at the company (12 men + 20 women = 32 employees).

$$\text{Probability(Woman wins prize)} = \frac{20}{32} = 62.5\%$$

So, the probability that a woman will win the prize is 62.5%.

CHECK YOUR KNOWLEDGE

Match each word to its definition.

1. Outcome

2. Complement

3. Probability

4. Event

A. The likelihood that something will happen

B. Possible result of an action

C. The opposite of an event

D. Any outcome or group of outcomes

Find the probability using the spinner.

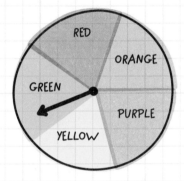

5. What is the probability of landing on green?

6. What is the probability of not landing on green?

7. What is the probability of landing on green or purple?

Find the probability using the phrase "Great Wall of China."

8. If a letter is randomly chosen, what is the probability of choosing the letter A?

9. If a letter is randomly chosen, what is the probability of choosing a vowel?

10. If a letter is randomly chosen, what is the probability of choosing a B?

ANSWERS

CHECK YOUR ANSWERS

1. B

2. C

3. A

4. D

5. $\frac{1}{5}$ or 20%

6. $1 - \frac{1}{5} = \frac{4}{5}$ or 80%

7. $\frac{2}{5}$ or 40%

8. $\frac{3}{16}$ or 18.75%

9. $\frac{6}{16}$ or 37.5%

10. 0%

Unit 6

The Coordinate Plane and Functions

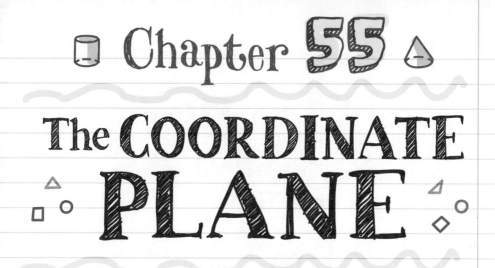

Chapter 55

The COORDINATE PLANE

A **COORDINATE PLANE** is a flat surface formed by the intersection of two lines or **AXES**: the horizontal line, known as the **X-AXIS**, and the vertical line, known as the **Y-AXIS**. The x- and y-axes intersect (cross) at the **ORIGIN**.

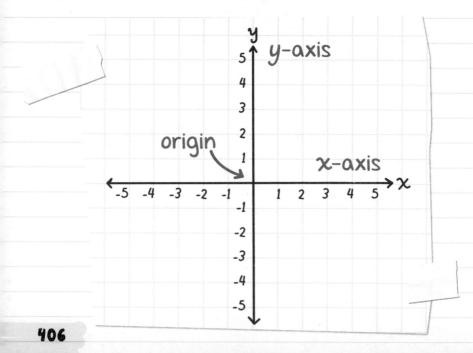

An ordered pair gives the coordinates (exact location) of a POINT. They are called an "ordered pair" because the order matters. The x-coordinate always comes first, then the y-coordinate, like so: (x, y). The x- and y-coordinates are separated by a comma and surrounded by parentheses.

EXAMPLE: The x-coordinate of the origin is 0, and the y-coordinate of the origin is also 0. So, the ordered pair of the origin is (0, 0).

X {

If the x-coordinate is **POSITIVE**, move **RIGHT** from the origin.
If the x-coordinate is **NEGATIVE**, move **LEFT** from the origin.
If the x-coordinate is **ZERO**, you **STAY** at the origin.

Y {

If the y-coordinate is **POSITIVE**, move **UP** from the origin.
If the y-coordinate is **NEGATIVE**, move **DOWN** from the origin.
If the y-coordinate is **ZERO**, you **STAY** at the origin.

Plot the point (4, 6).

For the *x*-coordinate: start at the origin,
then move 4 spaces to the right on the *x*-axis.

Next, apply the *y*-coordinate: move 6 spaces up
on the *y*-axis.

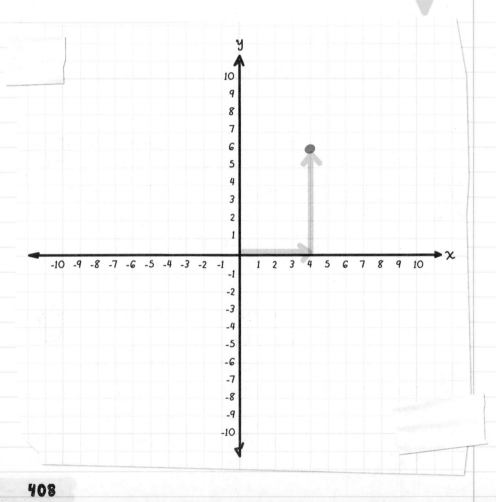

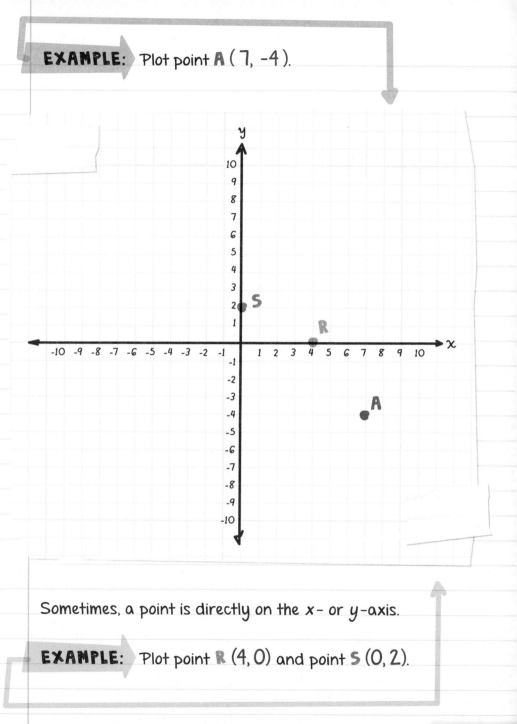

Sometimes, a point is directly on the x- or y-axis.

EXAMPLE: Plot point **R** (4, 0) and point **S** (0, 2).

The coordinate plane is divided into four **QUADRANTS**.

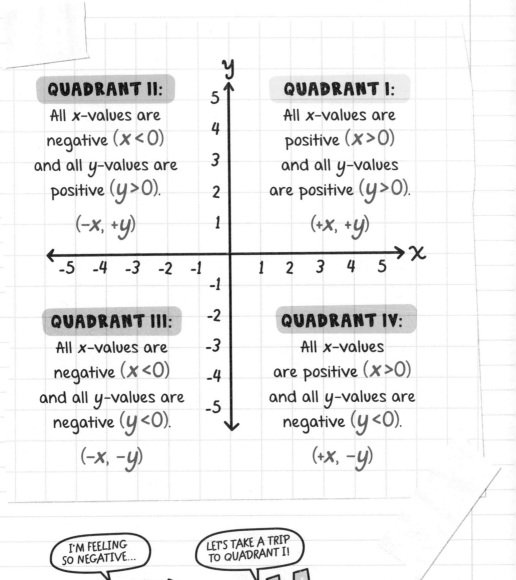

QUADRANT II:

All x-values are negative ($x < 0$) and all y-values are positive ($y > 0$).

$(-x, +y)$

QUADRANT I:

All x-values are positive ($x > 0$) and all y-values are positive ($y > 0$).

$(+x, +y)$

QUADRANT III:

All x-values are negative ($x < 0$) and all y-values are negative ($y < 0$).

$(-x, -y)$

QUADRANT IV:

All x-values are positive ($x > 0$) and all y-values are negative ($y < 0$).

$(+x, -y)$

I'M FEELING SO NEGATIVE...

LET'S TAKE A TRIP TO QUADRANT I!

DISTANCE

If two points have the same x-coordinate or the same
y-coordinate, we can find the distance between the points.
First, find the difference of the two different coordinates
by using subtraction. Next, calculate the absolute value of
that number.

EXAMPLE: Point **A** is located at $(2, 9)$. Point **B** is located
at $(5, 9)$. What is the distance between Points **A** and **B**?

Point **A** and Point **B** share the same y-coordinate (which is
9), so we simply find the difference of the x-coordinates,
which is

$5 - 2 = 3$ (or $2 - 5 = -3$).

Next, we calculate the absolute value of that number ($|3|$
or $|-3|$), which is 3.

I herefore, Point **A** and Point **B** are 3 units apart.

If you plot Points **A** and **B**, then draw a line to connect them,
you will get a horizontal line because the y-coordinates are
the same. The same method works if the x-coordinates
are the same.

EXAMPLE: Point P is located at $(5\frac{1}{4}, -\frac{2}{3})$.

Point Q is located at $(5\frac{1}{4}, -1\frac{3}{4})$. What is the distance between Point P and Point Q?

Because Point P and Point Q share the same x-coordinate (which is $5\frac{1}{4}$), we first find the difference of the y-coordinates, which is:

$$-\frac{2}{3} - \left(-1\frac{3}{4}\right) = -\frac{2}{3} + 1\frac{3}{4} = -\frac{8}{12} + \frac{21}{12} = \frac{13}{12} = 1\frac{1}{12}.$$

Next, we calculate the absolute value of that number, which is $1\frac{1}{12}$.

Therefore, Point P and Point Q are $1\frac{1}{12}$ units apart.

If you plot points P and Q, then draw a line to connect them, you will get a vertical line because the x-coordinates are the same.

AND THEREFORE AREN'T ON A VERTICAL OR HORIZONTAL LINE

But what if you need to find the distance between two points that <u>don't</u> share a coordinate? You can use this distance formula:

$$d = \sqrt{(x_2 - x_1)^2 + (y_2 - y_1)^2}$$

THE SUBSCRIPTS JUST SHOW THAT THERE IS A FIRST POINT AND A SECOND POINT—IT DOESN'T MATTER WHICH POINT YOU CALL FIRST OR SECOND, ONLY THAT YOU KEEP THEM SEPARATE.

EXAMPLE: Point **D** is located at $(11, -2)$. Point **E** is located at $(7, -5)$. What is the distance between Points **D** and **E**?

First, assign the values of the first and second coordinates.
$x_1 = 11, \; y_1 = -2; \; x_2 = 7, \; y_2 = -5$

Then, plug the values into the formula.

$d = \sqrt{(7 - 11)^2 + (-5 - -2)^2}$ ← ORDER OF OPERATIONS COMES IN HANDY HERE.

$d = \sqrt{(-4)^2 + (-3)^2}$

$d = \sqrt{16 + 9}$

$d = \sqrt{25}$

$d = 5$

Therefore, Point **D** and Point **E** are 5 units apart.

CHECK YOUR KNOWLEDGE

1. What quadrant is $(-5, 9)$ in?

2. What quadrant is $(4, -6)$ in?

3. What quadrant is $(8, 20)$ in?

4. What quadrant is $(-3, -7)$ in?

5. What are the coordinates of point **A**?

6. What are the coordinates of point **B**?

7. What are the coordinates of point **C**?

8. Plot **Q** $(-4, 8)$.

9. Plot **R** $(0, -6)$.

10. The coordinates of Point G are $(7, -2)$. The coordinates of Point H are $(7, 10)$. What is distance between Point G and Point H?

11. The coordinates of Point S are $(\frac{2}{5}, 9\frac{1}{8})$. The coordinates of Point T are $(-5\frac{7}{10}, 9\frac{1}{8})$. What is the distance between Point S and Point T?

12. The coordinates of Point K is $(2, 0)$. The coordinates of Point L is $(8, 8)$. What is the distance between Points K and L?

ANSWERS

CHECK YOUR ANSWERS

1. II
2. IV
3. I
4. III
5. (4,3)
6. (2,-2)
7. (-2,0)
8. and 9.

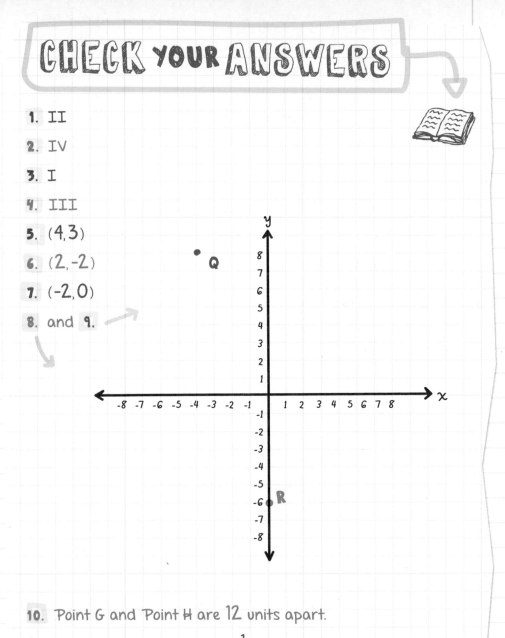

10. Point G and Point H are 12 units apart.

11. Point S and Point T are $6\frac{1}{10}$ units apart.

12. Point K and Point L are 10 units apart.

Chapter 56

RELATIONS, LINES,
○ ◁ ◻ ◇ AND △ ○ ◻ ◁
FUNCTIONS

A **RELATION** is a set of ordered pairs (like the *x*- and *y*-coordinates are in a "relationship"). In a relation, all of the *x*-coordinates are called the **DOMAIN**, and all of the *y*-coordinates are called the **RANGE**.

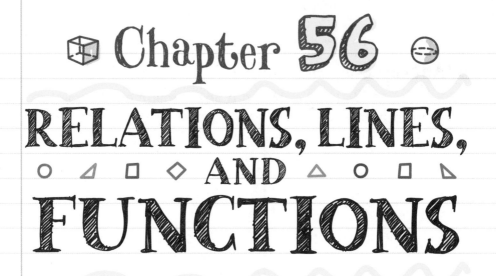

EXAMPLE: Name the domain and range for this relation: $(-5, -3)\ (-2, 0)\ (1, 3)\ (4, 6)\ (7, 9)$.

DOMAIN (all the *x*-values): $\{-5, -2, 1, 4, 7\}$
RANGE (all the *y*-values): $\{-3, 0, 3, 6, 9\}$

ALWAYS LIST THE DOMAIN AND RANGE IN NUMERICAL ORDER.

Sometimes, when we are given several ordered pairs, we can connect them by drawing a straight line through all the points.

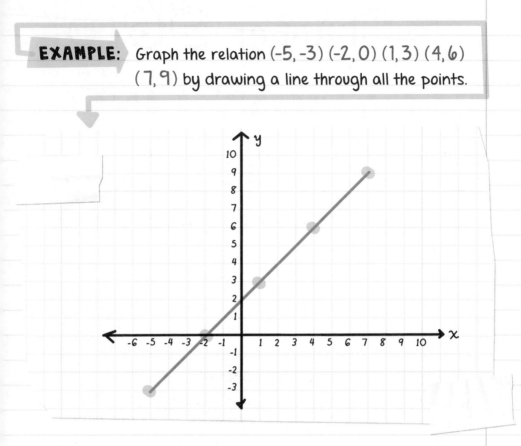

A relation can be any kind of relationship between sets of numbers, but **FUNCTIONS** are a kind of relationship where there is only one y-value for each x-value. In other words, a function is a kind of relationship where none of the x-values repeat. In the example above, none of the x-values repeat, so this line represents a **FUNCTION**.

You can easily determine if a relation is a function by graphing it and doing a **VERTICAL LINE TEST**. Just draw a vertical line on the graph—if your vertical line ever

↳ OR TWO!

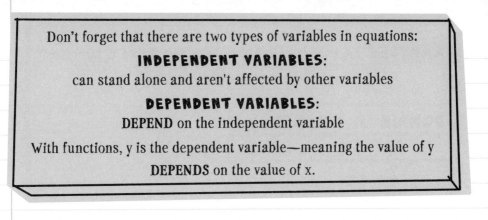

Don't forget that there are two types of variables in equations:

INDEPENDENT VARIABLES:
can stand alone and aren't affected by other variables

DEPENDENT VARIABLES:
DEPEND on the independent variable

With functions, y is the dependent variable—meaning the value of y **DEPENDS** on the value of x.

touches two points of the relation, it's not a function. In other words, the vertical line test proves that none of the *x*-values repeat, and a relation is a function if none of the domain numbers (*x*-coordinates) repeat.

EXAMPLE:

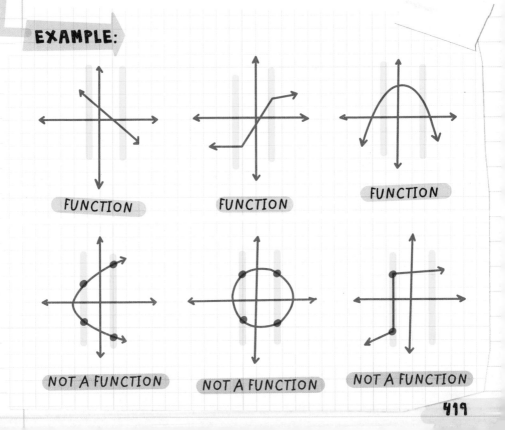

FUNCTION

FUNCTION

FUNCTION

NOT A FUNCTION

NOT A FUNCTION

NOT A FUNCTION

EXAMPLE: Is the relation shown in the table a function? Graph it to check your answer.

DOMAIN (x)	RANGE (y)
−4	8
−2	4
0	0
2	−4
4	−8

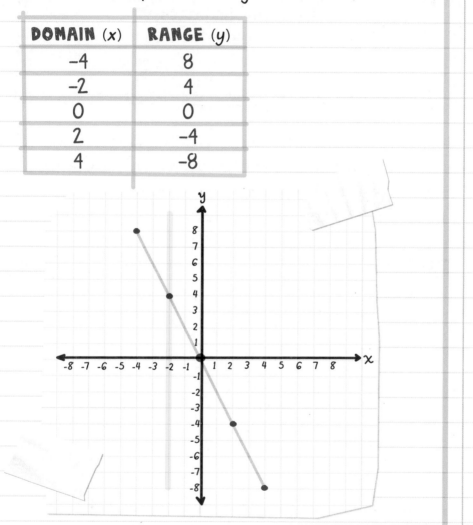

Is this a function? Yes, because all of the values in the domain are different. Does it pass the vertical line test? Yes!

EXAMPLE: Is the relation shown in the table a function? Graph it to check your answer.

DOMAIN (x)	RANGE (y)
−5	3
−5	6
−2	3
1	5
4	2
4	6

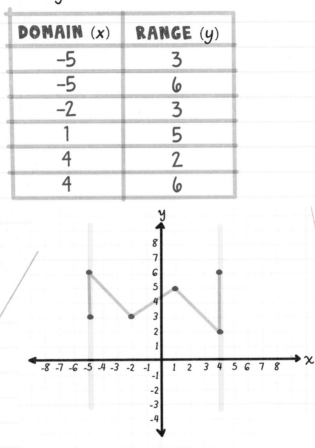

Is this a function? No, because there are values in the domain that repeat.

Does it pass the vertical line test? No. A vertical line can touch two or more points, so this is NOT a function.

INPUT and OUTPUT

This is what a function looks like algebraically: $y = x + 1$. The **INPUT** refers to all of the x-values (the domain) that can be substituted in the formula for x. The **OUTPUT** refers to all of the y-values (the range) that result *after* we input the x-values and simplify. If we have the function, we can create an **INPUT/OUTPUT CHART** to get all the values we need in order to graph the function.

> **INPUT** IS THE INDEPENDENT VARIABLE.
>
> **OUTPUT** IS THE DEPENDENT VARIABLE.

EXAMPLE: Graph $y = x + 1$.

INPUT (x)	FUNCTION: $y = x+1$	OUTPUT (y)	ORDERED PAIR (x,y)
-2	$y = -2 + 1$	-1	$(-2, -1)$
-1	$y = -1 + 1$	0	$(-1, 0)$
0	$y = 0 + 1$	1	$(0, 1)$
1	$y = 1 + 1$	2	$(1, 2)$
2	$y = 2 + 1$	3	$(2, 3)$

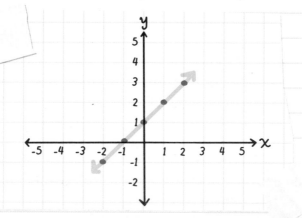

We don't need to be given any input values, because we can choose any value—each input creates a unique output, and they all represent the function. However, it is a good idea to pick input values that are easy to calculate.

EXAMPLE: Graph $y = -2x + 3$.

INPUT (x)	FUNCTION: $y = -2x + 3$	OUTPUT (y)	ORDERED PAIR (x, y)
-2	$y = -2(-2) + 3$	7	$(-2, 7)$
0	$y = -2(0) + 3$	3	$(0, 3)$
4	$y = -2(4) + 3$	-5	$(4, -5)$

Because we could pick any values for **x**, we connect the points and draw arrows on each end of the line to show that the inputs and outputs continue in both directions. Every point on the line is an input and an output.

Sometimes, a function has the input and output on the same side of the equal sign. When this happens, we simply rearrange the equation to solve for the "output." In other words, isolate the y on one side of the equal sign.

EXAMPLE: Graph $y - 3x = -4$.

$y - 3x = -4$ (We need to isolate y, so we add $3x$ to both sides.)

$y - 3x + 3x = -4 + 3x$

$y = 3x - 4$ (Because $3x$ and -4 are not like terms, we can't combine them and simplify this function any further. But now we can rearrange it so it's in standard function format and make an input/output chart.)

INPUT (x)	FUNCTION: $y = 3x - 4$	OUTPUT (y)	ORDERED PAIR (x, y)
-1	$y = 3(-1) - 4$	-7	$(-1, -7)$
0	$y = 3(0) - 4$	-4	$(0, -4)$
1	$y = 3(1) - 4$	-1	$(1, -1)$

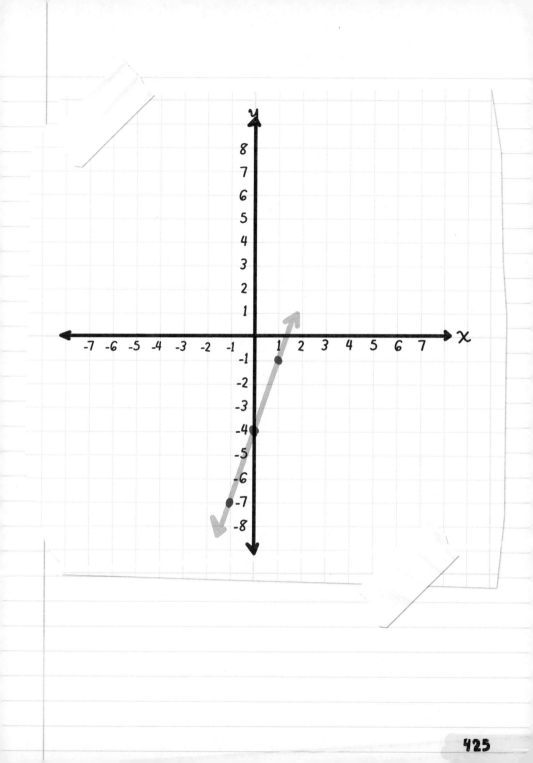

CHECK YOUR KNOWLEDGE

1. What numbers make up the domain of this relation:
   (7, 5) (-3, 2) (1, -1) (4, -6) (-2, 4)?

2. What numbers make up the range of the relation in the question above?

3. Is the relation in question 1 a function? Why or why not?

4. Graph the relation shown in this table:

DOMAIN (x)	RANGE (y)
-9	-3
-6	-1
-3	1
0	3
3	5

5. Complete the input/output chart and graph $y = x + 2$.

INPUT (x)	FUNCTION: $y = x + 2$	OUTPUT (y)	ORDERED PAIR (x, y)
-2			
0			
3			

6. Complete the input/output chart and graph $y = -3x + 1$.

INPUT (x)	FUNCTION: $y = -3x + 1$	OUTPUT (y)	ORDERED PAIR (x, y)
-1			
0			
2			

7. Complete the input/output chart and graph $y - x = 5$.

INPUT (x)	FUNCTION: $y - x = 5$	OUTPUT (y)	ORDERED PAIR (x, y)
-4			
0			
1			

8. Complete the input/output chart and graph $y + 2x = -4$.

INPUT (x)	FUNCTION: $y + 2x = -4$	OUTPUT (y)	ORDERED PAIR (x, y)
-4			
0			
1			

ANSWERS

CHECK YOUR ANSWERS

1. Domain: {-3, -2, 1, 4, 7}
2. Range: {-6, -1, 2, 4, 5}
3. Yes, because none of the x-values (in the domain) repeat.
4.

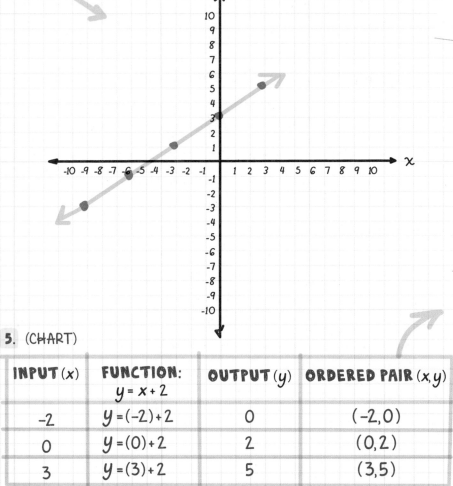

5. (CHART)

INPUT (x)	FUNCTION: y = x + 2	OUTPUT (y)	ORDERED PAIR (x, y)
-2	y = (-2) + 2	0	(-2, 0)
0	y = (0) + 2	2	(0, 2)
3	y = (3) + 2	5	(3, 5)

5. (GRAPH)

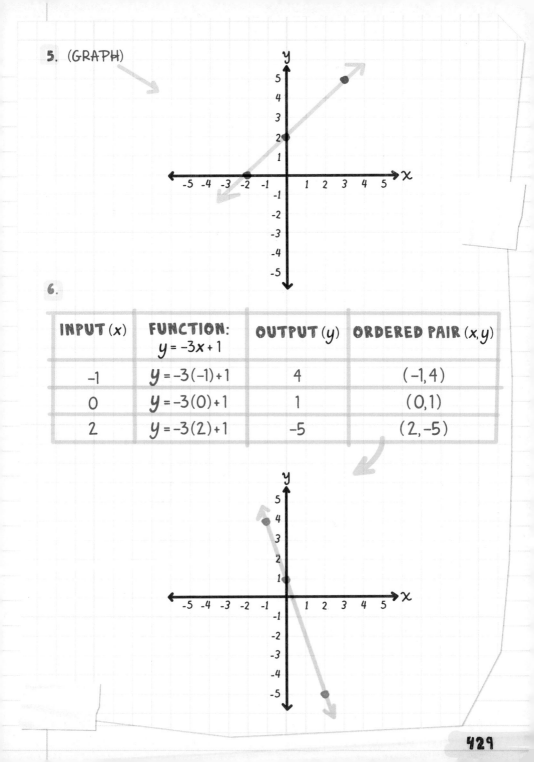

6.

INPUT (x)	FUNCTION: $y = -3x + 1$	OUTPUT (y)	ORDERED PAIR (x,y)
–1	$y = -3(-1) + 1$	4	(–1, 4)
0	$y = -3(0) + 1$	1	(0, 1)
2	$y = -3(2) + 1$	–5	(2, –5)

7.

INPUT (x)	FUNCTION: $y-x=5$ $y=x+5$	OUTPUT (y)	ORDERED PAIR (x, y)
−4	$y = (−4) + 5$	1	(−4, 1)
0	$y = (0) + 5$	5	(0, 5)
1	$y = (1) + 5$	6	(1, 6)

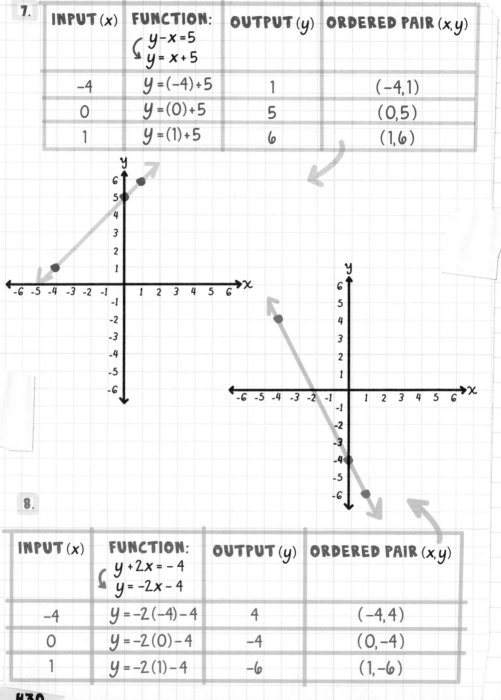

8.

INPUT (x)	FUNCTION: $y+2x=-4$ $y=-2x-4$	OUTPUT (y)	ORDERED PAIR (x, y)
−4	$y = −2(−4) − 4$	4	(−4, 4)
0	$y = −2(0) − 4$	−4	(0, −4)
1	$y = −2(1) − 4$	−6	(1, −6)

Chapter 57

SLOPE

SLOPE is commonly referred to as the steepness of a line. More specifically, slope is a number that is a ratio that describes the tilt of a line:

$$\text{SLOPE} = \frac{\text{RISE}}{\text{RUN}}$$

↕ **RISE** is how much a line goes up or down.

↔ **RUN** is how much a line moves left or right.

EXAMPLE: A line with a slope of $\frac{2}{3}$

RISE - 2
RUN = 3

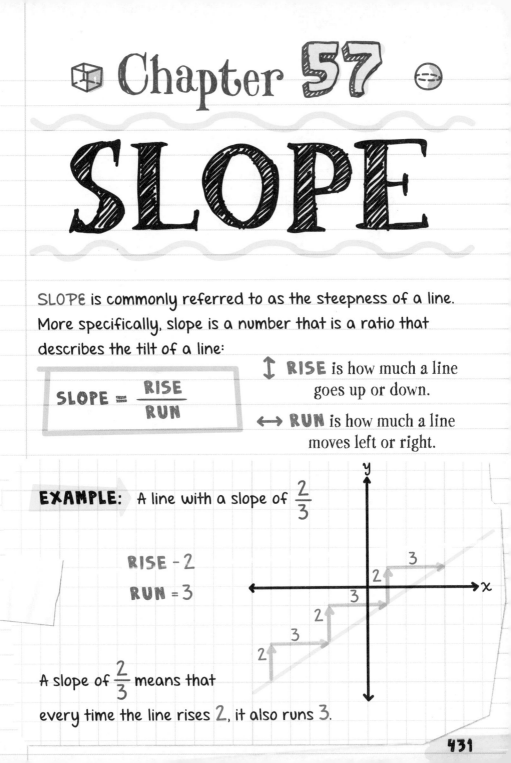

A slope of $\frac{2}{3}$ means that every time the line rises 2, it also runs 3.

Another way to understand slope is that it represents **UNIT RATE**, or a ratio that shows the units a line rises per 1 line it runs.

The previous example shows that a slope of $\frac{2}{3}$ means that every time the line runs 3, it also rises 2 because:

$$\text{SLOPE} = \frac{\text{RISE}}{\text{RUN}} = \frac{2}{3}, \text{ so rise} = 2 \text{ and run} = 3.$$

But another way to see it is:

$$\text{SLOPE} = \frac{\text{RISE}}{\text{RUN}} = \frac{\frac{2}{3}}{1}$$

This says: For every time a line runs 1, it rises $\frac{2}{3}$.
Look closely at the graph and you can see this ratio as well.

TYPES of SLOPE

We can use the graphs to compare two different relationships by comparing the slopes. The larger the slope, the faster the rate.

EXAMPLE:
Bob walks an average of 3 blocks per minute, and Jane walks an average of 5 blocks per minute.

Use the graphs to determine who walks faster.

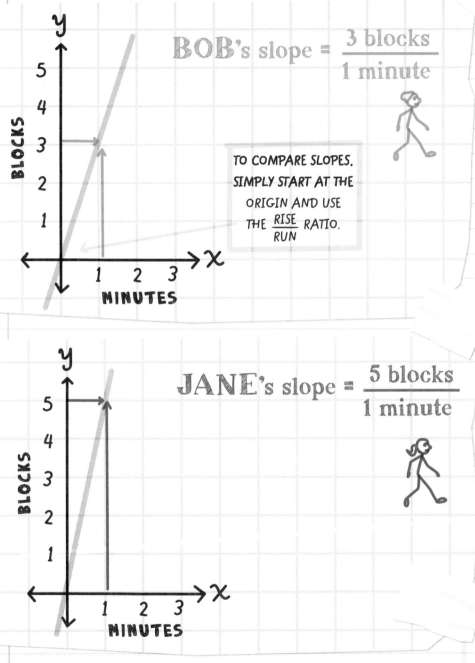

BOB's slope = $\dfrac{3 \text{ blocks}}{1 \text{ minute}}$

TO COMPARE SLOPES,
SIMPLY START AT THE
ORIGIN AND USE
THE $\dfrac{\text{RISE}}{\text{RUN}}$ RATIO.

JANE's slope = $\dfrac{5 \text{ blocks}}{1 \text{ minute}}$

Because the slope of Jane's speed is steeper than the slope of Bob's speed, it means that her speed is faster.

Remember the different types of slope by imagining someone skating on them from left to right (the same direction we read).

There are four types of slope:

1. POSITIVE SLOPE:

rises from left to right

2. NEGATIVE SLOPE:

falls from left to right

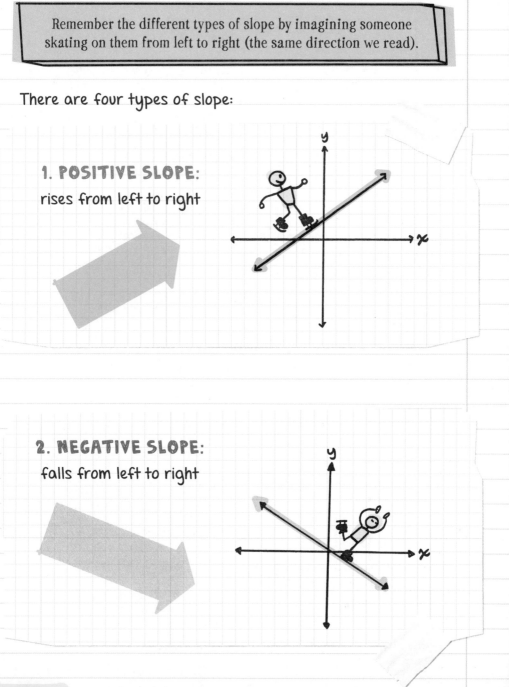

3. ZERO SLOPE:

is horizontal because the rise is 0, and 0 divided by any number is 0

4. UNDEFINED SLOPE:

is a vertical line because the run is 0, and any number divided by 0 is undefined

5 THINGS YOU NEED TO KNOW ABOUT SLOPE:

1. Any time you move **UP**, that is a **POSITIVE RISE**.

2. Any time you move **DOWN**, that is a **NEGATIVE RISE**.

3. Any time you move **RIGHT**, that is a **POSITIVE RUN**.

4. Any time you move **LEFT**, that is a **NEGATIVE RUN**.

5. The slope is the **SAME** everywhere on a **STRAIGHT LINE**.

FINDING the SLOPE of a LINE

To **FIND THE SLOPE OF A LINE**, pick any two points on the line. Starting at the point farthest to the left, draw a right triangle that connects the two points and uses the line as the hypotenuse. How many units did you go up or down? That is your rise. How many units did you go left or right? That is your run. Put your rise over your run, and you have the slope.

EXAMPLE: Find the slope of the line.

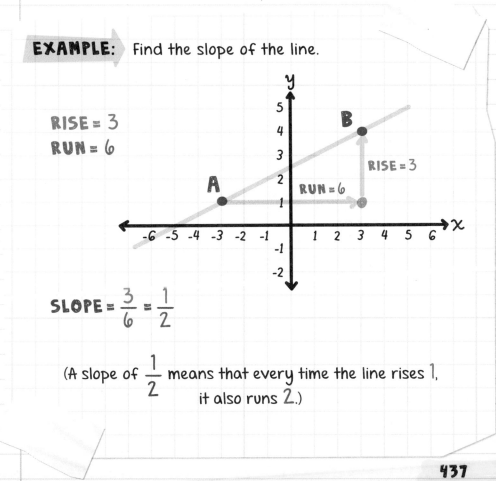

RISE = 3
RUN = 6

SLOPE = $\frac{3}{6}$ = $\frac{1}{2}$

(A slope of $\frac{1}{2}$ means that every time the line rises 1, it also runs 2.)

EXAMPLE: Use a slope triangle to find the slope of the line.

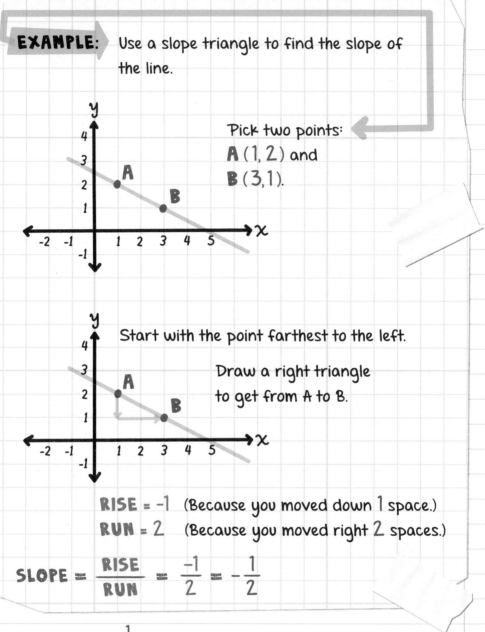

Pick two points:
A (1, 2) and
B (3, 1).

Start with the point farthest to the left.

Draw a right triangle to get from A to B.

RISE = -1   (Because you moved down 1 space.)

RUN = 2   (Because you moved right 2 spaces.)

$$\text{SLOPE} = \frac{\text{RISE}}{\text{RUN}} = \frac{-1}{2} = -\frac{1}{2}$$

(The slope is $-\frac{1}{2}$ everywhere on the line.
Any time you rise -1 and run 2, you'll be back on the line.)

There is also a **FORMULA FOR SLOPE** that you can use when you know two points on a line:

$$\left\{\quad \text{slope} = \frac{\text{the change in } y}{\text{the change in } x} \quad \text{or} \quad m = \frac{y_2 - y_1}{x_2 - x_1} \quad\right\}$$

EXAMPLE: Find the slope of the line that goes through $(2, 3)$ and $(4, 6)$.

1. Label each given value as (x_1, y_1) and (x_2, y_2).
   $x_1 = 2$, $y_1 = 3$; $x_2 = 4$, $y_2 = 6$

2. Use the slope formula and substitute the values:

$$m = \frac{y_2 - y_1}{x_2 - x_1} = \frac{6 - 3}{4 - 2} = \frac{3}{2}$$

$$\text{SLOPE} = \frac{3}{2}$$

EXAMPLE: Find the slope of the line that goes through $(-5, 6)$ and $(-2, -6)$.

$$m = \frac{y_2 - y_1}{x_2 - x_1} = \frac{-6 - 6}{-2 - (-5)} \quad \frac{-6 + -6}{-2 + 5} = \frac{-12}{3} = -4$$

$$\text{SLOPE} = -4$$

You can also graph a line if you know only one point and the slope. You have all the information you need—a starting point, the number of units it rises, and the number of units it runs.

EXAMPLE: Draw the line that goes through $(0, -4)$ and has a slope of $\frac{2}{3}$.

Begin by plotting the given point $(0, -4)$.

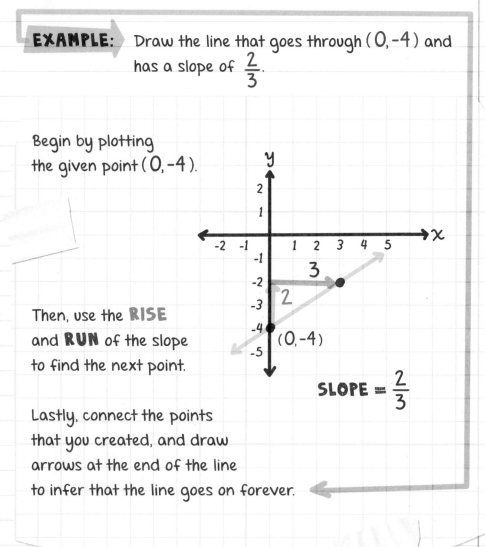

Then, use the **RISE** and **RUN** of the slope to find the next point.

$$\text{SLOPE} = \frac{2}{3}$$

Lastly, connect the points that you created, and draw arrows at the end of the line to infer that the line goes on forever.

1. Is the slope positive, negative, zero, or undefined?

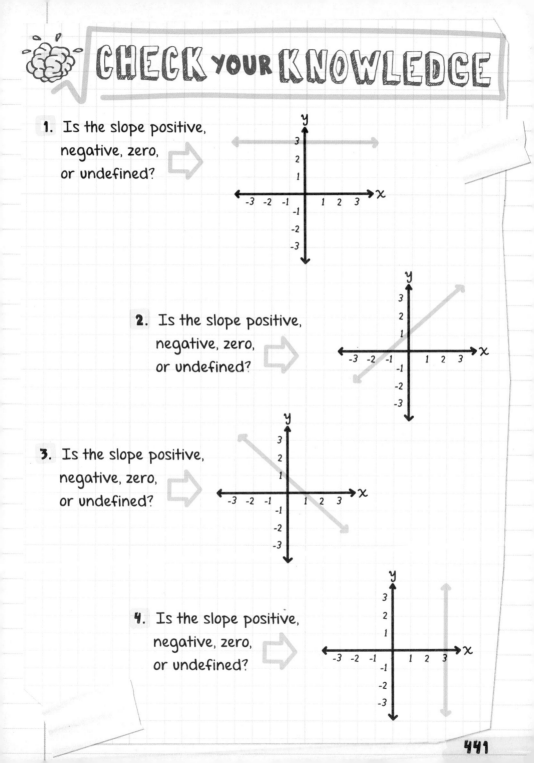

2. Is the slope positive, negative, zero, or undefined?

3. Is the slope positive, negative, zero, or undefined?

4. Is the slope positive, negative, zero, or undefined?

5. Use a slope triangle to find the slope of this line:

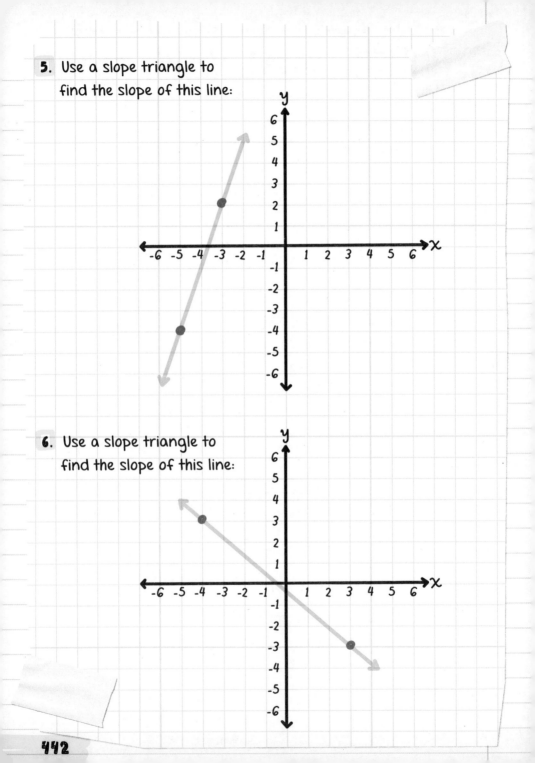

6. Use a slope triangle to find the slope of this line:

7. Use the slope formula to find the slope of the line that passes through the points $(2, 8)$ and $(5, 7)$.

8. Use the slope formula to find the slope of the line that passes through the points $(-3, 2)$ and $(-6, 10)$.

9. Draw the line that goes through $(3, 5)$ and has a slope of 4.

10. Draw the line that goes through $(6, -2)$ and has a slope of 0.

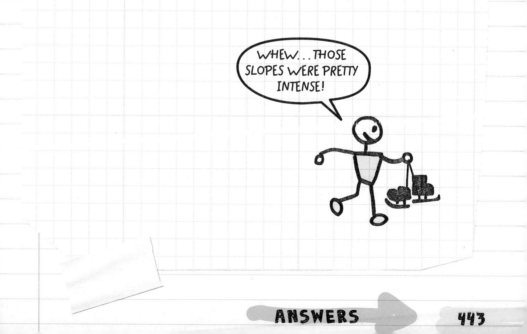

WHEW... THOSE SLOPES WERE PRETTY INTENSE!

ANSWERS

CHECK YOUR ANSWERS

1. Zero

2. Positive

3. Negative

4. Undefined

5. Slope = $\dfrac{6}{2}$ = 3

2

6

6. Slope = $-\dfrac{6}{7}$

−6

7

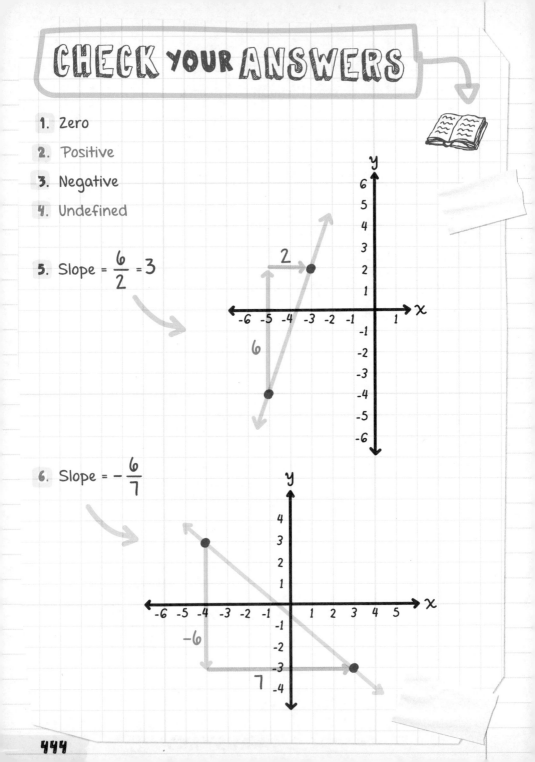

7. $m = \dfrac{7-8}{5-2} = -\dfrac{1}{3}$

8. $m = \dfrac{10-2}{-6+3} = \dfrac{8}{-3} = -\dfrac{8}{3}$

9.

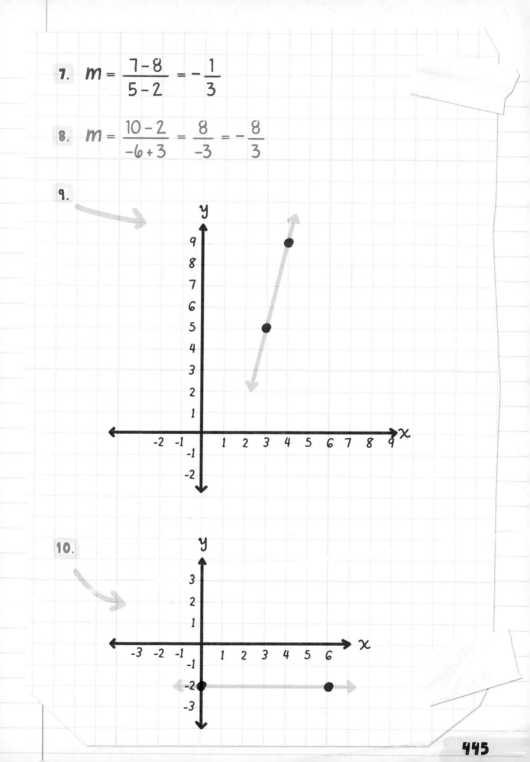

10.

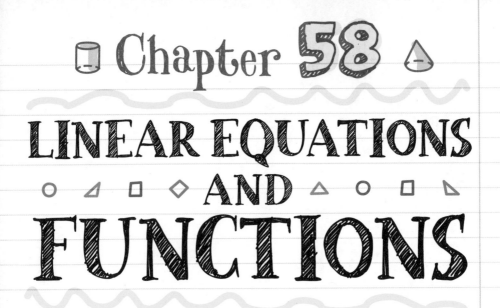

Chapter 58

LINEAR EQUATIONS AND FUNCTIONS

A **LINEAR EQUATION** is an equation whose graph is a line. A linear equation always has the form:

$$y = mx + b$$

y represents every y-value on the line, m represents the slope (the ratio of $\frac{RISE}{RUN}$), and b represents the **Y-INTERCEPT** (where a line crosses the y-axis). If you know the y-intercept, you know the value of y at the point where the line crosses the y-axis, and, therefore, you also know the x-value there because it is always 0! If you know both the y-intercept and the slope of a line, you can graph the line.

Because the graph of a linear equation is a straight line, this means that all linear equations are functions...except for vertical lines!

EXAMPLE: Graph $y = 2x + 1$.

The equation of a linear function is $y = mx + b$, so in this case:

$$m = \frac{2}{1}$$
$$b = 1$$

First, plot the y-intercept (in this equation, where $y = 1$ and $x = 0$). From there, we know from the slope ($\frac{2}{1}$) that we must rise 2 and run 1. Then we continue to plot points until we have a line.

Lastly, we connect the points and draw an arrow on the ends of the line to show that it keeps going in both directions.

The equation of a linear function is $y = mx + b$, so in this case:

$b = -3$

$m = \dfrac{1}{2}$

Pay close attention to positive and negative symbols so you don't mistakenly plot the wrong point!

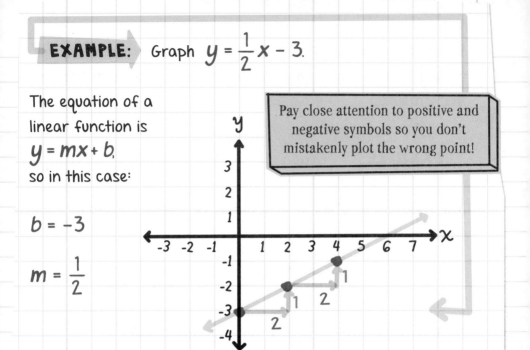

EXAMPLE: Graph $y = x$.

The equation of a linear function is $y = mx + b$, so in this case:

$b = 0$

$m = 1$ or $\dfrac{1}{1}$

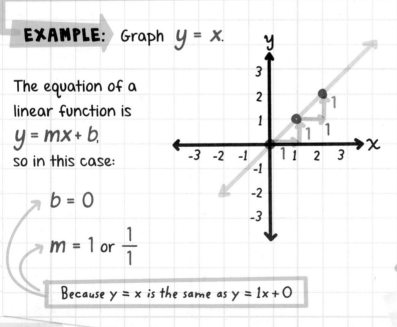

Because $y = x$ is the same as $y = 1x + 0$

Even if the given equation doesn't look like this: $y = mx + b$, we can manipulate it so y is isolated on one side of the equal sign.

EXAMPLE: Graph $y + x = 4$.

$y + x = 4$
$y + \cancel{x} - \cancel{x} = 4 - x$
$y = 4 - x$ (We can put the $-x$ before the $+4$, so it is in $y = mx + b$ form.)

$y = -x + 4$ (Now we know the y-intercept and slope is $\frac{-1}{1}$.)

$m = -1$

$b = 4$

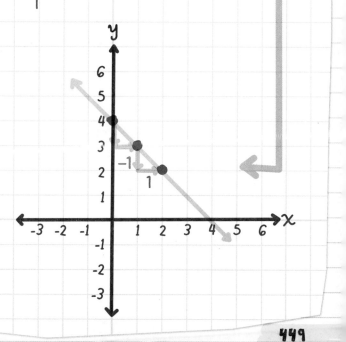

EXAMPLE: Graph $2y - 4x - 2 = 0$.

$2y - 4x - 2 = 0$

$2y - 4x - \cancel{2} + \cancel{2} = 0 + 2$

> Think: How can I get y isolated on one side of the equal sign?

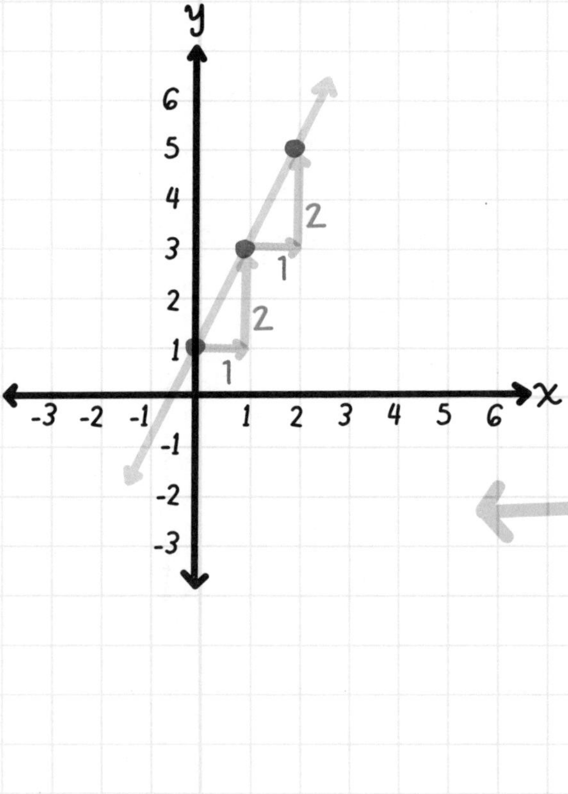

$2y - 4x = 2$

$2y - \cancel{4x} + \cancel{4x} = 2 + 4x$

$2y = 4x + 2$

$\dfrac{\cancel{2}y}{\cancel{2}} = \dfrac{4x}{2} + \dfrac{2}{2}$

$y = 2x + 1$

$m = \dfrac{2}{1}$

$b = 1$

SHORTCUT ALERT! Any time you have an equation that looks like: "y = (a number)," plot a point on the y-axis at that number, and trace a horizontal line going through the point.

EXAMPLE: Graph $y = 2$.

Every point on this line has a y-coordinate equal to 2: (0,2) (1,2) (2,2), etc.

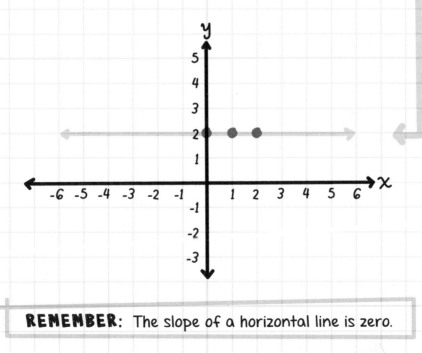

REMEMBER: The slope of a horizontal line is zero.

Similarly, any time you have an equation that looks like "**x** = (a number)," plot a point on the x-axis at that number and trace a vertical line going through the point.

EXAMPLE: Graph **x** = -5.

Every point on this line has an x-coordinate equal to -5.

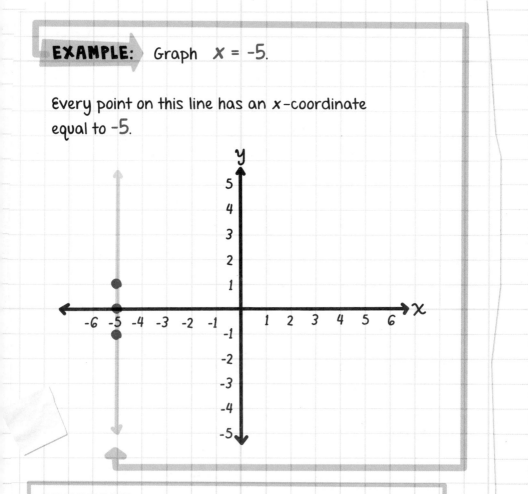

REMEMBER: The slope of a vertical line is undefined.

CHECK YOUR KNOWLEDGE

1. What is the slope and y-intercept of $y = 2x + 3$?

2. What is the slope and y-intercept of $y = -\dfrac{2}{3}x + 1$?

3. What is the slope and y-intercept of $y = \dfrac{5}{6}x$?

4. What is the slope and y-intercept of $y + x = -2$?

5. Graph $y = \dfrac{1}{2}x - 3$.

6. Graph $y = -3x + 7$.

7. Graph $y + 2x = 0$.

8. Graph $3y = 9x - 6$.

9. Graph $y = -5$.

10. Graph $x = 6$.

ANSWERS

CHECK YOUR ANSWERS

1. Slope = $\frac{2}{1}$, y-intercept = $(0, 3)$

2. Slope = $-\frac{2}{3}$, y-intercept = $(0, 1)$

3. Slope = $\frac{5}{6}$, y-intercept = $(0, 0)$

4. Slope = $-\frac{1}{1}$, y-intercept = $(0, -2)$

5.

6.

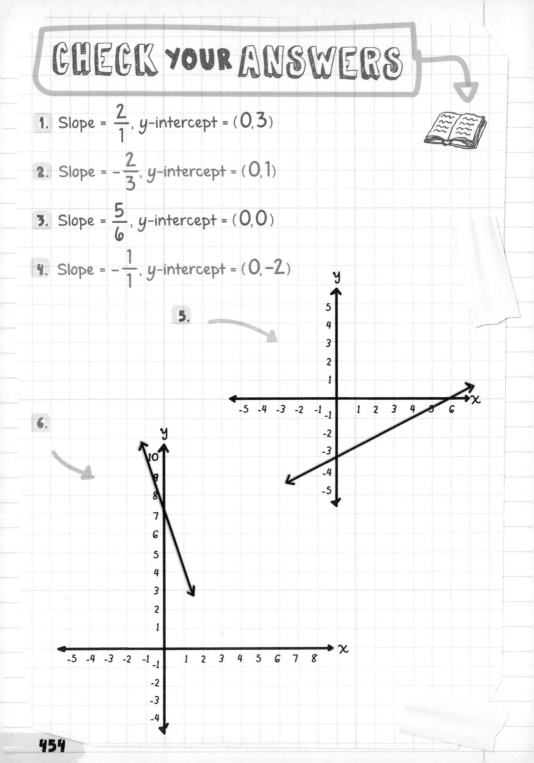

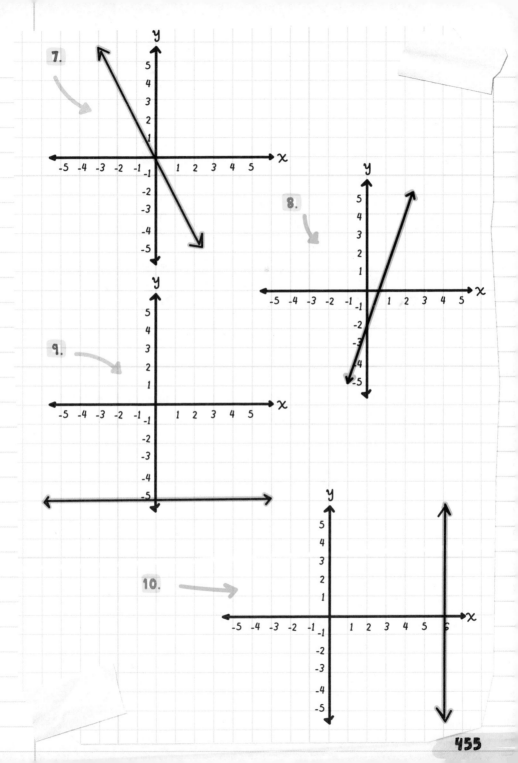

7.

8.

9.

10.

455

Chapter 59

SIMULTANEOUS LINEAR EQUATIONS AND FUNCTIONS

But why stop at one line? We can take two linear equations and study them together, such as:

$$\begin{cases} ax + by = c \\ dx + ey = f \end{cases}$$

This is known as **SIMULTANEOUS LINEAR EQUATIONS**. Because each of the linear questions represents a line, we can ask, "If I draw two lines, where do they intersect?" The process of finding the answer is called **SOLVING SIMULTANEOUS LINEAR EQUATIONS**. There are three ways of doing it.

GRAPHING

We can solve simultaneous equations by graphing each linear equation and then finding where they intersect.

EXAMPLE: Graph the simultaneous equations to find the solution.

$$\begin{cases} x + y = 5 \\ 2x - y = 4 \end{cases}$$

First rewrite each of the equations into the $y = mx + b$ form in order to graph each equation better.

We can change the first equation from $x + y = 5$ to $y = -x + 5$, and change the second equation from $2x - y = 4$ to $y = 2x - 4$.

Then, we graph the equations by using the y-intercept and slope from each.

From the graph, we can see that the two lines intersect at $(3, 2)$.

So, the solution to the simultaneous equation is $(3, 2)$.

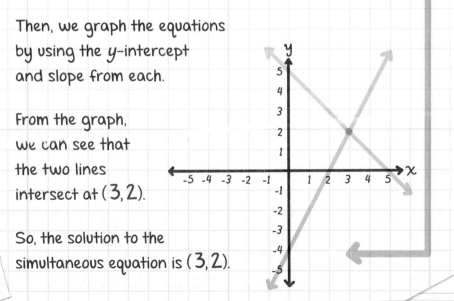

EXAMPLE: Graph the simultaneous equations to find the solution.

$$\begin{cases} 2x + y = -2 \\ 2x + y = 3 \end{cases}$$

In order to graph these more easily, change the first equation from $2x + y = -2$ to $y = -2x - 2$, and change the second equation from $2x + y = 3$ to $y = -2x + 3$.

Then, we graph the two equations.

There are no intersection points, so there is **NO SOLUTION** to the simultaneous equations.

How can there be **NO** solution? Let's look back at the original two linear equations. The first linear equation is $2x + y = -2$ and the second linear equation is $2x + y = 3$. In other words, the equations tell us that the expression $2x + y$ will equal −2 and 3 AT THE SAME TIME. Of course, this logically doesn't make sense because something cannot equal two different numbers! That's why there is no solution to these simultaneous equations.

EXAMPLE: Graph the simultaneous equations to find the solution.

$$\begin{cases} 4x - 2y = 6 \\ 2x - y = 3 \end{cases}$$

We can change the first equation from $4x - 2y = 6$ to $y = 2x - 3$, and change the second equation from $2x - y = 3$ to $y = 2x - 3$.

Graphing the two equations, we realize that they are the exact same line!

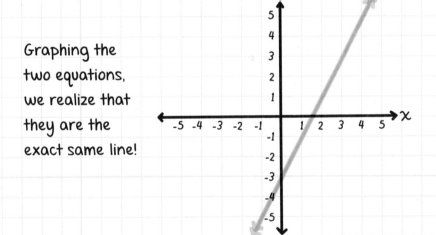

In this case, we can see that the two lines overlap each other and intersect at every point along the line, so there are an **INFINITE NUMBER OF SOLUTIONS** to the simultaneous equations.

SUBSTITUTION METHOD

We can also use algebra to solve simultaneous linear equations—one way is known as the **SUBSTITUTION METHOD.** In the substitution method, we find the solution by rewriting one equation and then *substituting* it into the other equation.

EXAMPLE: Solve the simultaneous equations by using the substitution method.

$$\begin{cases} 4x + y = 7 \ ① \\ 3x + 2y = 9 \ ② \end{cases}$$ First, number your equations.

Then, rewrite equation ① as: $y = -4x + 7$

and substitute it into equation ②: $3x + 2(-4x + 7) = 9$

Now we can solve for x: $3x - 8x + 14 = 9$
$$-5x = -5$$
$$x = 1$$

Substituting $x = 1$ into either ① or ②, or $y = -4x + 7$, we find that $y = 3$,

so the solution is $(x, y) = (1, 3)$.

> You can plug either the x- or y-value into both original equations to check your work.

**EXAMPLE:** Solve the simultaneous equations by using the substitution method.

$$\begin{cases} -2x + 6y = 1 \;\; ① \\ x - 4y = 2 \;\; ② \end{cases}$$

We can rewrite equation ② as: $x = \underbrace{4y + 2}$

and substitute it
into equation ①: $-2(4y + 2) + 6y = 1$

Now we can solve for y: $\begin{aligned} -8y - 4 + 6y &= 1 \\ -2y &= 5 \\ y &= -\frac{5}{2} \end{aligned}$

Substituting $y = -\frac{5}{2}$ into either ① or ②,

or $x = 4y + 2$, we find that $x = -8$,

so the solution is: $(x, y) = (-8, -\frac{5}{2})$.

ADDITION METHOD

The third way to solve simultaneous equations is by using the **ADDITION METHOD**. The goal of the addition method is to eliminate either the x or y variable by adding their opposite. First, we multiply all the terms of one equation by a constant that will get one of the variables to add up to zero. Next, add the two equations together, in order to eliminate a variable, and then solve the simultaneous equations.

EXAMPLE: Solve the simultaneous equations by using the addition method.

$$\begin{cases} 4x - y = -7 & \text{①} \\ -3x + 2y = 9 & \text{②} \end{cases}$$

First, number the equations.

Then, multiply each term in equation ① by 2 and call it equation ①':

$$8x - 2y = -14 \quad \text{①'}$$

WE MULTIPLY BY 2 BECAUSE THEN -2y IN ①' WILL CANCEL OUT 2y IN ② IN THE NEXT STEP.

Now add equation ①' and equation ② together:

$$\begin{cases} 8x - 2y = -14 & \text{①'} \\ -3x + 2y = 9 & \text{②} \end{cases}$$

$$8x + (-3x) + (-2y) + 2y = -14 + 9$$
$$5x = -5$$
$$x = -1$$

OR TRY ALL THREE IF YOU WANT TO TRIPLE-CHECK YOUR WORK.

Substituting $x = -1$ into either ①, ②, or ①', we find that $y = 3$,

so the solution is: $(x, y) = (-1, 3)$.

We can multiply the terms of both equations if that is what is necessary to solve the problem. Just find the least common multiple of the x's or the y's and multiply each term accordingly to eliminate the variable.

EXAMPLE: Solve by using the addition method.

$$\begin{cases} 2x + 5y = 3 & ① \\ 3x + 4y = 1 & ② \end{cases}$$

The LCM of $2x$ and $3x$ is $6x$. Therefore, we must multiply equation ① by 3 and call it equation ①':

$$6x + 15y = 9 \quad ①'$$

Next, multiply equation ② by -2 and call it equation ②':

$$-6x - 8y = -2 \quad ②'$$

Now add equation ①' and equation ②' together:

$$6x + 15y = 9 \quad ①'$$
$$-6x - 8y = -2 \quad ②'$$

$$6x + (-6x) + 15y + (-8y) = 9 + (-2)$$

$$\begin{cases} 7y = 7 \\ y = 1 \end{cases}$$

Substituting $y = 1$ into either ①, ②, ①', or ②', we find that, $x = -1$, so the solution is: $(x, y) = (-1, 1)$.

1. Solve the simultaneous equations by using the graphing method:

$$\begin{cases} x + y = 3 \\ 2x + y = 7 \end{cases}$$

2. Solve the simultaneous equations by using the graphing method:

$$\begin{cases} -x + y = 4 \\ x + y = 2 \end{cases}$$

3. Solve the simultaneous equations by using the graphing method:

$$\begin{cases} x + 2y = 0 \\ x - y = 6 \end{cases}$$

4. Solve the simultaneous equations by using the graphing method:

$$\begin{cases} -4x + 3y = 6 \\ 2x - 4y = 2 \end{cases}$$

5. Solve the simultaneous equations by using either the addition method or the substitution method:

$$\begin{cases} x - y = 9 \\ x + y = 7 \end{cases}$$

6. Solve the simultaneous equations by using either the addition method or the substitution method:

$$\begin{cases} x + y = 10 \\ 2x - y = -4 \end{cases}$$

7. Solve the simultaneous equations by using either the addition method or the substitution method:

$$\begin{cases} 3x - 2y = 10 \\ 2x + 3y = 11 \end{cases}$$

8. Solve the simultaneous equations by using either the addition method or the substitution method:

$$\begin{cases} 5x - 3y = 9 \\ -x + y = -2 \end{cases}$$

ANSWERS

CHECK YOUR ANSWERS

1. Solution: (4, -1)

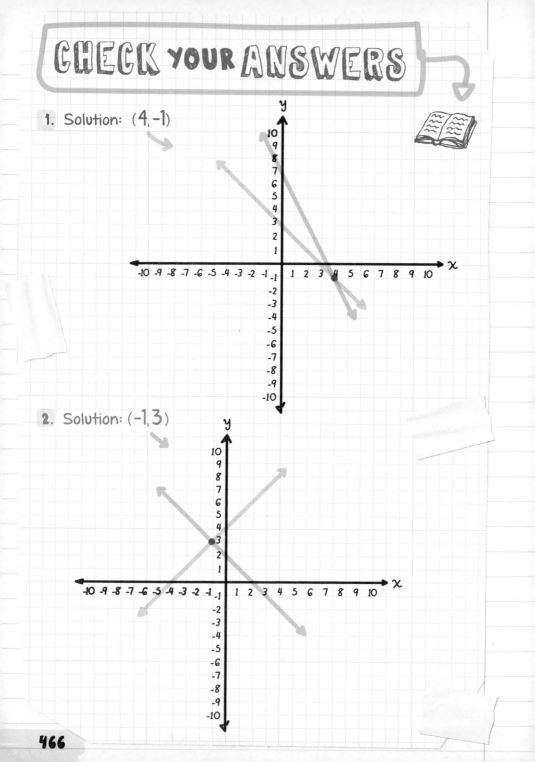

2. Solution: (-1, 3)

3. Solution: = $(4, -2)$

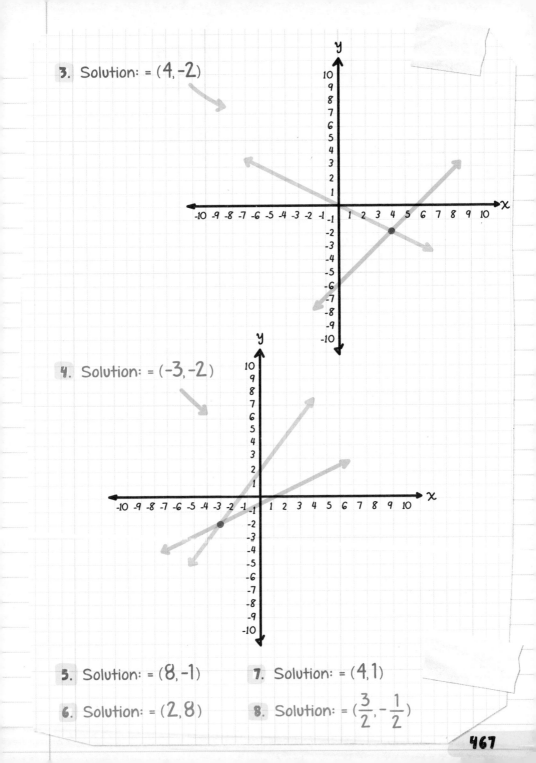

4. Solution: = $(-3, -2)$

5. Solution: = $(8, -1)$

6. Solution: = $(2, 8)$

7. Solution: = $(4, 1)$

8. Solution: = $(\frac{3}{2}, -\frac{1}{2})$

Chapter 60
NONLINEAR
FUNCTIONS

NONLINEAR FUNCTIONS are NOT straight lines when they are graphed, and they are NOT in the form $y = mx + b$. One example of a nonlinear function is a **QUADRATIC FUNCTION**. In a quadratic function, the input variable (x) is squared like so: x^2. The result is a **PARABOLA**, which is a U-shaped curve.

EXAMPLE: Create an input/output chart and graph $y = x^2$.

INPUT (x)	FUNCTION: $y = x^2$	OUTPUT (y)	COORDINATE POINTS (x,y)
-3	$y = (-3)^2$	9	(-3, 9)
-2	$y = (-2)^2$	4	(-2, 4)
-1	$y = (-1)^2$	1	(-1, 1)
0	$y = (0)^2$	0	(0, 0)
1	$y = (1)^2$	1	(1, 1)
2	$y = (2)^2$	4	(2, 4)
3	$y = (3)^2$	9	(3, 9)

Create an input/output chart and graph $y = -2x^2 + 1$.

INPUT (x)	FUNCTION: $y = -2x^2 + 1$	OUTPUT (y)	COORDINATE POINTS (x,y)
-2	$y = -2(-2)^2 + 1$ $y = -2(4) + 1$ $y = -8 + 1$ $y = -7$	-7	(-2, -7)
-1	$y = -2(-1)^2 + 1$ $y = -2(1) + 1$ $y = -2 + 1$ $y = -1$	-1	(-1, -1)
0	$y = -2(0)^2 + 1$ $y = -2(0) + 1$ $y = 0 + 1$ $y = 1$	1	(0, 1)
1	$y = -2(1)^2 + 1$ $y = -2(1) + 1$ $y = -2 + 1$ $y = -1$	-1	(1, -1)
2	$y = -2(2)^2 + 1$ $y = -2(4) + 1$ $y = -8 + 1$ $y = -7$	-7	(2, -7)

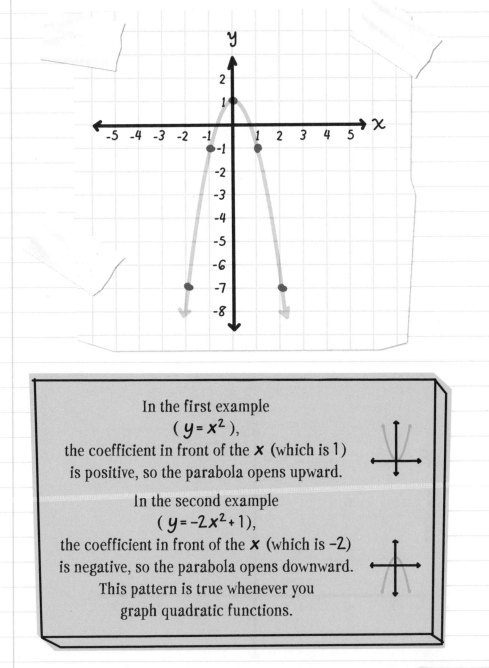

In the first example
($y = x^2$),
the coefficient in front of the **x** (which is 1)
is positive, so the parabola opens upward.

In the second example
($y = -2x^2 + 1$),
the coefficient in front of the **x** (which is –2)
is negative, so the parabola opens downward.
This pattern is true whenever you
graph quadratic functions.

Another example of a nonlinear function is an **ABSOLUTE VALUE FUNCTION**. When graphed, the result is shaped like a "V."

EXAMPLE: Create an input/output chart and graph $y = |x|$.

INPUT (x)	FUNCTION: $y = |x|$	OUTPUT (y)	COORDINATE POINTS (x,y)
-2	$y = |-2|$	2	(-2, 2)
-1	$y = |-1|$	1	(-1, 1)
0	$y = |0|$	0	(0, 0)
1	$y = |1|$	1	(1, 1)
2	$y = |2|$	2	(2, 2)

Create an input/output chart
and graph $y = -|x| + 1$.

INPUT (x)	FUNCTION: $y = -|x| + 1$	OUTPUT (y)	COORDINATE POINTS (x, y)
-2	$y = -|-2| + 1$ $y = -2 + 1$ $y = -1$	-1	(-2, -1)
-1	$y = -|-1| + 1$ $y = -1 + 1$ $y = 0$	0	(-1, 0)
0	$y = -|0| + 1$ $y = 0 + 1$ $y = 1$	1	(0, 1)
1	$y = -|-1| + 1$ $y = -1 + 1$ $y = 0$	0	(1, 0)
2	$y = -|-2| + 1$ $y = -2 + 1$ $y = -1$	-1	(2, -1)

1. Complete the input/output chart and graph $y = x^2 + 1$.

INPUT (x)	FUNCTION: $y = x^2 + 1$	OUTPUT (y)	COORDINATE POINTS (x,y)
-2			
-1			
0			
1			
2			

2. Complete the input/output chart and graph $y = -2x^2$.

INPUT (x)	FUNCTION: $y = -2x^2$	OUTPUT (y)	COORDINATE POINTS (x,y)
-2			
-1			
0			
1			
2			

3. Complete the input/output chart and graph $y = |x| + 2$.

INPUT (x)	FUNCTION: $y = |x| + 2$	OUTPUT (y)	COORDINATE POINTS (x,y)
3			
-1			
0			
2			
4			

4. Complete the input/output chart and graph $y = -|x| - 1$.

INPUT (x)	FUNCTION: $y = -|x| - 1$	OUTPUT (y)	COORDINATE POINTS (x,y)
-5			
-3			
0			
2			
5			

ANSWERS ⟶ 475

1.

INPUT (x)	FUNCTION: $y = x^2 + 1$	OUTPUT (y)	COORDINATE POINTS (x,y)
–2	$y = (-2)^2 + 1$ $y = 4 + 1$ $y = 5$	5	(–2, 5)
–1	$y = (-1)^2 + 1$ $y = 1 + 1$ $y = 2$	2	(–1, 2)
0	$y = (0)^2 + 1$ $y = 0 + 1$ $y = 1$	1	(0, 1)
1	$y = (1)^2 + 1$ $y = 1 + 1$ $y = 2$	2	(1, 2)
2	$y = (2)^2 + 1$ $y = 4 + 1$ $y = 5$	5	(2, 5)

2.

INPUT (x)	FUNCTION: $y = -2x^2$	OUTPUT (y)	COORDINATE POINTS (x,y)
-2	$y = -2(-2)^2$ $y = -2(4)$ $y = -8$	-8	(-2, -8)
-1	$y = -2(-1)^2$ $y = -2(1)$ $y = -2$	-2	(-1, -2)
0	$y = -2(0)^2$ $y = -2(0)$ $y = 0$	0	(0, 0)
1	$y = -2(1)^2$ $y = -2(1)$ $y = -2$	-2	(1, -2)
2	$y = -2(2)^2$ $y = -2(4)$ $y = -8$	-8	(2, -8)

3.

INPUT (x)	FUNCTION: $y = \lvert x \rvert + 2$	OUTPUT (y)	COORDINATE POINTS (x,y)
-3	$y = \lvert -3 \rvert + 2$ $y = 3 + 2$ $y = 5$	5	(-3, 5)
-1	$y = \lvert -1 \rvert + 2$ $y = 1 + 2$ $y = 3$	3	(-1, 3)
0	$y = \lvert 0 \rvert + 2$ $y = 0 + 2$ $y = 2$	2	(0, 2)
2	$y = \lvert 2 \rvert + 2$ $y = 2 + 2$ $y = 4$	4	(2, 4)
4	$y = \lvert 4 \rvert + 2$ $y = 4 + 2$ $y = 6$	6	(4, 6)

4.

INPUT (x)	FUNCTION: y = -|x|-1	OUTPUT (y)	COORDINATE POINTS (x,y)
-5	$y=-\|-5\|-1$ $y=-(5)-1$ $y=-6$	-6	(-5,-6)
-3	$y=-\|-3\|-1$ $y=-(3)-1$ $y=-4$	-4	(-3,-4)
0	$y=-\|0\|-1$ $y=-(0)-1$ $y=-1$	-1	(0,-1)
2	$y=-\|2\|-1$ $y=-(2)-1$ $y=-3$	-3	(2,-3)
5	$y=-\|5\|-1$ $y=-(5)-1$ $y=-6$	-6	(5,-6)

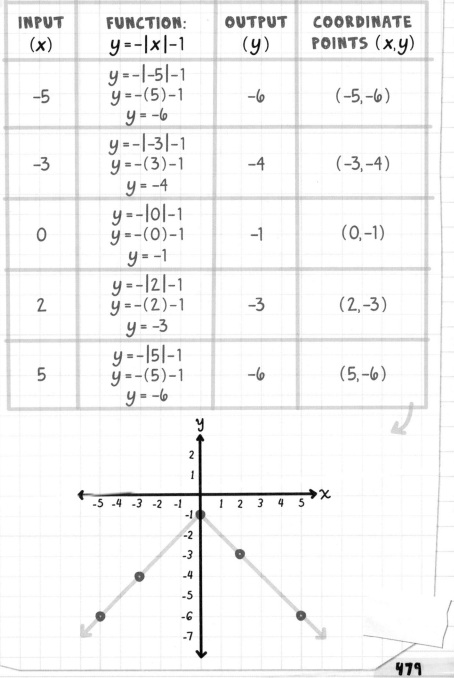

Chapter 61

POLYGONS AND THE COORDINATE PLANE

Besides plotting points, drawing lines, and creating various other graphs, we can also use the coordinate plane to draw shapes. We just plot points and connect them with lines.

> **EXAMPLE:**
> Plot the points (2,-3), (4,-3), (4,1), and (2,1).
> Then identify the shape that is formed by the points.

First plot the points:

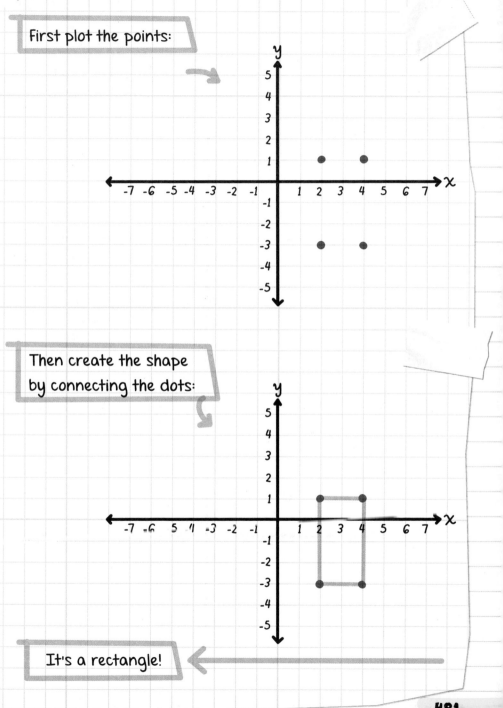

Then create the shape by connecting the dots:

It's a rectangle!

EXAMPLE: Plot the points (-2,3), (2,3), (0,-3), (4,0), and (-4,0). Then identify the shape that is formed by the points.

First plot the points:

Then connect the dots:

The points create a pentagon.

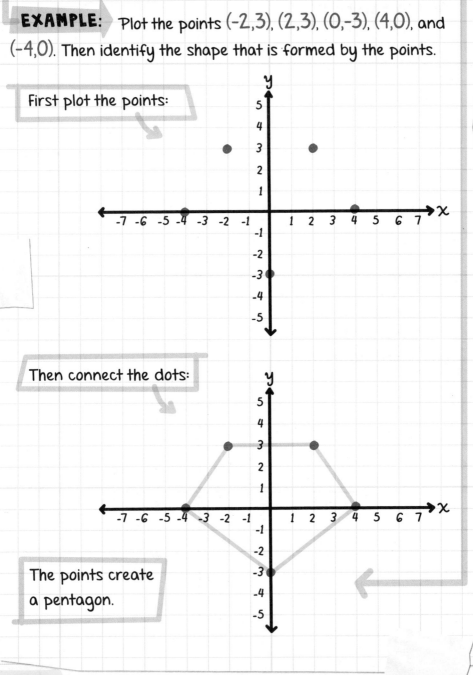

DON'T FORGET: We can find the length of the side of a figure if the *x*-coordinate or the *y*-coordinate is the same. So, we can solve problems related to shapes on a coordinate plane.

EXAMPLE: A square is plotted on a coordinate plane. Three of its vertices are **A** (1,-3), **B** (5,-3), and **C** (1, 1). What are the coordinates of point **D**, the 4th vertex?

First, plot points **A**, **B**, and **C** on the coordinate plane:

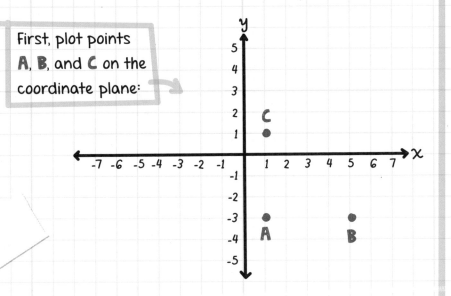

Because we know a square has four equal sides, we only have to find the length of one side.

Because Point **A** and Point **B** share the same *y*-coordinate, we can calculate the distance between the two points by finding the difference of the *x*-coordinates, which is $5 - 1 = 4$.

Therefore, the distance between Point **C** and Point **D** must also be 4 units, and the distance between Point **B** and Point **D** must also be 4 units.

So, the coordinates for Point **D** are (5, 1).

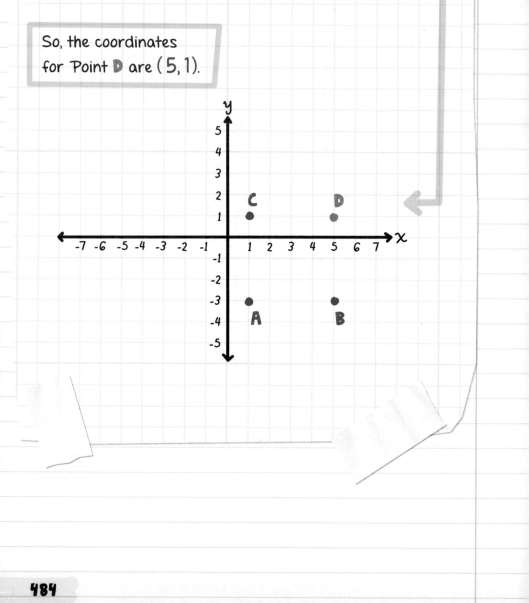

CHECK YOUR KNOWLEDGE

1. Plot the points $(1,-3)$, $(5,2)$, and $(7,-2)$. Then identify the shape that is formed by the points.

2. Plot the points $(-3,1)$, $(1,2)$, $(-2,-3)$, and $(2,-2)$. Then identify the shape that is formed by the points.

3. Plot the points $(-1,2)$, $(2,-1)$, $(1,4)$, and $(4,1)$. Then identify the shape that is formed by the points.

4. Plot the points $(1,0)$, $(1,4)$, $(3,2)$, $(3,4)$, $(-1,2)$, and $(-1,0)$. Then identify the shape that is formed by the points.

5. A square is plotted on a coordinate plane. Three of its vertices are at **A** $(-5,4)$, **B** $(2,4)$, and **C** $(2,-3)$. What are the coordinates of Point **D**, the 4th vertex?

6. A rectangle is plotted on a coordinate plane. Three of its vertices are at **A** $(1,3)$, **B** $(3,-2)$, and **C.** $(3,3)$. What are the coordinates of Point **D**, the 4th vertex?

7. A square is plotted on the coordinate plane. Three of its vertices are at **A** $(2,4)$, **B** $(-2,4)$, and **C** $(2,0)$. What are the coordinates of Point **D**, the 4th vertex?

8. A rectangle is plotted on the coordinate plane. Three of its vertices are at **A** $(-5,-2)$, **B** $(-5,3)$, and **C** $(6,3)$. What are the coordinates of Point **D**, the 4th vertex?

ANSWERS

CHECK YOUR ANSWERS

1. The shape is a triangle.

2. The shape is a square.

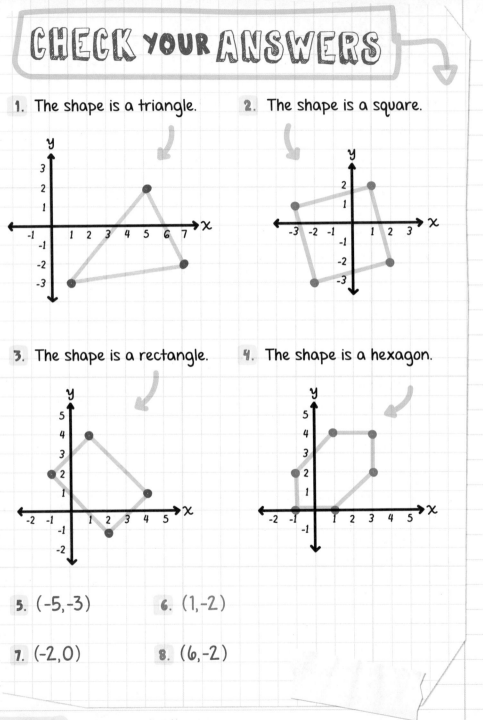

3. The shape is a rectangle.

4. The shape is a hexagon.

5. (-5,-3)

6. (1,-2)

7. (-2,0)

8. (6,-2)

🎲 Chapter 62 🎲

TRANSFORMATIONS

TRANSFORMATIONS

TRANSFORMATIONS

Besides plotting points and shapes, we can also use the coordinate plane to work with shapes and figures. A **TRANSFORMATION** is a change of position or size of a figure. When we transform a figure, we create a new figure that is related to the original.

TRANSLATIONS

One type of transformation is a **TRANSLATION**, which is a transformation that moves all the figure's points the same distance and direction. However, the orientation and size remain the same. The newly translated figure is called the **IMAGE**, and the new points are written with a **PRIME SYMBOL** (').

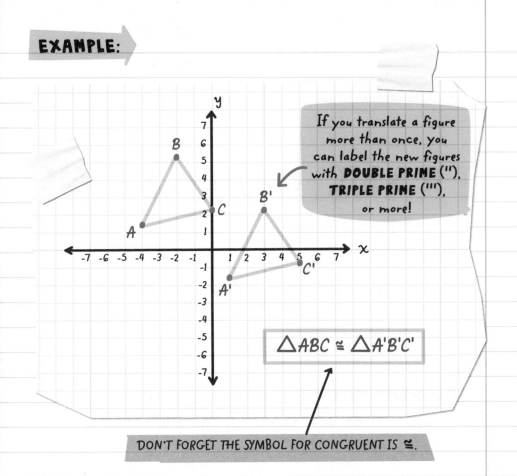

If you translate a figure more than once, you can label the new figures with **DOUBLE PRIME** ("), **TRIPLE PRIME** ("'), or more!

$$\triangle ABC \cong \triangle A'B'C'$$

DON'T FORGET THE SYMBOL FOR CONGRUENT IS ≅.

These congruent triangles have corresponding sides that are the same length and corresponding angles that are the same number of degrees. They are simply plotted on different parts of the coordinate plane, so only the locations of the triangles are different.

To do a translation, move each point according to the given criteria.

EXAMPLE: Given $\triangle ABC$, translate it as follows: $(x + 4, y + 3)$.

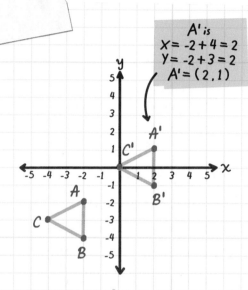

A' is
$x = -2 + 4 = 2$
$y = -2 + 3 = 2$
$A' = (2, 1)$

First, write the original coordinates.

Then calculate each translated point by adding 4 units to the x-value $(x + 4)$ and then adding 3 units to the y-value $(y + 3)$.

ORIGINAL	IMAGE
A (–2, –2)	A' (2, 1)
B (–2, –4)	B' (2, –1)
C (–4, –3)	C' (0, 0)

Lastly, plot and label the image as $A'B'C'$.

If it's a simple translation like this, you can simply move each point by counting the units on the coordinate plane. If it's more complex, you can calculate the translation separately and then plot your new points.

489

EXAMPLE: Given the polygon *LMNO*, translate it as follows: $(x - 3, y + 6)$.

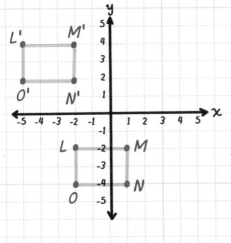

First, write the original coordinates.

Then calculate each translated point by subtracting 3 units from the x-value $(x - 3)$, and then adding 6 units to the y-value $(y + 6)$.

Lastly, plot and label the image as *L'M'N'O'*.

ORIGINAL	IMAGE
L (–2,–2)	L' (–5, 4)
M (1, –2)	M' (–2, 4)
N (1, –4)	N' (–2, 2)
O (–2, –4)	O' (–5, 2)

REFLECTION

A **REFLECTION** is a transformation that flips a figure over a **LINE OF SYMMETRY**—if you fold the paper at the line of symmetry, the original and the image would match exactly.

EXAMPLES:

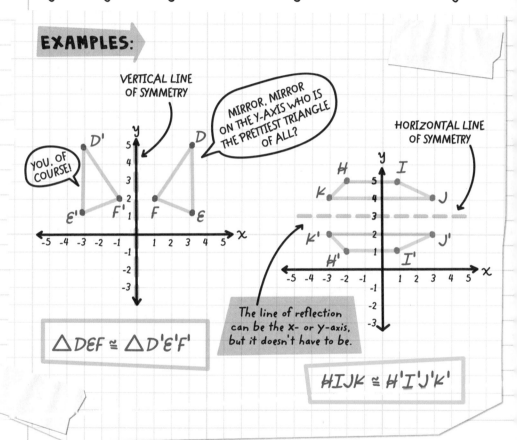

VERTICAL LINE OF SYMMETRY

MIRROR, MIRROR ON THE Y-AXIS WHO IS THE PRETTIEST TRIANGLE OF ALL?

YOU, OF COURSE!

HORIZONTAL LINE OF SYMMETRY

The line of reflection can be the x- or y-axis, but it doesn't have to be.

$\triangle DEF \cong \triangle D'E'F'$

$HIJK \cong H'I'J'K'$

In both of the reflections above, the original figure and its image are congruent. The original figure and its image are also the same distance away from the line of symmetry, so we can say that they are **EQUIDISTANT** from the line of symmetry.

To do a reflection, move each point according to the given criteria.

EXAMPLE: Given $\triangle EFG$, reflect the shape over the x-axis.

It's easier to work point by point than to move the whole figure at once.

4 UNITS AWAY FROM THE REFLECTION LINE

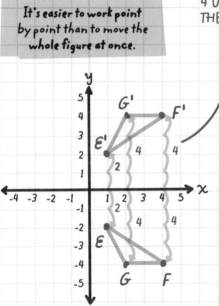

First, count how many units each point is away from the line of symmetry (in this case, the x-axis) and draw the reflected point the same distance away on the other side.

Lastly, plot and label the image as $E'F'G'$.

ORIGINAL	IMAGE
E (1, -2)	E' (1, 2)
F (4, -4)	F' (4, 4)
G (2, -4)	G' (2, 4)

SHORTCUT: When a figure is reflected across the x-axis, the sign of the y-value will simply change to the opposite.

EXAMPLE: Given the polygon *HIJK*, reflect the shape over the *y*-axis.

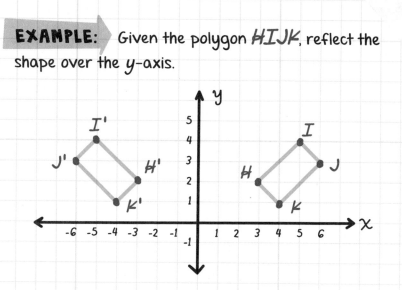

First, count how many units each point is away from the reflection line (the *y*-axis) and position the reflected point the same distance away on the other side.

Lastly, plot and label the new image as *H'I'J'K'*.

ORIGINAL	IMAGE
H (3, 2)	H' (−3, 2)
I (5, 4)	I' (−5, 4)
J (6, 3)	J' (−6, 3)
K (4, 1)	K' (−4, 1)

SHORTCUT: When a figure is reflected across the *y*-axis, the sign of the *x*-value will simply change to the opposite.

DILATION

A **DILATION** is a transformation that enlarges or reduces a figure by a **SCALE FACTOR**. The scale factor is the amount by which you stretch or shrink the original figure. When you change the size of a figure, there is a **CENTER OF DILATION**, which is the fixed point in the coordinate plane around which the figure expands or contracts.

EXAMPLE:

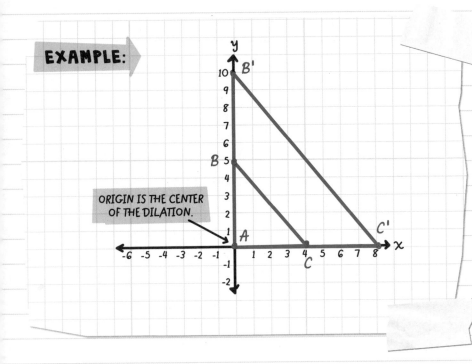

ORIGIN IS THE CENTER OF THE DILATION.

In the above figure ABC, side AB has a length of 5 units and side AC has a length of 4 units. If ABC is enlarged by a scale factor of 2 to make $AB'C'$, side AB' has a length of 10 units and side AC' has a length of 8 units.

$AB'C'$ is twice as large as ABC. The two triangles are also similar because the corresponding angles are congruent and the sides are proportional.

When you enlarge a figure, the scale factor is greater than 1.

When you shrink a figure, the scale factor is less than 1. ←

Usually, when a dilation is done on a coordinate plane, the origin (0,0) is the center of dilation. If the center of dilation is the origin, simply multiply the coordinates of the original shape by the given scale factor, k:

$$(x, y) \rightarrow (xk, yk)$$

Then plot your new shape.

THIS MEANS THE NEW DILATED OBJECT WILL LITERALLY BE A FRACTION OF THE ORIGINAL SIZE.

WHEN YOU ENLARGE A FIGURE, THINK ABOUT HOW A SHADOW GETS BIGGER AS THE LIGHT SOURCE GETS FARTHER AWAY.

Given the polygon *EFGH*, draw the dilation image with the center of dilation at the origin and a scale factor of 3.

ORIGINAL	SCALE FACTOR	IMAGE
E (1, 3)	• 3	E' (3, 9)
F (3, 3)	• 3	F' (9, 9)
G (3, 1)	• 3	G' (9, 3)
H (2, 1)	• 3	H' (6, 3)

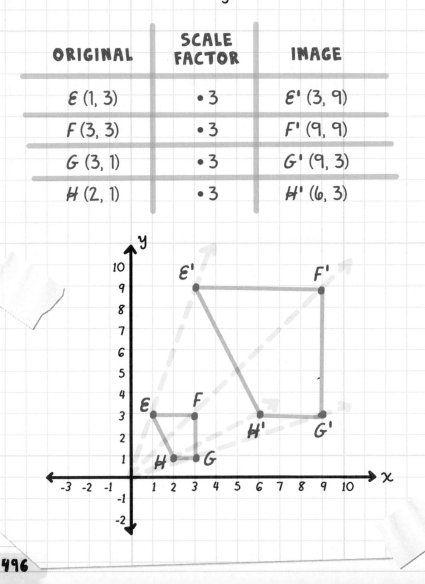

You can check your answer by connecting the corresponding points (for example, E to E') and extending the line beyond the two points. If the line intersects at the origin, your answer is correct.

EXAMPLE: Given $\triangle LMN$, draw the dilation image with the center of dilation at the origin and a scale factor of $\frac{1}{2}$.

ORIGINAL	SCALE FACTOR	IMAGE
L (−2, 6)	$\cdot \frac{1}{2}$	L' (−1, 3)
M (−2, 2)	$\cdot \frac{1}{2}$	M' (−1, 1)
N (−6, 4)	$\cdot \frac{1}{2}$	N' (−3, 2)

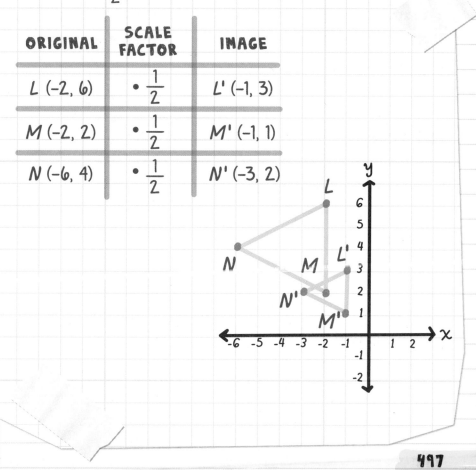

ROTATION

A **ROTATION** is a transformation that turns a figure around

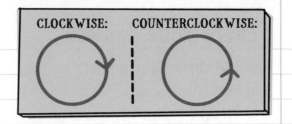

a fixed point called the **CENTER OF ROTATION**. The number of degrees that the figure turns is called the **ANGLE OF ROTATION**. The criteria tell us the degrees that the shape moves, whether the shape moves **CLOCKWISE** or **COUNTERCLOCKWISE**, and the center of rotation. A rotation does not change the size or shape of the figure. This means the image after the rotation is congruent to the original figure.

EXAMPLE:

NOTICE POINT **C** DID NOT MOVE. IT IS THE CENTER OF THE ROTATION.

If you measure $\angle ACA'$, you will find that A' moved $90°$ in a counterclockwise direction.

If you measure $\angle BCB'$, you will find that B' moved $90°$ in a counterclockwise direction.

$\triangle ABC \cong \triangle A'B'C$

So this means that *ABC* was rotated 90° in a counterclockwise direction to form *A'B'C*. Also, the two triangles are congruent—the corresponding sides are the same length and the corresponding angles are the same degrees.

Rotations can also be performed on a coordinate plane. Usually, the origin (0,0) will be the center of rotation.

EXAMPLE: Rotate △*ABC* 90° clockwise.

THIS COULD ALSO BE A 270° COUNTERCLOCKWISE ROTATION—YOU END UP AT THE SAME PLACE.

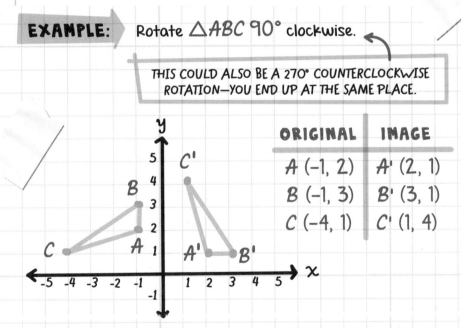

ORIGINAL	IMAGE
A (–1, 2)	A' (2, 1)
B (–1, 3)	B' (3, 1)
C (–4, 1)	C' (1, 4)

What happened? The *x*- and *y*-coordinates swapped places and then took the appropriate signs for quadrant I.

SHORTCUT: Every time a figure rotates 90°, the figure moves one quadrant and the coordinates swap places and take the signs of the quadrant.

QUADRANT II
(–x, +y)

QUADRANT I
(+x, +y)

QUADRANT III
(–x, –y)

QUADRANT IV
(+x, –y)

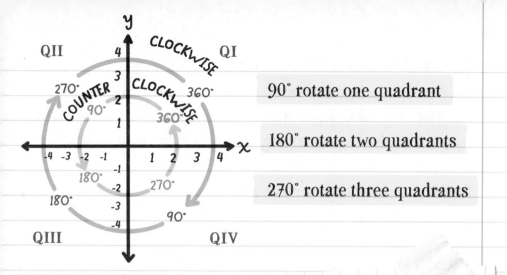

QII

QI

CLOCKWISE

270°

COUNTER

CLOCKWISE

360°

90°

360°

180°

270°

180°

90°

QIII

QIV

90° rotate one quadrant

180° rotate two quadrants

270° rotate three quadrants

EXAMPLE: Rotate △ABC 180° clockwise.

Rotate each point 180° or two quadrants clockwise
(the coordinates swap twice).

SO, BACK TO THE
ORIGINAL POSITION

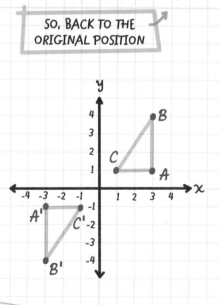

A is (3, 1), so A' is (−3,−1).
Both coordinates are
negative because A' will
be in QIII.

B is (3, 4), so B' is (−3, −4)
because B' will be in QIII.

C is (1, 1), so C' is (−1, −1)
because C' will be in QIII.

EXAMPLE: Rotate △ABC 270° clockwise.

Rotate each point three quadrants clockwise (the coordinates swap three times).

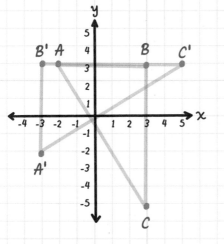

A is (-2, 3), so A' is (-3, -2). Both are negative because A' will be in QI.

B is (3, 3), so B' is (-3, 3) because B' will be in QII.

C is (3, -5), so C' is (5, 3) because C' will be in QI.

EXAMPLE: Graph the △ABC and its image after a rotation of 90° counterclockwise. | ONE QUADRANT TO THE LEFT |

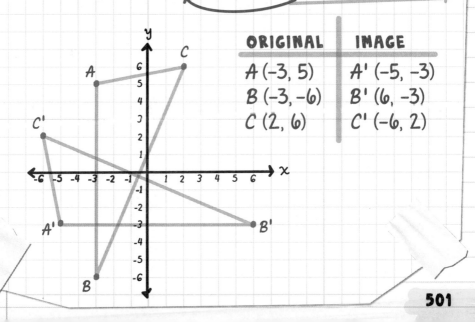

ORIGINAL	IMAGE
A (-3, 5)	A' (-5, -3)
B (-3, -6)	B' (6, -3)
C (2, 6)	C' (-6, 2)

CHECK YOUR KNOWLEDGE

1. Graph a polygon with the following points: A (−4, 2), B (−2, 2), C (−2, −1), and D (−4, −1). Then translate it as follows: $(x + 6, y − 3)$.

2. Graph a polygon with the following points: E (3, 5), F (4, 1), and G (2, 4). Then translate it as follows: $(x − 3, y − 4)$.

3. Graph a polygon with the following points: P (−2, 4), Q (−3, 1), and R (−4, 3). Then reflect the shape over the x-axis.

4. Graph a polygon with the following points: S (1, 2), T (4, 4), U (4, −2), and V (2, −2). Then reflect the shape over the y-axis.

5. Graph a triangle with the following points: A (−2, −6), B (2, 8), and C (2, −4). Then dilate it by a scale factor of $\frac{1}{2}$.

6. Graph the quadrilateral with the following points: A (−2, −6), B (−2, −3), C (4, 3), and D (4, −6). Then rotate it $180°$ clockwise around the origin (the center of rotation).

7. Graph a polygon with the following points: H (1, 2), I (3, 2), J (3, –3), and K (1, –3). Then rotate it counterclockwise by 90° around the origin (the center of rotation).

8. Graph a polygon with the following points: L (–4, 4), M (–2, 4), N (–2, 1), and O (–5, 1). Then rotate it counterclockwise by 180° around the origin (the center of rotation).

ANSWERS

1.

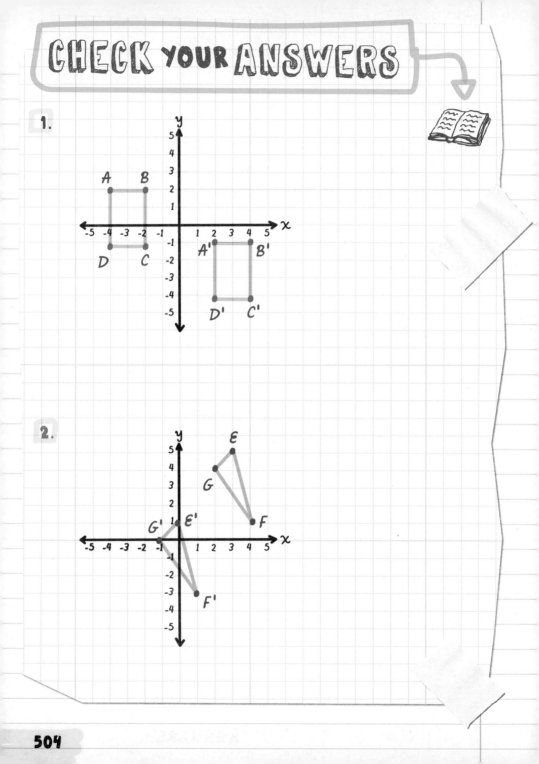

2.

3.

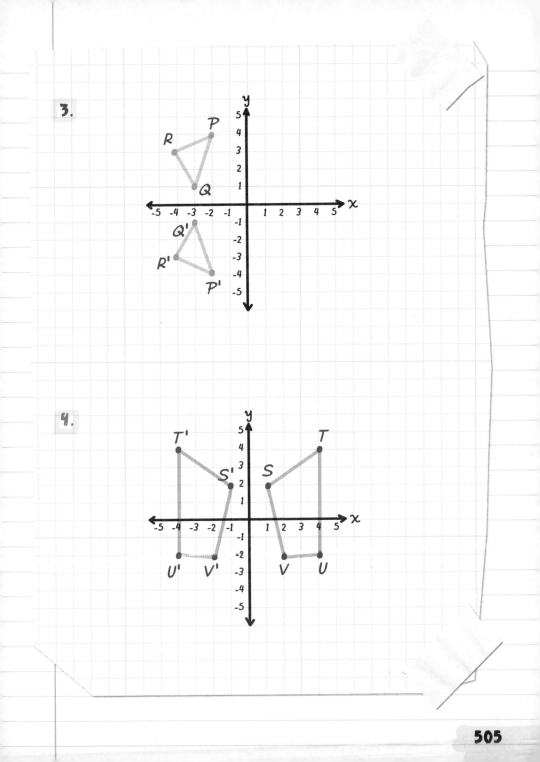

4.

5.

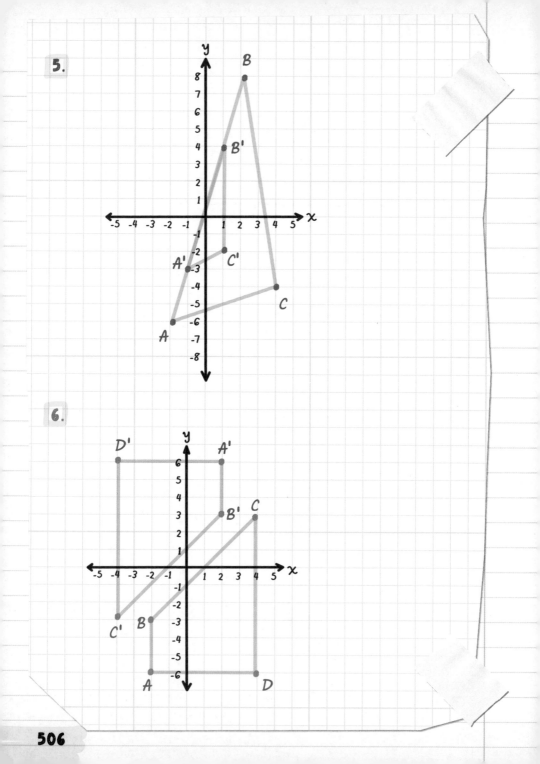

6.

7.

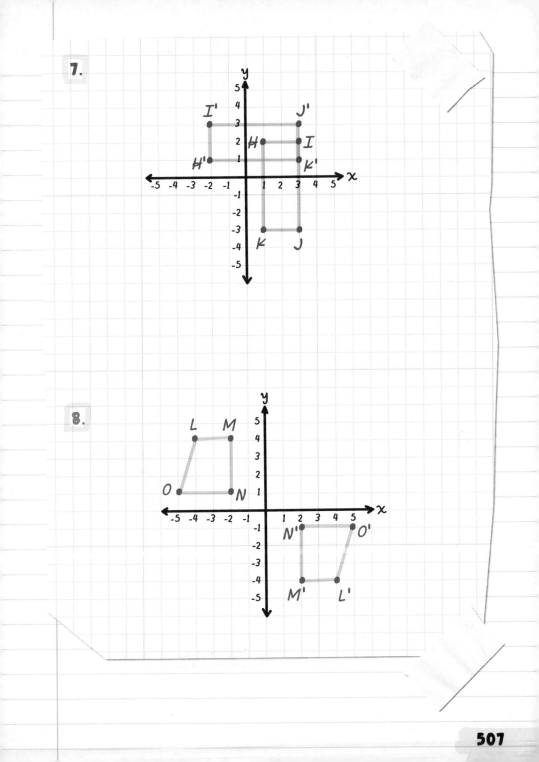

8.

Chapter 63

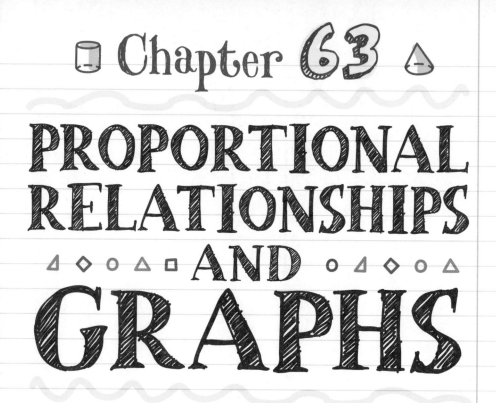

PROPORTIONAL RELATIONSHIPS AND GRAPHS

PROPORTIONAL RELATIONSHIPS

We can use math to make predictions about the future! By using a table or graph, we can show a trend.

MATH IS BETTER THAN A FORTUNE-TELLER!

TRY A GRAPH

EXAMPLE: An art student is trying to calculate how many tubes of paint he will need for his mural. If he is using 6 tubes every 4 days, how many tubes would he use in 8 days? How many tubes would he use in 10 days?

First, use the given info to create a table:

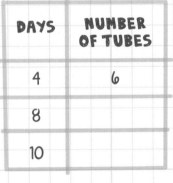

DAYS	NUMBER OF TUBES
4	6
8	
10	

Then, using the ratio 4 days: 6 tubes, find the missing numbers by making proportions for each scenario:

FOR THE SCENARIO OF 8 DAYS:

Let x represent the number of tubes needed for 8 days.

$$\frac{4}{6} = \frac{8}{x}$$

$$4x = 48$$

$$x = 12$$

ANSWER: For 8 days, 12 tubes are needed.

FOR THE SCENARIO OF 10 DAYS:

Let x represent the number of tubes needed for 10 days.

$$\frac{4}{6} = \frac{10}{x}$$

$$4x = 60$$

$$x = 15$$

ANSWER: For 10 days, 15 tubes are needed.

Next, use the information in the completed table to create a graph and predict the future! "Days" are your x-values, and "Number of Tubes" are your y-values.

DAYS	NUMBER OF TUBES
4	6
8	12
10	15

First, plot the points we know on a coordinate graph.
Then draw a line through these points.

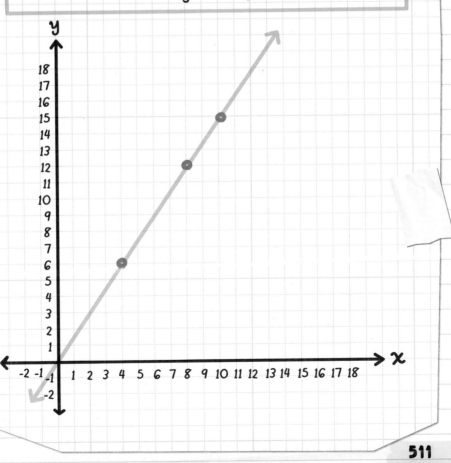

We can see from the graph that they form a straight line. We can also see that the graph goes through the origin (0,0). Therefore, we can make this observation: Whenever we graph data and it forms a straight line and the line goes through the origin, we can say that two quantities are in a **PROPORTIONAL RELATIONSHIP**.

AS ONE AMOUNT GETS BIGGER OR SMALLER, THE OTHER AMOUNT WILL ALSO GET BIGGER OR SMALLER BY THE SAME RATIO.

EXAMPLE: Larry jogs 4 miles in 2 days and 12 miles in 4 days. Is this a proportional relationship?

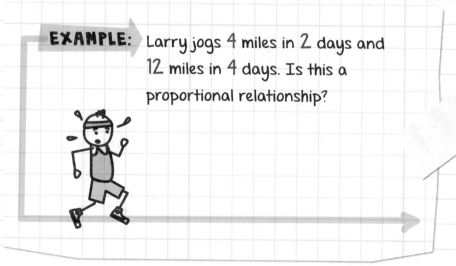

Let's put these two data points on a table and then graph it:

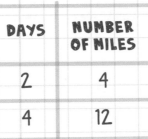

DAYS	NUMBER OF MILES
2	4
4	12

When we draw a straight line, we see...

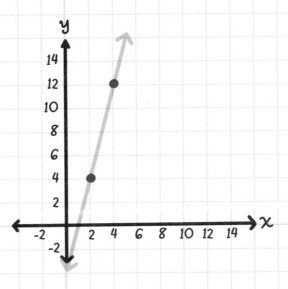

...that the line does NOT go through the origin, so we know that it is NOT a proportional relationship.

UNIT RATE

We can also use tables and graphs to find the **UNIT RATE**, which is the rate at which something is completed during 1 unit of measurement. We just have to study the line we draw on the graph.

EXAMPLE: In 3 minutes, Sandra can climb 9 flights of steps. Use a graph to find the unit rate.

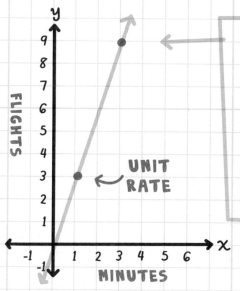

We can find the unit rate by plotting the point we know and drawing a line through it and the origin. Let the x-axis represent minutes and the y-axis represent flights.

We can also find the answer to this by making a ratio:

Let X represent the number of flights she climbs in 1 minute.

$$\frac{3}{9} = \frac{1}{x}$$

$$3x = 9$$

$$x = 3$$

Sandra climbs 3 flights in 1 minute.

514

CHECK YOUR KNOWLEDGE

1. In 3 seconds, Mary Lou answers 1 question. In 6 seconds, she answers 2 questions. Use this information to answer each of the following questions.

(A) Complete the missing parts in the table below.

TIME (SECONDS)	NUMBER OF QUESTIONS
3	
6	
9	

(B) Use your table to plot the points on a graph.

(C) Based on your graph or table, is this a proportional relationship?

2. In 4 minutes, Bob reads 4 pages. Use a graph to find his unit rate.

ANSWERS

CHECK YOUR ANSWERS

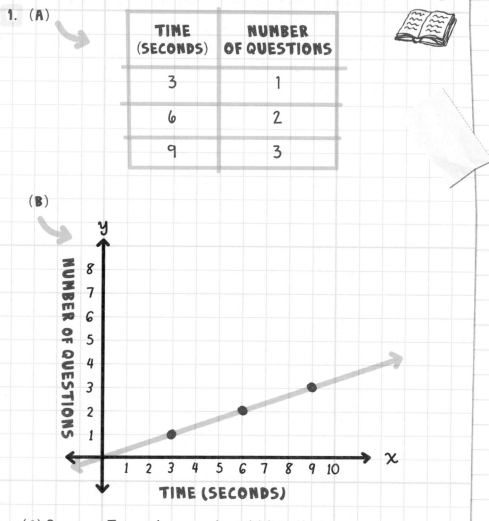

1. **(A)**

TIME (SECONDS)	NUMBER OF QUESTIONS
3	1
6	2
9	3

(B)

(C) Because I can draw a straight line that passes through all the points and also goes through the origin, it is a proportional relationship.

2. Bob's unit rate is 1 page per minute.

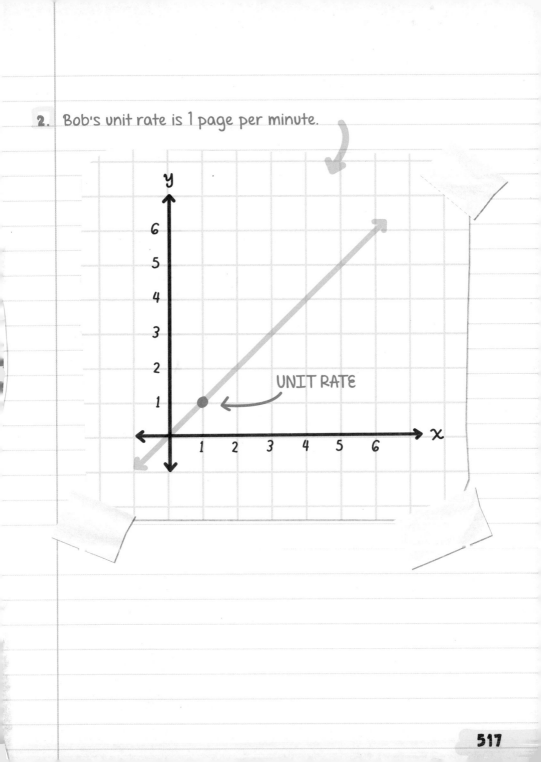

UNIT RATE

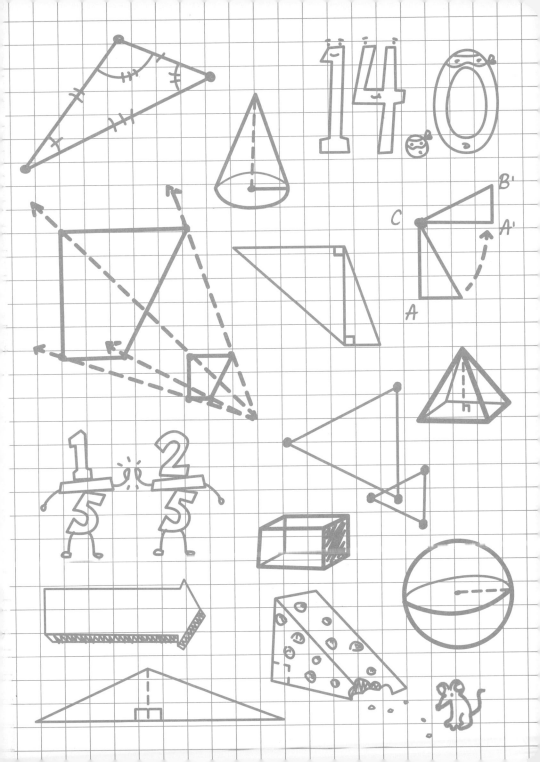